JN233744

A COURSE IN MODERN JAPANESE
[REVISED EDITION]
VOLUME ONE

名古屋大学日本語教育研究グループ 編
**Japanese Language Education
Research Group, Nagoya University**

名古屋大学出版会
The University of Nagoya Press

この教科書には別売ＣＤがあります。
最寄りの書店または小会宛ご注文ください。
◆ＣＤ×３枚組，定価(本体 4,800 円＋税)

There is a set of 3 CDs which accompanies this textbook.
You can order this set from your nearest bookshop or from
The University of Nagoya Press.
◆ The set of 3 CDs is 4,800 yen plus tax.

はじめに

　A Course in Modern Japanese [Revised Edition]（CMJ-R）はゼロから日本語を学ぶ学習者のための教科書です。1983 年に名古屋大学出版会から出版された初級日本語教科書 A　Course　in　Modern Japanese（CMJ）の改訂版です。

　CMJ は大学での研究を生活の中心におく留学生の日本語入門書として作られました。日本で研究生活を送るために、文法の基礎をしっかり学習するとともに日常生活で出会う場面での会話を学ぶことをねらったものでした。本書はこのねらいを基本的には引き継いでいます。しかし、この間の言語教育の成果を取り入れ、運用能力をいっそう高めるための改訂を加えました。

　名古屋大学留学生センター（現名称）では、CMJ を作成してから 20 年近く、実際には毎期毎期少しずつ手を加えながら、教育活動を続けてまいりました。それらをもとにまとめたのが本書です。2 年ほど前から本格的に改訂作業に取り組み、前書に対する学習者の要望、意見を取り入れ、よりわかりやすく、しかし、量が多くならないように、そしてコミュニケーション能力を身につけることができるよう、工夫を重ねました。

　登場人物をはじめ、本書には前書を引き継いでいる部分があります。こころよく改訂を承知してくださった、前書の執筆者の方々に感謝申し上げます。

　また、試作版を使用し、日々の作業でも協力くださった名古屋大学留学生センターの同僚の先生方、多くの質問や意見をくださった名古屋大学の日本語研修コース、NUPACE の学習者のみなさんに感謝いたします。

　最後に、出版を勧めてくださった名古屋大学出版会、煩雑な形式の本書を出版に至るまでお世話くださった同出版会の村井美恵子氏に、心からお礼申し上げます。

2002 年 2 月

編者一同

Preface

A Course in Modern Japanese [Revised Edition] (CMJ-R) is a textbook for complete beginners of the Japanese language. It is a revised edition of the textbook, A Course in Modern Japanese (CMJ), first published by The University of Nagoya Press in 1983.

CMJ was originally created as an introductory textbook for international students based on carrying out day-to-day life and research activities on the university campus. Its main aims were for the student to learn conversations for dealing with situations in everyday life as well as gaining a good understanding of the basic grammar of Japanese, in order to carry out research activities in Japan. This book continues with these aims as the main focus. However, it has been revised to take account of current language teaching practices and to further improve proficiency in using Japanese.

The Education Center for International Students (ECIS) at Nagoya University (the current name) has carried out language teaching for the last 20 years, since the creation of CMJ, continually updating the teaching methods and materials each year. This book represents the product of these improvements. Revision of the original book began 2 years ago, taking into acount feedback and comments from students who used CMJ, and it has been revised to make it easier to use without increasing the volume of material to be covered, and to be able to acquire communicative competentce in Japanese. There are parts of the book which have not changed from the original CMJ, such as the characters who appear in the materials.

Here, we would like to thank the many people who created the original CMJ for allowing us to make these changes. Furthermore, we would like to thank our colleagues in the ECIS, who used the textbook in class and helped us with the revision of the textbook as well as students from the Japanese language training course and NUPACE language programs at Nagoya University, who gave us plenty of feedback and comments on the test versions of the revised edition.

Finally, we would sincerely like to thank The University of Nagoya Press, who suggested that we publish this revised edition, and in particular Ms. Mieko Murai of The University of Nagoya Press who played a large role in bringing this text to publication.

February 2002
The Editors

About This Textbook

I Objectives and Goals

This textbook is an introductory textbook aimed at learners of Japanese as a foreign language who have no prior experience of the language. In particular, we have chosen conversational situations and vocabulary which learners will encounter in their daily life, study and research on a university campus.

This textbook has the following as its goals:

To acquire communicative proficiency in Japanese by acquiring an ability to speak and listen to Japanese,

To systematically learn the basic grammar of Japanese,

To learn basic Kanji characters, acquire the ability to read Japanese and build a foundation to go on and study Japanese at intermediate and advanced levels.

II Structure of this textbook

1. Number of lessons
20 lessons
(Vol. 1 : Lesson 1〜Lesson 10,　Vol. 2 : Lesson 11〜Lesson 20)

2. The structure of each lesson
(1)　Dialogue
　　　Discourse Practice and Activity
(2)　Vocabulary List
(3)　Notes on Grammar
(4)　Notes on Discourse
(5)　Drill
(6)　Aural comprehension
(7)　Reading comprehension
(8)　Kanji Practice

(1) Dialogue

We pick up on situations which international students are likely to meet in their daily life at university. We aim for natural conversation using the spoken language. We want you to practice the conversations paying attention to the sound patterns appropriate to each situation. After practicing the conversation we would like you to practice further by changing the situation to fit your own situation. The new grammar which is used in each conversation is explained in the Notes on Grammar. Some discourse patterns and expressions are explained in Notes on Discourse.

There are supplementary conversations in some of the lesssons. We would like you to practice them as much as necessary depending on the time available and the time of the classes.

From Lesson 7 **Discourse Practice and Activity** section follows the Dialogue section.

This section should be practiced after studying the Drills and Dialogues for each lesson.

As for the Discourse Practices, practice them so that you are able to carry out the conversations in real situations by placing yourself in that situation, or changing the situation to fit your own situation. It is necessary to practice using real movements.

The activity section is where you can enjoy communicating by practicing all the Japanese you have learnt so far, in free exercises.

(2) Vocabulary List

This provides the new vocabulary that appears in the Dialogue and Drills.

There are also lessons in which **Additional Vocabulary** is given as needed. We recommend that you learn these words.

Related Vocabulary is also given as and when required. This is for reference only.

(3) Notes on Grammar

This explains the new grammar for each lesson. The example sentences use vocabulary already learnt as much as possible, and makes the grammar as easy to understand as possible. An English translation is given and when a literal meaning is given the sign (Lit.) is provided. Up to Lesson 5 Romanization is used to lessen the burden of learning the readings of Kanji and Hiragana.

(4) Notes on Discourse

In the discourse and expressions used in the Dialogues there are points that are not explained in the Notes on Grammar, so these have been added as particular points to be noted for learning.

(5) Drill

There are three types of Drills : "Structure," "Usage" and "Let's Talk."

Structure drills are for remembering the form of the grammar points introduced in that lesson.

Usage drills provide short conversation examples illustrating how that grammar point is used. These are intended to help you to be able to use these grammar patterns in real situations.

Let's Talk drills are provided, as needed, in order to talk about yourself freely using the grammar points.

Oral practice should be carried out until you can smoothly say the sentences and conversations, grasping the sound patterns of Japanese, after understanding the meaning of the sentence. Cue words are given but we urge you to use substitution which suits your situation. With the Usage Drills it is desirable that the learner continues with the conversation freely. The symbols used in the drills have the following meanings.

① Symbols used in the title
   N：noun　　V：verb　　A：adjective　　いA：い adjective　　なA：な adjective
   Adv：adverb　　S：sentence
   ～ ：Various types of words from the word types above can be inserted.

② Symbols used in examples
   _____ ：represents where a cue word should be substituted.
   .... ：shows that the learner should make a substitution as required by themselves.
   ～～～ ：shows that a new sentences should be made using the cue word, in parenthesis
   （　）.

③ Others

For vocabulary that is not given in the vocabulary list and has not yet been learnt, the English is given in parenthesis (　).

We have provided useful words which can be used in a drill even though they are not included in the drill, as a cue in the box ....

(6) Aural comprehension

It is divided into Sections Ⅰ, Ⅱ and Ⅲ.

Section I is listening for the content of the conversation. Among these (A) (B) and (C) are conversations using the grammar learnt up to that lesson, and are for understanding the content of the conversation as well as for listening for small points. (D) is a little more difficult and is used for listening to the overall content of the conversation, which may include grammar and vocabulary which have yet to be learnt.

Section II is for listening to numbers. Listening is focused on numbers which have counters attached to them.

Section III is focus listening and is practice at listening for specific information within a conversation. Unlearnt grammar, vocabulary and expressions may be included in this section. First, do not try to hear all the sounds but just try to grasp the meaning and story of the conversation and answer the questions. You should try to answer in Japanese. Conversations are recorded at normal speed, so at the beginning you may find it difficult to tune your ears to the conversations. However, it is essential for you to be able to comprehend real spoken Japanese.

In Section I the conversation contains grammar used in that lesson, so it is not so difficult to listen to after studying the Dialogue. Section II and III do not have to be carried out in this order. A script for the aural comprehension is available with the CD.

(7) Reading Comprehension

This is written using the grammar learnt up to that lesson. Most of the topics are about things relevant to student life or Japanese culture and society, etc. Although it is written using introductory grammar, it aims to stimulate the intellectual needs of the learner as far as possible.

It is extremely important to grasp the content of the Reading Comprehension. By answering the questions at the end of each passage it is possible to grasp the overall understanding of the passage.

Lessons after Lesson 8 are presented in the written style. Furthermore, in Vol.2 **Three Clues to Reading Comprehension** are introduced as a bridge to reading at the intermediate level. Depending on the topic there will be a large number of new words used. Lines are given under these words and there are word lists provided. These words are not required to study this textbook, but are given as supplementary vocabulary.

(8) Kanji Practice

Selection of Kanji :

300 kanji, 15 in each lesson, have been selected from kanji vocabulary which correspond to Level 3 of the Japan Foundation Japanese Language Proficiency Test and kanji vocabulary that is needed for carrying out daily activities on campus.

Ordering of Kanji:

From Lesson 1 to 4 basic kanji are introduced so that learners from non-kanji countries can understand the radical system and the way kanji were formed. From Lesson 5 onwards in order to aid memorisation, related kanji are presented.

New Kanji : Not all of the readings for the kanji are given. The readings have been chosen from their use in the textbook and in relation to Level 3 of the Japan Foundation Japanese Language Proficiency Test.

Essential Words : Compulsory kanji vocabulary using kanji in that lesson.

Words : These are words which do not have to be learnt but it is desirable to know them.

Reading Practice : Practice in reading sentences (However, up to Lesson 3 just words) using the kanji learnt. The sentences use grammar that has been learnt up to that lesson.

A highlighted kanji indicates a kanji that is not among the 300 essential kanji for this course.

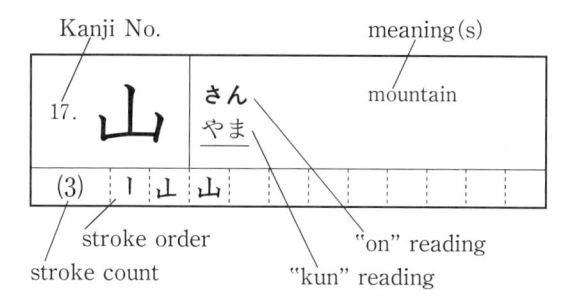

```
Kanji No.        meaning(s)
                              
17.  山    さん      mountain
          やま
(3)  丨 凵 山
stroke order
stroke count       "on" reading
                  "kun" reading
```

3. The learning order for each lesson (Example)

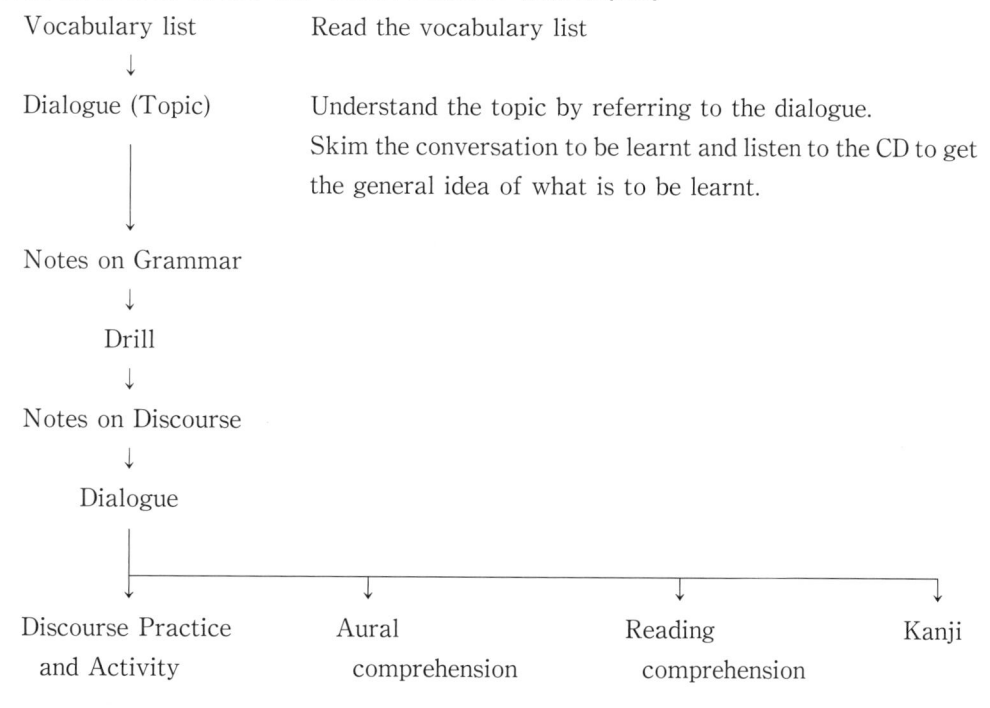

Vocabulary list   Read the vocabulary list
↓
Dialogue (Topic)   Understand the topic by referring to the dialogue.
                         Skim the conversation to be learnt and listen to the CD to get
                         the general idea of what is to be learnt.
↓
Notes on Grammar
↓
Drill
↓
Notes on Discourse
↓
Dialogue
↓
Discourse Practice   Aural   Reading   Kanji
and Activity   comprehension   comprehension

4. Example schedule for using the textbook in class

We estimate that the time needed to study the text (vol. 1 and vol. 2) is 300 classroom hours. The following gives some example times for study in class (1 class = 90 minutes). This schedule assumes that the student has prepared for the class.

Drill	2〜3 classes
Dialogue, Discourse Practice	2〜3 classes
Activity	1〜2 classes
Kanji	1 class
Aural comprehension	0.5〜1 class
Reading comprehension	0.5〜1 class

About the CD

In this textbook 🔊 is used to indicate there is recorded material for this section. The following sections are recorded on the CD.

- Pronunciation

For each lesson

- Dialogue
- Drill

    Structure Drill : Example and Substitution 1 and 2 (However the whole of Lesson 1 is recorded.)

    Usage Drill : Example

- Aural Comprehension Ⅰ, Ⅱ, Ⅲ

About notation used in the textbook

1) From Lesson 1 to Lesson 5
    - Hiragana is used for katakana reading. However it is not used in the Drill and Notes on Grammar sections.
    - Romanization using the Hepburn system is used in the example sentences in Notes on Grammar, Notes on Discourse. (Double vowels are written like "aa," "oo" in this textbook.)
2) Interjections such as "うーん", "えー" are used.
3) Kanji notation : as a rule kanji notation follows that for "Kyooiku Kanji." It conforms to *Hikkei Yooji Yoogo Jiten ver.4* (Sanseido, 2000) (『必携用字用語辞典第四版』(三省堂, 2000)) and *Asahi Shinbun Yoogo no Tebiki* (Asahi shinbunsha, 1997) (『朝日新聞用語の手引き』(朝日新聞社, 1997)).
4) The stroke order given for each kanji conforms to *Atarashii Kokugo Hyooki Handbook ver.4* (Sanseido, 2001) (『新しい国語表記ハンドブック』第4版 (三省堂, 2001)).
5) In the Reading Comprehension section furigana (hiragana for kanji reading) is gradually omitted for kanji vocabulary already learnt. For example, all the kanji in Lesson 1-5 have furigana. However, in Lesson 6 all the kanji learnt in Lesson 1-5 have no furigana, and in Lesson 7 all the kanji up to Lesson 6 have no furigana, and so on.

CONTENTS

はじめに　i

About This Textbook　iii

Pronunciation and Writing System　xv

Lesson 1 1

Dialogue　大学で　1
　1-1　On the way to class (1)／1-2　At lunch time (2)
　1-3　In the Co-op cafeteria (2)／1-4　In the classroom (3)

Vocabulary List　4

Notes on Grammar　7
　I　Verbal sentences (7)／II　Verbs (8)／III　Particles：へ, で, と (11)
　IV　Question sentences (12)／V　Particles：は and も (14)
　VI　Classification of particles (16)
　VII　Time expressions：きのう, きょう, あした (17)
　VIII　Omission of some noun phrases in a sentence (17)
　IX　Numerals and some numbers (1) (18)

Notes on Discourse　22
　I　はい (22)／II　そうですか (22)

Drill　24

Aural Comprehension　31

Reading Comprehension　32

Kanji Practice　33

Lesson 2 35

Dialogue　しょうかい　35
　2-1　In front of the Ryuugakusee Center (35)／2-2　Introducing each other (36)
　2-3　Introducing oneself (36)

Vocabulary List 37
    Related Vocabulary (University Terminology) (40)
Notes on Grammar 42
    I Noun sentences (42)／II Alternative questions (44)
    III Demonstrative pronouns (1) (45)／IV Group 1 particles：の，から，に (48)
    V Question word：いつ (51)／VI Prefixes：お- and ご- (52)
Notes on Discourse 53
    I カナダですか (53)／II じゃ、また (53)／III 失礼します (54)
Drill 55
Aural Comprehension 60
Reading Comprehension 61
Kanji Practice 62

Lesson 3 64

Dialogue パーティーで 64
    3-1 Asking what is going on lately (64)／3-2 Asking about food (65)
Vocabulary List 66
Notes on Grammar 68
    I Adjective sentences (68)／II Invitation or suggestion (73)
    III Extended predicate：んです (1) (74)／IV Group 3 particles：ね and よ (75)
    V Adverbs：とても，少し，ちょっと，あまり (76)／VI Conjunction：でも (77)
    VII Question words：どう and どんな (77)
    VIII Omission of the particles：は，が，を (78)
Notes on Discourse 79
    I ちょっと (79)
Drill 81
Aural Comprehension 86
Reading Comprehension 87
Kanji Practice 88

Lesson 4 90

Dialogue いろいろな建物 90
    4-1 On campus (90)／4-2 Asking where the classroom is (91)
    4-3 Looking for Lwin at the laboratory (91)
    4-Supplement デパートの売り場で (93)
Vocabulary List 94

Notes on Grammar 97
    I Location of a thing or a person (97)
    II Substitution：の as a substitute for a noun (100)
    III Substitution：です as a substitute for a verb (101)
    IV Demonstrative pronouns (2)：それ and その (103)
    V Question words：いくら and いくつ (104)／VI Conjunctions：じゃ and では (104)
    VII Numerals and some numbers (2) (105)

Notes on Discourse 107
    I そうですね (107)／II すみません (107)／III あのう (108)／IV ええと (109)

Drill 110
Aural Comprehension 117
Reading Comprehension 118
Kanji Practice 119

Lesson 5 121

Dialogue　地下鉄に乗る 121
    5-1 On the way to Motoyama Station (121)
    5-2 Asking about the bus to Nagoya Port from the bus terminal (122)

Vocabulary List 123

Notes on Grammar 125
    I Question words＋か or も (125)／II Group 1 particles：で，を，まで (127)
    III Conjunctive particle (Group 4 particle)：が (128)
    IV Question word：どうやって (129)
    V Words for approximate amounts：ぐらい／くらい (130)／VI Conjunction：そして (130)

Notes on Discourse 132
    I そうですねえ (132)／II ちょっとうかがいますが (132)

Drill 133
Aural Comprehension 138
Reading Comprehension　カーリンさんの日記（diary） 139
Kanji Practice 140

Lesson 6 142

Dialogue　図書館で 142
    6-1 At the library counter (142)／6-2 In front of the copy machine (143)

Vocabulary List 144

Notes on Grammar 146
    I Expressions of request or polite command (146)

II　Expression of the speaker's and the hearer's desire (148)
　　III　Extended meaning of the verb あります (151) / IV　Suffix：かた (152)
　　V　Verb modifiers：こう，そう，ああ，どう (153)
　　VI　Words for temporal sequence：まず，それから，最後に (153)
　　VII　Group 1 particle：に (154)

Notes on Discourse　155
　　I　〜たいんですが (155) / II　ここですね (156)

Drill　157
Aural Comprehension　161
Reading Comprehension　メール　162
Kanji Practice　163

Lesson 7 165

Dialogue　郵便局で　165
　　7-1　After class (165) / 7-2　Sending a parcel by airmail (166)
　　7-Supplement　事務室で (168)
　Discourse Practice and Activity　Inviting／Speech　169

Vocabulary List　170
Notes on Grammar　173
　　I　The -て form of -い adjectives, -な adjectives, and noun＋です (173)
　　II　Function and usages of the -て form (174) / III　V-てきます (175)
　　IV　Conjunction：それから (175) / V　Group 4 particles：から and が (175)
　　VI　Group 1 particles：に and で (177) / VII　Numbers as adverbs (178)

Notes on Discourse　179
　　I　いいですね (179) / II　お願いします (180) / III　これでいいですか (180)

Drill　181
Aural Comprehension　186
Reading Comprehension　手紙　187
Kanji Practice　189

Lesson 8 191

Dialogue　体の調子　191
　　8-1　At the hospital (191) / 8-2　On campus (192)
　　8-3　Making an appointment with the dentist (193)
　Discourse Practice and Activity　Telling your symptom　194

Vocabulary List　195

Related Vocabulary (Names of Parts of the Body) (198)
Additional Vocabulary (Adjectives (1)) (199)
Notes on Grammar 200
    I The non-polite form (200)
    II Usages of the non-polite form according to grammatical rules (203)
    III 〜ほうがいい／〜ほうがいいです (205)／IV Suffix：-すぎる／-すぎます (206)
    V Group 4 particles：けど，けれど，けれども (207)
Notes on Discourse 208
    I はっ (208)／II ルインです (208)
Drill 209
Aural Comprehension 216
Reading Comprehension 数字のイメージ 217
Kanji Practice 218

Lesson 9 220

Dialogue 研究室で 220
    9-1 About Lwin's presentation (220)
    9-2 Asking permission to miss a Japanese language class (221)
  Discourse Practice and Activity Asking Permission 222
Vocabulary List 223
    Additional Vocabulary (Time Expressions) (225)
Notes on Grammar 226
    I Nominalizing particle：の (226)／II Negative -て form (228)
    III Permission, prohibition, obligation (228)／IV Particles：ので and だけ (230)
    V でしょうか (231)／VI Conjunction：それで (232)
Notes on Discourse 233
    I ちょっとよろしいでしょうか (233) II 〜んですが、〜てもいいでしょうか (233)
Drill 235
Aural Comprehension 241
Reading Comprehension ゼミの発表 242
Kanji Practice 243

Lesson 10 245

Dialogue お茶を飲みながら話す 245
    10-1 About Alice's family (245)／10-2 About daily life (246)
  Discourse Practice and Activity Interview 248

Vocabulary List 249
    Additional Vocabulary (family members) (252)

Notes on Grammar 253
    Ⅰ V-ている (253)／Ⅱ Giving and receiving verbs (1)：あげる，くれる，もらう (255)
    Ⅲ Construction：〜-たり〜-たりする (258)／Ⅳ Particles：でも，とか，しか (259)
    Ⅴ でしょう(1) (260)／Ⅵ Expressions：〜でいいです and 〜がいいです (261)
    Ⅶ Demonstrative pronouns (3)：あれ，あの，あそこ (262)／Ⅷ Family terms (262)

Notes on Discourse 264
    Ⅰ そうですか (264)／Ⅱ 大変でしょうね (264)

Drill 266
Aural Comprehension 273
Reading Comprehension 年賀状 274
Kanji Practice 276

Appendix
Japanese Conjugation Patterns (1) (280)
Numbers (Numerals + Counters) (Lesson 1〜10) (282)

Vocabulary Index (Lesson 1〜10) 285
Index for Notes on Grammar (Lesson 1〜10) 294
Index for Kanji Strokes (Lesson 1〜10) 298

Pronunciation and Writing System

I Pronunciation

1. Basic sounds (1)

Table 1 shows the basic sounds of the Japanese language. Each box represents one sound in the Japanese syllable system. Unlike alphabets such as that of the English language, Japanese has so-called "syllable based" units as shown in Table 1. These are considered to be the smallest sounds by Japanese speakers. Each box has its own letter as shown later. Except for the second row, each box, numbered from 1 to 44, is actually composed of two sounds (consonant + vowel). The sounds from 1 to 5 are vowels, and are the most important elements of all 44 boxes. Combinations of boxes make up words, phrases, and sentences.

Now, let's listen to the sounds from 1 to 44. What is important is to listen to each sound repeatedly without saying anything for the first step. Refer to Table 1 above.

Table 1 Basic sounds(1)

	a	i	u	e	o
φ	1	2	3	4	5
k	6	7	8	9	10
s	11	12	13	14	15
t	16	17	18	19	20
n	21	22	23	24	25
h	26	27	28	29	30
m	31	32	33	34	35
y	36	×	37	×	38
r	39	40	41	42	43
w	44	×	×	×	×
					45

1) Boxes 1 to 5

Please make sure that box 3 is pronounced with lips unrounded. Consequently, boxes 8, 13, 18, 23, 28, 33, 37, and 41 which contain the same vowel as in box 3 should be pronounced in the same manner.

2) Boxes 6 to 10

3) Boxes 11 to 15

Please note that box 12 is not the same sound as is inferred by the combination of $[s]+[i]$.

4) Boxes 16 to 20

Boxes 17 and 18 are different from the combinations of $[t]+[i]$ and $[t]+[u]$ respectively.

5) 🔊 Boxes 21 to 25
6) 🔊 Boxes 26 to 30

Box 27 is easy to understand if compared with box 12. Box 28 is produced with the lips.

7) 🔊 Boxes 31 to 35
8) 🔊 Boxes 36, 37, and 38
9) 🔊 Boxes 39 to 43

For the sounds in this row, the lower surface of the tongue is used to touch the roof of the front mouth area briefly.

10) 🔊 Box 44

The lips should not be rounded.

The sound of Box 45 is explained later.

2. Basic sounds (2)

Next, let's examine Table 2.

Table 2 shows other basic sounds where [g], [z], and [d] are the voiced counterparts of [k], [s], and [t] of Table 1, respectively. [b] and [p] are also related in a similar manner.

11) 🔊 Boxes 46 to 50
12) 🔊 Boxes 51 to 55

Boxes 52 and 53 should be listened to carefully.

13) 🔊 Boxes 56 to 60

Boxes 57 and 58 are the same sounds as in boxes 52 and 53, respectively.

14) 🔊 Boxes 61 to 65
15) 🔊 Boxes 66 to 70

Table 2 Basic sounds(2)

	a	i	u	e	o
g	46	47	48	49	50
z	51	52	53	54	55
d	56	57	58	59	60
b	61	62	63	64	65
p	66	67	68	69	70

3. Sounds in Tables 3 and 4

Tables 3 and 4 show another type of basic sounds which are called "twisted sounds." Please note that the first component of each row in both Tables 3 and 4, a consonant, is the same sound as the consonant in the third column of the corresponding rows in Tables 1 and 2. For example, the first component sound in boxes 77 to 79 is the same as that in box 17 of Table 1.

16) 🔊 Boxes 71 to 73
17) 🔊 Boxes 74 to 76
18) 🔊 Boxes 77 to 79
19) 🔊 Boxes 80 to 82
20) 🔊 Boxes 83 to 85
21) 🔊 Boxes 86 to 88
22) 🔊 Boxes 89 to 91

Table 3 Twisted sounds(1)

	a	u	o
ky	71	72	73
sy	74	75	76
ty	77	78	79
ny	80	81	82
hy	83	84	85
my	86	87	88
ry	89	90	91

23) 🔊 Boxes 92 to 94
24) 🔊 Boxes 95 to 97
25) 🔊 Boxes 98 to 100
26) 🔊 Boxes 101 to 103

Table 4 Twisted sounds(2)

	a	u	o
gy	92	93	94
zy	95	96	97
by	98	99	100
py	101	102	103

4. Special sounds

There are three types of special sounds, each represented by a special letter.

(a) Box 45 in Table 1 is the first type of special sound and represents a variety of nasal sounds that vary depending on the sounds which follow it. This means that box 45 cannot be pronounced in isolation and does not occur in the initial position of any word. This is also the case for the other two special sounds. Let's examine the various sound qualities of box 45. The number cited corresponds to the box number in each table.

27) 🔊 Ex.1 [19+45+68+39] "a Japanese dish," [54+45+63] "all," [10+45+31] "comma"

　　　Ex.2 [19+45+20] "tent," [20+45+56] "flew," [32+45+21] "everyone"

　　　Ex.3 [19+45+7] "weather," [40+45+50] "apple"

　　　Ex.4 [11+45] "three"

　　　Ex.5 [16+45+2] "unit"

In spite of its variety of sounds, there is only one letter for box 45.

(b) The second type of special sound is the so-called "choked sound." As explained above, this sound does not occur in the initial position of words and the quality differs depending on sounds which follow it. Table 5 shows all the sounds that follow the choked sound. The box number for this sound would be 104. Please note that this sound has two different qualities as mentioned above. Please listen to some of the words containing a choked sound.

28) 🔊 Ex.1 [17+104+15] "nitrogen," [51+104+12] "magazine"

In the words in Ex.1, boxes such as 11, 12, 13, 14, 15, 74, 75, or 76 follow the choked sound 104. On the other hand, the words in Ex.2 contain one of the boxes other than those mentioned above following the choked sound.

29) 🔊 Ex.2 [32+104+6] "three days," [31+104+20] "mat," [10+104+68] "cup," [10+104+17] "this way," [32+104+18] "three," [43+104+101+8] "600"

(c) The last type of special sounds is a long vowel. This sound is a prolongation of each of the vowels listed from 1 to 5 in Table 1.

30) 🔊 Ex.1 [5+61+1+11+45] "old lady"

　　　Ex.2 [22+2+11+45] "elder brother"

Table 5 Boxes following the choked sound

	a	i	u	e	o
k	6	7	8	9	10
s	11	12	13	14	15
t	16	17	18	19	20
p	66	67	68	69	70
ky	71	×	72	×	73
sy	74	×	75	×	76
ty	77	×	78	×	79
py	101	×	102	×	103

Ex.3 [8+3+7] "air"
Ex.4 [4+4+46] "movie"
Ex.5 [65+5+12] "cap"

The writing rules for long vowels will be introduced in a later section. As noted earlier, each of these special sounds cannot be pronounced in isolation and is always pronounced together with a preceding box. This is a very important characteristic which contributes to the specific rhythm of Japanese utterances.

5. Devocalization

Words are produced by combining some boxes as explained above. However, some sounds are modified due to a preceding and a following sound. Please listen to some examples.

31) 🔊 Ex.1 [1+12+16] "tomorrow"
          Ex.2 [19+13+20] "test"

Box 2, which should be contained in box 12, cannot be heard in the above example 1. Similarly, box 3 which is contained in box 8 is not perceived in the second example. This phenomenon is called the devocalization of vowels, and specifically indicates that boxes 7, 8, 12, 13, 17, 18, 27 and 28 lose the vowel quality they contain.

6. Pitch Accent

Another important aspect of the pronunciation of words in Japanese is pitch accent. Japanese pitch patterns vary with dialect. Here we will use the Tokyo dialect to explain pitch.

As mentioned previously, many words contain more than two boxes. As a result, there are relative height differences in pitch between the boxes. Depending on the number of boxes a word contains, specific pitch patterns are produced in the Tokyo dialect. There are three basic patterns for an accent fall. The accent fall refers to the drop of pitch which occurs between two boxes.

The basic three patterns of pitch are as follows :
(a) The accent fall occurs between the first and the second box.
(b) The accent fall is absent.
(c) The accent fall occurs somewhere between the second and the last boxes if a word contains more than three boxes. (note : Some words have an accent fall on the last box. In such cases, the accent fall cannot be detected unless the words are followed by another word, such as a particle.) If a word contains three boxes, the accent fall is automatically between the second and the last box.

Now, first listen to two-box and three-box nonsense words containing the sound from box 31. A real Japanese word follows each of the nonsense words. Please note that two-box words can have only two patterns of (a) or (b), and that three-box words can have one of the three patterns (a), (b), or (c), as explained above.

32) 🔊 two-box words (「 ¬ 」indicates an accent fall.)

(a) $[3\bar{1}+31][\bar{1}+34]$ "rain," (b) $[31+31][1+34]$ "candy"

33) ◀⦁ three-box words
(a) $[3\bar{1}+31+31][3\bar{4}+46+24]$ "glasses"
(b) $[31+31+31][11+6+21]$ "fish"
(c) $[31+3\bar{1}+31][16+3\bar{1}+50]$ "egg"

It is recommended that you listen to the patterns repeatedly in order to produce and distinguish them correctly. These patterns are definitely a basis for naturalness of utterances in Japanese.

II Writing System

1. Basic letters(1)

Table 6 shows the basic letters called HIRAGANA(left) and KATAKANA(right) which correspond to each box in Table 1. KATAKANA letters are especially used to write foreign names such as those of persons, countries, and things, etc. In Table 6, a roman letter writing, called the Hepburn system, is added in the upper part of each box.

There are two rules which should be remembered in using the letters in Table 6.
(a) For box 5 sound, there are two kinds of letters. One is 「お」 as shown in box 5, and the other is 「を」 in box 5′ which is used to indicate a particle.
(b) When 「は」 and 「へ」 are used as particles, their pronunciation should be same as boxes 44 and 4, respectively.

Table 6 Basic HIRAGANA and KATAKANA(1)

	a	i	u	e	o
φ	1 a あ ア	2 i い イ	3 u う ウ	4 e え エ	5 o お オ
k	6 ka か カ	7 ki き キ	8 ku く ク	9 ke け ケ	10 ko こ コ
s	11 sa さ サ	12 shi し シ	13 su す ス	14 se せ セ	15 so そ ソ
t	16 ta た タ	17 chi ち チ	18 tsu つ ツ	19 te て テ	20 to と ト
n	21 na な ナ	22 ni に ニ	23 nu ぬ ヌ	24 ne ね ネ	25 no の ノ
h	26 ha は ハ	27 hi ひ ヒ	28 fu ふ フ	29 he へ ヘ	30 ho ほ ホ
m	31 ma ま マ	32 mi み ミ	33 mu む ム	34 me め メ	35 mo も モ
y	36 ya や ヤ	×	37 yu ゆ ユ	×	38 yo よ ヨ
r	39 ra ら ラ	40 ri り リ	41 ru る ル	42 re れ レ	43 ro ろ ロ
w	44 wa わ ワ	×	×	×	5′ o を ヲ
					45 n ん ン

2. Basic letters (2)

Table 7 shows the letters representing the boxes in Table 2.

The letters 46 to 65, which are voiced counterparts, have " ゛ " on each of the corresponding letters in Table 6. For letters 66 to 70, there is a " ゜ " attatched to the corresponding letters of the same table.

Table 7 Basic HIRAGANA and KATAKANA(2)

	a	i	u	e	o
g	46 ga が ガ	47 gi ぎ ギ	48 gu ぐ グ	49 ge げ ゲ	50 go ご ゴ
z	51 za ざ ザ	52 ji じ ジ	53 zu ず ズ	54 ze ぜ ゼ	55 zo ぞ ゾ
d	56 da だ ダ	57 ji ぢ ヂ	58 zu づ ヅ	59 de で デ	60 do ど ド
b	61 ba ば バ	62 bi び ビ	63 bu ぶ ブ	64 be べ ベ	65 bo ぼ ボ
p	66 pa ぱ パ	67 pi ぴ ピ	68 pu ぷ プ	69 pe ぺ ペ	70 po ぽ ポ

3. Letters for Tables 8 and 9

The letters in Tables 8 and 9 correspond to the boxes in Tables 3 and 4, respectively. For the twisted sounds, the small letters 「や、ゆ、よ」 are attached.

Table 8 Twisted sounds(1)

	a	u	o
ky	71 kya きゃ キャ	72 kyu きゅ キュ	73 kyo きょ キョ
sy	74 sha しゃ シャ	75 shu しゅ シュ	76 sho しょ ショ
ty	77 cha ちゃ チャ	78 chu ちゅ チュ	79 cho ちょ チョ
ny	80 nya にゃ ニャ	81 nyu にゅ ニュ	82 nyo にょ ニョ
hy	83 hya ひゃ ヒャ	84 hyu ひゅ ヒュ	85 hyo ひょ ヒョ
my	86 mya みゃ ミャ	87 myu みゅ ミュ	88 myo みょ ミョ
ry	89 rya りゃ リャ	90 ryu りゅ リュ	91 ryo りょ リョ

Table 9 Twisted sounds(2)

	a	u	o
gy	92 gya ぎゃ ギャ	93 gyu ぎゅ ギュ	94 gyo ぎょ ギョ
zy	95 ja じゃ ジャ	96 ju じゅ ジュ	97 jo じょ ジョ
by	98 bya びゃ ビャ	99 byu びゅ ビュ	100 byo びょ ビョ
py	101 pya ぴゃ ピャ	102 pyu ぴゅ ピュ	103 pyo ぴょ ピョ

4. The letters for the special sounds

The three types of special sounds have their own letters.

(a) Box 45 in Table 1 is the first type of special sound which represents a wide variety of nasal sounds depending on the sound which follows it. However, there is only letter to represent all of those sounds : it is 「ん」 in HIRAGANA writing.

Let's show some of the examples explained in ◀◉ 27) using the HIRAGANA and KATA-KANA writing system.

27) ◀◉ Ex.1 [19+45+68+39] "a Japanese dish" てんぷら (tenpura)
    Ex.2 [19+45+20] "tent" テント (tento)
    Ex.3 [19+45+7] "weather" てんき (tenki)
    Ex.4 [11+45] "three" さん (san)
    Ex.5 [16+45+2] "unit" たんい (tan'i)

(b) The second type of special sound is the so-called "choked sound." There is also only one letter for this sound, that is, a small 「っ」. Let's see some of examples in HIRAGANA.

28) ◀◉ Ex.1 [17+104+15] "nitrogen" ちっそ (chisso)
29) ◀◉ Ex.2 [32+104+6] "three days" みっか (mikka)

(c) The last type of special sound is a long vowel. The rules for changing this sound into HIRAGANA are a bit more complicated than for the other two special sounds.

Let's look again at the examples cited previously.

30) ◀◉ Ex.1 [5+61+1+11+45] "old lady" おばあさん (obaasan)
    Ex.2 [22+2+11+45] "elder brother" にいさん (niisan)
    Ex.3 [8+3+7] "air" くうき (kuuki)
    Ex.4 [4+4+46] "movie" えいが (eega)
    Ex.5 [65+5+12] "cap" ぼうし (booshi)

Please note that example 1 has the letter 「あ」 as a long vowel since the vowel contained in the preceding box is the [a]-sound of 「ば」. The same rule is applied to examples 2 and 3. In other words, if the preceding box contains an [i]-sound or [u]-sound, then the corresponding letter for vowel lengthening should be 「い」 or 「う」 respectively.

On the other hand, if a preceding box contains an [e] or [o]-sound, then the letter for a long vowel is also 「い」 or 「う」, respectively. There are, however, some exceptions to these cases. That is, if a preceding box has an [e]-sound, there are a few words where the letter 「え」 is used as in the following example.

Ex.4′ [5+24+4+11+45] "elder sister" おねえさん (oneesan)

The same exception exists for some words in which the preceding box has the [o]-sound. In such words, the letter 「お」 is used.

Ex.5′ [10+5+40] "ice" こおり (koori)

In KATAKANA orthography, long vowels are transcribed by the symbol 「ー」 as in the example below.

Ex.6 [10+5+20] "coat" コート (kooto)

Lesson 1

Dialogue 大学(だいがく)で

1-1 On the way to class

Alice meets Lwin on the way to the classroom.
They are talking about preparation for today's class.

アリス： おはようございます。
ルイン： あ、アリスさん、おはようございます。
アリス： きのう教科書(きょうかしょ)を読(よ)みましたか。
ルイン： はい、読(よ)みました。
アリス： テープ(てぃぷ)は聞(き)きましたか。
ルイン： いいえ、聞(き)きませんでした。

1-2 At lunch time

ルイン　　：　アリスさん。
アリス　　：　はい。
ルイン　　：　食堂へ行きますか。
アリス　　：　ええ。
ルイン　　：　カーリンさんは。
カーリン　：　わたしは行きません。

1-3 In the Co-op cafeteria

At the counter Lwin orders food and waits for it.

ルイン　　　：　魚フライ定食、お願いします。
食堂の人　　：　はい。
　　　　　　　（Handing the food to Lwin）
　　　　　　　はい、どうぞ。

◇　　　　◇　　　　◇

レジの人　　：　390円いただきます。
ルイン　　　：　はい。
レジの人　　：　ありがとうございました。

1-4　In the classroom

カーリン：　ルインさん、何を食べましたか。
ルイン　：　魚フライ定食とサラダを食べました。
カーリン：　アリスさんは。
アリス　：　わたしも魚フライ定食を食べました。
カーリン：　あ、そうですか。サラダも食べましたか。
アリス　：　いいえ、サラダは食べませんでした。

Vocabulary List

⟨ ⟩: dictionary form
┐: accent fall (for words only)

Dialogue

1-1

だいがく	大学	university
で		[Group 1 particle for action place]
あ┐りす	アリス	Alice [personal name]
おはようございます。		Good morning.
あ		Oh
る┐いん	ルイン	Lwin [personal name]
〜さん		Mr., Ms.
きのう		yesterday
きょうか┐しょ	教科書	textbook
を		[Group 1 particle for direct object]
よみま┐す⟨よ┐む⟩（〜が〜を）	読みます⟨読む⟩	to read
か		[Group 3 particle for question sentences]
はい。		Yes.
て┐いぷ	テープ	tape
は		[Group 2 particle for topic]
ききま┐す⟨きく⟩（〜が〜を）	聞きます⟨聞く⟩	to listen
いいえ。		No.

1-2

しょくどう	食堂	cafeteria
へ		to [Group 1 particle for direction]
いきま┐す⟨いく⟩（〜が〜へ）	行きます⟨行く⟩	to go
ええ。		Yes.
か┐あрин	カーリン	Karin [personal name]
わたし		I

1-3

さかなふらいて┐いしょく	魚フライ定食	fried fish set meal
おねがいします。	お願いします。	Please.

しょくどうのひと	食堂の人	staff of cafeteria
はい、どうぞ。		Here it is.
どうぞ		please
れじ	レジ	cashier
れじのひと	レジの人	staff at cash register
さんびゃくきゅうじゅう	390	390
えん	円	yen
いただきます。		Please. [Lit. I would like to receive....]
ありがとうございました。		Thank you very much.

1-4

なに	何	what
たべます （～が～を）〈たべる〉	食べます 〈食べる〉	to eat
と		and [Group 1 particle]
さらだ	サラダ	salad
も		too [Group 2 particle]
そうですか。		I see.

Drill

が		[Group 1 particle for indicating actor]
ほん	本	book
かんじ	漢字	Chinese character
しんぶん	新聞	newspaper
ざっし	雑誌	magazine
にほんご	日本語	Japanese language
べんきょうします（～が～を）〈べんきょうする〉	勉強します 〈勉強する〉	to study
ひらがな		"hiragana"
かたかな		"katakana"
ぶんぽう	文法	grammar
らじお	ラジオ	radio
しいでぃい	CD	compact disc
おんがく	音楽	music
さんどいっち	サンドイッチ	sandwich
かれいらいす	カレーライス	curry
けんきゅうしつ	研究室	professor's office, laboratory

としょかん	図書館	library
りゅうがくせいかいかん	留学生会館	International Students' House
どこ		where
あした		tomorrow
きょう		today
だれ		who
ばんばん	バンバン	[personal name]
なろん	ナロン	[personal name]
します〈する〉　(〜が〜を)		to do
ごはん		meal, rice
てれび	テレビ	television
みます〈みる〉　(〜が〜を)	見ます〈見る〉	to see, to watch
こうひい	コーヒー	coffee
のみます〈のむ〉 (〜が〜を)	飲みます〈飲む〉	to drink
かいかん	会館	(International Students') House

Notes on Grammar

I Verbal sentences

There are three types of simple sentences in Japanese: a verbal sentence (Lesson 1), a noun sentence (Lesson 2), and an adjective sentence (Lesson 3). In this lesson verbal sentences will be introduced.

The following are examples of typical Japanese verbal sentences.

Examples
1. アリスさんが 行きます。(Arisu san ga ikimasu.)
   Alice will go.
2. アリスさんが 来ます。(Arisu san ga kimasu.)
   Alice will come.
3. ルインさんが 本を 読みます。(Ruin san ga hon o yomimasu.)
   Lwin reads a book.
4. アリスさんが テープを 聞きます。
   (Arisu san ga teepu o kikimasu.)
   Alice is going to listen to the tape.
5. ルインさんが アリスさんを 先生に しょうかいします。
   (Ruin san ga Arisu san o sensee ni shookai shimasu.)
   Lwin introduces Alice to a teacher.

From the five examples above, you may draw some conclusions. They are:
(1) All these sentences end with a word ending in -ます(masu).
(2) All of words ending with -ます(masu) are verbs. (See this Lesson, Notes on Grammar II.) All the sentences above end in a verb.
(3) All verbs are preceded by at least two words (Examples 1 and 2), アリスさん (Arisu san) "Alice," and が(ga). アリスさん(Arisu san) is a noun and が(ga) is a particle. As you can see, nouns are followed by a particle. This applies to 本を(hon o) in Example 3, テープを(teepu o) in Example 4, アリスさんを(Arisu san o) and 先生に(sensee ni) in Example 5. These units will be called a noun phrase in this textbook.
(4) Japanese verbal sentences consist of one or more noun phrases+a verb in this

order. The number of noun phrases is determined by the meaning of the verb.

(5) Particles are those small words which never change their form and are used with a noun which precedes them. For further details, see this Lesson, Notes on Grammar VI.

(6) For many learners of Japanese, the selection of a particle is confusing. However, as is shown in the above examples, が (ga) is added to a noun which indicates the person who does something, を (o) is added to a noun which indicates the thing which an actor does and に (ni) is added to a noun which indicates the person who is the recipient of the action. This knowledge will help you select an appropriate particle. But this does not apply to the following case.

アリスさんが　ルインさんに　会います。

(Arisu san ga Ruin san ni aimasu.)

Alice will meet Lwin.

会います (aimasu) is a verb which takes が (ga) and に (ni), although some learners may expect を (o) instead of に (ni). It is advisable to memorize verbs with their appropriate particles. In the vocabulary lists in this textbook, each verb is shown with particles, as shown here.

Japanese verb	(particles)	English equivalent
食べます (tabemasu)	(〜が〜を) (〜 ga〜 o)	to eat
会います (aimasu)	(〜が〜に) (〜 ga〜 ni)	to meet

II Verbs

A Classification of verbs

Verbs are classified into three types. All verbs are shown in their dictionary form which is cited in a language dictionary.

1. **Group 1 verbs, or verbs ending in -eru or -iru**

   食べる (taberu)　　ねる (neru)　　見る (miru)　　起きる (okiru)
   to eat　　　　　　to sleep　　　　to see　　　　to get up

2. **Group 2 verbs, or verbs ending in -u**

   読む (yomu)　　聞く (kiku)　　行く (iku)　　買う (kau)
   to read　　　　to listen to　　to go　　　　to buy

3. Irregular verbs

来る(kuru)　　　する(suru)
to come　　　　to do

B Polite form of verbs

The verbal form ending with -ます(masu) is called the polite form(-ます form). It is used between persons who are not close friends. It shows deference, respect, etc. Learners are expected to use this form when they talk to superiors. The polite form is obtained from the dictionary form of a verb in the following way.

1. Formation rule of the -ます(masu) form

(1) Group 1 verbs, or verbs ending in **-eru** or **-iru**

　　Drop -る(ru) and add -ます(masu).

† Table of the polite form of Group 1 verbs †

Dictionary form	Polite form	English equivalent
たべる (taberu)	たべます(tabemasu)	to eat
ねる (neru)	ねます(nemasu)	to go to bed
みる (miru)	みます(mimasu)	to see, look at
おきる (okiru)	おきます(okimasu)	to get up

(There are some exceptions such as かえる(kaeru) "return," which is a Group 2 verb.)

(2) Group 2 verbs, or verbs ending in **-u**

　　Change **-u** to **-i** and add -ます(masu).

† Table of the polite form of Group 2 verbs †

Dictionary form	Polite form	English equivalent
よむ(yomu)	よみます(yomimasu)	to read
きく(kiku)	ききます(kikimasu)	to listen, hear
いく(iku)	いきます(ikimasu)	to go
かう(kau)	かいます(kaimasu)	to buy

(3) Irregular verbs

† Table of the polite form of Irregular verbs †

Dictionary form	Polite form	English equivalent
くる (kuru)	きます (kimasu)	to come
する (suru)	します (shimasu)	to do

2. Conjugation of the -ます(masu) form

Verbs ending in -ます(masu) are used to describe a habitual action or an action in the future. For the negative form of verbs ending in -ます(masu), change -ます(masu) to -ません(masen). What has already happened can be described by verbs ending in -ました(mashita) instead of -ます(masu). For the negative form of verbs ending in -ました(mashita), drop -ました(mashita) and add -ませんでした(masen deshita).

† Table of the polite form of verbs †

-ます (masu)	-ません (masen)	-ました (mashita)	-ませんでした (masen deshita)
たべます to eat (tabemasu)	たべません (tabemasen)	たべました (tabemashita)	たべませんでした (tabemasen deshita)
みます to see (mimasu)	みません (mimasen)	みました (mimashita)	みませんでした (mimasen deshita)
よみます to read (yomimasu)	よみません (yomimasen)	よみました (yomimashita)	よみませんでした (yomimasen deshita)
ききます to listen (kikimasu)	ききません (kikimasen)	ききました (kikimashita)	ききませんでした (kikimasen deshita)
きます to come (kimasu)	きません (kimasen)	きました (kimashita)	きませんでした (kimasen deshita)
します to do (shimasu)	しません (shimasen)	しました (shimashita)	しませんでした (shimasen deshita)

Examples

1. ルインさんが食堂へ行きません。
   (Ruin san ga shokudoo e ikimasen.)
   Lwin won't/doesn't go to the cafeteria.

2. ルインさんがテープを聞きました。
   (Ruin san ga teepu o kikimashita.)
   Lwin listened to the tape.

3. アリスさんが日本語を勉強しませんでした。
   (Arisu san ga Nihongo o benkyoo shimasen deshita.)
   Alice didn't study Japanese.

Since verbs ending in -ました(mashita) or -ませんでした(masen deshita) describe a completed action, this form of verb will be called the perfective form of verbs in this textbook. On the other hand, verbs ending in -ます(masu) or -ません(masen) will be called the imperfective form of verbs in this textbook, because they describe an action not completed.

† Table of the conjugation of the polite form of verbs †

	Affirmative form	Negative form
Imperfective form	Verb-ます(masu)	Verb-ません(masen)
Perfective form	Verb-ました(mashita)	Verb-ませんでした(masen deshita)

III Particles : へ(e), で(de), と(to)

A へ(e)

へ(e) indicates the direction towards which an actor moves. へ(e) is used with verbs like 行きます(ikimasu) "to go," 来ます(kimasu) "to come," 帰ります(kaerimasu) "to return," etc.

Examples
1. ルインさんが食堂へ行きます。(Ruin san ga shokudoo e ikimasu.)
   Lwin goes to the cafeteria.
2. アリスさんが留学生会館へ帰りました。
   (Arisu san ga ryuugakuseekaikan e kaerimashita.)
   Alice went back to the International Students' House.
3. きのう大学へ来ました。(Kinoo daigaku e kimashita.)
   Someone* came to the university yesterday.

(*"Someone" may be the speaker.)

B で(de)

で(de) indicates the place where an action takes place.

Examples
1. 食堂で食べました。(Shokudoo de tabemashita.)
   Someone ate at the cafeteria.
2. 教室でテープを聞きました。(Kyooshitsu de teepu o kikimashita.)
   (教室：classroom)
   Someone* listened to the tape in the classroom.

(*"Someone" may be the speaker.)

C と(to)

と(to), different from が(ga), を(o), に(ni), へ(e) and で(de), connects two nouns, meaning "and."

Examples
1. ルインさんとアリスさん (Ruin san to Arisu san)
   Lwin and Alice
2. ルインさんとアリスさんが来ました。
   (Ruin san to Arisu san ga kimashita.)
   Lwin and Alice came.
3. 本と新聞 (hon to shinbun)
   a book and a newspaper
4. 本と新聞を読みました。(Hon to shinbun o yomimashita.)
   Someone* read a book and a newspaper.

(*"Someone" may be the speaker.)

IV Question sentences

A Yes - No questions

Examples
1. a. テープを聞きます。(Teepu o kikimasu.)
      Someone* is going to listen to the tape.
   b. テープを聞きますか。(Teepu o kikimasu ka.)
      Is someone* going to listen to the tape?
2. a. 新聞を読みました。(Shinbun o yomimashita.)
      Someone* read a newspaper.
   b. 新聞を読みましたか。(Shinbun o yomimashita ka.)
      Did someone* read a newspaper?

(*"Someone" may be the speaker in a., and the listener in b..)

In order to make a Yes-No question, the particle か(ka) is added to the end of a sentence, and is pronounced with a rising intonation.

Examples
1. 食堂へ行きましたか。(Shokudoo e ikimashita ka.)
   Did someone* go to the cafeteria?

2. あした大学へ行きますか。(Ashita daigaku e ikimasu ka.)
Is someone* going to the university tomorrow?

(*"Someone" may be the listener.)

In answering a Yes-No question positively, we say はい(hai) or ええ(ee) first and repeat the predicate. はい(hai) sounds more polite than ええ(ee). In answering a Yes-No question negatively, we say いいえ(iie) first and negate the predicate.

Examples

1. A：食堂へ行きますか。(Shokudoo e ikimasu ka.)
   Will you go to the cafeteria?
   B：はい、行きます。(Hai, ikimasu.)
   Yes, I will.
2. A：食堂へ行きますか。(Shokudoo e ikimasu ka.)
   Will you go to the cafeteria?
   B：いいえ、行きません。(Iie, ikimasen.)
   No, I won't.
3. A：きのうテープを聞きましたか。

   (Kinoo teepu o kikimashita ka.)
   Did you listen to the tape yesterday?
   B：はい、聞きました。(Hai, kikimashita.)
   Yes, I did.

B Questions with question words

Examples

a. アリスさんが新聞を読みました。

(Arisu san ga shinbun o yomimashita.)

Alice read a newspaper.

b. アリスさんが何を読みましたか。

(Arisu san ga nani o yomimashita ka.)

What did Alice read?

c. だれが新聞を読みましたか。(Dare ga shinbun o yomimashita ka.)
Who read a newspaper?

In order to make a question with question words: replace the noun which you want to know with an appropriate question word, and add か(ka) to the end of a sentence and pronounce it with a rising intonation.

The question word だれ(dare) means "who." 何(nani) means "what." どこ(doko) means "where." These question words are usually followed by Group 1 particles. (For the explanation of Group 1 particles, see this Lesson, Notes on Grammar VI.)

Examples
1. だれがテープを聞きましたか。(Dare ga teepu o kikimashita ka.)
   Who listened to the tape?
2. アリスさんをだれにしょうかいしましたか。
   (Arisu san o dare ni shookai shimashita ka.)
   Who did you introduce Alice to?

In answering a question with a question word, we say the required information first and repeat the predicate.

Examples
1. A：だれがテープを聞きましたか。
   (Dare ga teepu o kikimashita ka.)
   Who listened to the tape?
   B：アリスさんが聞きました。(Arisu san ga kikimashita.)
   Alice did.
2. A：何を食べましたか。(Nani o tabemashita ka.)
   What did you eat?
   B：サラダを食べました。(Sarada o tabemashita.)
   I ate salad.

V Particles：は(wa) and も(mo)

A は(wa)

は(wa) indicates the topic (or something to be talked about) of a sentence and means "as for."

Examples
1. 魚を食べました。(Sakana o tabemashita.)
   Someone* ate fish.
2. 魚が食べました。(Sakana ga tabemashita.)
   A fish ate something.
3. 魚は食べました。(Sakana wa tabemashita.)
   As for fish, someone* ate it./As for fish, it ate something.
   (*"Someone" may be the speaker.)

In the above examples, the same noun 魚 (sakana) "fish" and the same verb 食べました (tabemashita) "ate" are used in different sentences. The difference is the particle used in each sentence. 魚 (sakana) in Example 1 is the object of the action of eating because the particle used with it is を (o), the object-indicating particle. 魚 (sakana) in Example 2 is something which does the action of eating because of the particle が (ga), the actor-indicating particle. However, Example 3 cannot be interpreted in one specific way because the particle は (wa) does not give any information about the grammatical case. The two interpretations above are possible because 魚 (sakana) means either an animal which eats, or food which is to be eaten. The basic function of a は (wa)-phrase is to present the topic of a sentence or a conversation, and the rest of the sentence (or a series of sentences) give comments about the topic. The number of comments given about one topic cannot be limited. You can give as many comments as you like.

(Topic)	(Comment)
ルインさんは (Ruin san wa)	食堂へ行きました。(shokudoo e ikimashita.)
As for Lwin	went to the cafeteria.
	サラダを食べました。(sarada o tabemashita.)
	ate salad.
	アリスさんに会いました。(Arisu san ni aimashita.)
	met Alice.

Repeating the topic is usually unnecessary because both the speaker and the hearer know what they are talking about.

は (wa) is also used to show a contrast between two things, two actions, two events, etc.

Examples

1. A：きのうテープを聞きましたか。
    (Kinoo teepu o kikimashita ka.)
    Did you listen to the tape yesterday?
   B：いいえ。きょうは聞きます。(Iie. Kyoo wa kikimasu.)
    No. I'll do it today.
2. A：漢字を勉強しましたか。(Kanji o benkyoo shimashita ka.)
    Did you study kanji?
   B：いいえ。ひらがなは勉強しました。
    (Iie. Hiragana wa benkyoo shimashita.)
    No. I studied hiragana.

B も(mo)

も (mo) also indicates the topic and means "too" or "also" in a positive sentence and "either" in a negative sentence. も (mo), like は (wa), does not indicate any grammatical case.

Examples
1. ルインさんも食べました。(Ruin san mo tabemashita.)
   Lwin also ate something.
2. サラダも食べました。(Sarada mo tabemashita.)
   Someone* ate salad also.
3. ルインさんもサラダを食べました。
   　　　　　　　　　　　　　(Ruin san mo sarada o tabemashita.)
   Lwin also ate salad.
4. 本はカーリンさんが読みました。新聞もカーリンさんが読みました。
   (Hon wa Kaarin san ga yomimashita. Shinbun mo Kaarin san ga yomimashita.)
   As for the book, Karin read it. Karin read the newspaper also.
5. きのう行きました。きょうも行きます。
   　　　　　　　　　　　(Kinoo ikimashita. Kyoo mo ikimasu.)
   I went yesterday. I'll go today, too.

　　　　　　　　　　　　　　　　　(*"Someone" may be the speaker.)

VI Classification of particles

In this lesson you have learned three types of particles. が(ga), を(o), へ(e), に(ni), etc. will be called Group 1 particles in this textbook. These particles show a grammatical case, or a relationship between a noun and a verb in a sentence or a relationship between two nouns. は(wa), も(mo), etc. will be called Group 2 particles in this textbook, and the most fundamental function of these particles is to indicate the topic of a sentence. か(ka) and those which come at the end of a sentence will be called Group 3 particles in this textbook. They change a sentence into a question, or make a sentence more emphatic, etc. There are two more Groups of particles (Group 4 particles and Group 5 particles). They will be introduced later.

When Group 1 particles are used together with Group 2 particles, Group 1 particles come first and Group 2 particles follow them. However, there are no combinations such as が+は(ga+wa), が+も(ga+mo), or を+は(o+wa). Only は(wa) or も(mo) are used instead. 魚は食べました (Sakana wa tabemashita) is ambiguous because は (wa) can substitute for が (ga) or を (o).

Examples

1. 魚はだれが食べましたか。(Sakana wa dare ga tabemashita ka.)
   Who ate fish?
2. 食堂へはだれが行きましたか。
   (Shokudoo e wa dare ga ikimashita ka.)
   Who went to the cafeteria?
3. カーリンさんにも会いましたか。(Kaarin san ni mo aimashita ka.)
   Did you also meet Karin?

VII Time expressions: きのう (kinoo), きょう (kyoo), あした (ashita)

Time expressions are nouns which indicate time, such as きのう (kinoo) "yesterday," きょう (kyoo) "today" and あした (ashita) "tomorrow." They always precede the verb of a sentence.

Examples

1. 先生はきょう東京へ行きます。
   (Sensee wa kyoo Tookyoo e ikimasu.)
   Our teacher is going to Tokyo today.
2. あしたアリスさんは日本語を勉強します。
   (Ashita Arisu san wa Nihongo o benkyoo shimasu.)
   Alice will study Japanese tomorrow.
3. ルインさんはきのうテープを聞きました。
   (Ruin san wa kinoo teepu o kikimashita.)
   Lwin listened to the tape yesterday.

VIII Omission of some noun phrases in a sentence

Japanese people frequently omit those noun phrases which the speaker thinks the hearer knows or can understand from the context or the situation.

Example

A: 食堂へ行きますか。(Shokudoo e ikimasu ka.)
   Are you going to the cafeteria?
B: ええ、行きます。(Ee, ikimasu.)
   Yes, I am.

A：カーリンさんは。(Kaarin san wa.)
How about Karin?
B：行きません。(Ikimasen.)
No, she will not go.

In the example above, neither the first sentence nor the second sentence contains an actor who goes to the cafeteria. However, speaker A and speaker B know that the actor of the first sentence is あなた (anata) "you" and that of the second sentence is わたし (watashi) "I," because it is quite probable that the speaker is asking about the hearer. In such a situation it is preferable to omit あなた (anata) and わたし (watashi). Frequent use of あなた (anata) makes speech unnatural. Even when "you" (あなた: anata) must be used, あなた (anata) is avoided by Japanese native speakers, and instead of あなた (anata), the name of the person addressed is used. This applies to any subjects which can be understood from the context.

Examples
1. Karin：きのう大学へ来ましたか。(Kinoo daigaku e kimashita ka.)
   Did you come to the university yesterday?
   Lwin：いいえ、来ませんでした。(Iie, kimasen deshita.)
   No, I didn't.
2. Karin：ルインさんは東京へ行きましたか。
   (Ruin san wa Tookyoo e ikimashita ka.)
   Lwin, did you go to Tokyo?
   Lwin：いいえ、行きませんでした。カーリンさんは。
   (Iie, ikimasen deshita. Kaarin san wa.)
   No, I didn't. How about you, Karin?
   Karin：わたしも行きませんでした。
   (Watashi mo ikimasen deshita.)
   I didn't go either.

IX Numerals and some numbers (1)

Japanese numbers consist of a numeral and a counter in this order.
There are two types of numerals in Japanese; Type A numerals (Chinese origin) and Type B numerals (Japanese origin). In this lesson Type A numerals are introduced. For an explanation of Type B numerals, refer to Lesson 4, Notes on Grammar Ⅶ.
A counter is a suffix following a numeral. $1.00 is pronounced as one dollar in

English. "One dollar" is translated into Japanese as 1 ドル (ichidoru). Here, 1 (ichi) is a numeral meaning "one," and ドル (doru) is a counter meaning "dollar." This is the same as ¥1, which is pronounced as 1 円 (ichien). There are a lot of counters in Japanese. The counter to be used depends on the quality of what is counted. Learners are expected to memorize counters one by one.

A Numeral of Type A

0	れい (ree)		10	じゅう (juu)
	ぜろ (zero)			
1	いち (ichi)		11	じゅういち (juuichi)
2	に (ni)		12	じゅうに (juuni)
3	さん (san)		13	じゅうさん (juusan)
4	し (shi)		14	じゅうし (juushi)
	よん (yon)			じゅうよん (juuyon)
5	ご (go)		15	じゅうご (juugo)
6	ろく (roku)		16	じゅうろく (juuroku)
7	しち (shichi)		17	じゅうしち (juushichi)
	なな (nana)			じゅうなな (juunana)
8	はち (hachi)		18	じゅうはち (juuhachi)
9	きゅう (kyuu)		19	じゅうきゅう (juukyuu)
	く (ku)			じゅうく (juuku)
10	じゅう (juu)		100	ひゃく (hyaku)
20	にじゅう (nijuu)		200	にひゃく (nihyaku)
30	さんじゅう (sanjuu)		300	さん**びゃく** (sanbyaku)
40	よんじゅう (yonjuu)		400	よんひゃく (yonhyaku)
50	ごじゅう (gojuu)		500	ごひゃく (gohyaku)
60	ろくじゅう (rokujuu)		600	**ろっぴゃく** (roppyaku)
70	ななじゅう (nanajuu)		700	ななひゃく (nanahyaku)
80	はちじゅう (hachijuu)		800	**はっぴゃく** (happyaku)
90	きゅうじゅう (kyuujyuu)		900	きゅうひゃく (kyuuhyaku)
1000	せん (sen)		10000	いちまん (ichiman)
2000	にせん (nisen)		20000	にまん (niman)
3000	さん**ぜん** (sanzen)		30000	さんまん (sanman)
4000	よんせん (yonsen)		40000	よんまん (yonman)
5000	ごせん (gosen)		50000	ごまん (goman)

6000	ろくせん(rokusen)		60000	ろくまん(rokuman)
7000	ななせん(nanasen)		70000	ななまん(nanaman)
8000	はっせん(hassen)		80000	はちまん(hachiman)
9000	きゅうせん(kyuusen)		90000	きゅうまん(kyuuman)

- -

100000　じゅうまん(juuman)　　　1000000　ひゃくまん(hyakuman)

question word：いくつ(ikutsu)

Examples
- 21　にじゅういち(nijuuichi)
- 101　ひゃくいち(hyakuichi)
- 144　ひゃくよんじゅうよん(hyakuyonjuuyon)
- 1528　せんごひゃくにじゅうはち(sengohyakunijuuhachi)
- 65300　ろくまんごせんさんびゃく(rokumangosensanbyaku)
- 974000　きゅうじゅうななまんよんせん(kyuujuunanamanyonsen)

B Some numbers

1. Japanese currency Yen：～円(en)

- 1円　いちえん(ichien)
- 2円　にえん(nien)
- 3円　さんえん(sanen)
- 4円　よえん(yoen)
- 5円　ごえん(goen)
- 6円　ろくえん(rokuen)
- 7円　ななえん(nanaen)
- 8円　はちえん(hachien)
- 9円　きゅうえん(kyuuen)
- 10円　じゅうえん(juuen)

question word：いくら(ikura)/何円　なんえん(nan'en)

Examples
- 50円　ごじゅうえん(gojuuen)
- 600円　ろっぴゃくえん(roppyakuen)
- 8370円　はっせんさんびゃくななじゅうえん(hassensanbyakunanajuuen)
- 10429円　いちまんよんひゃくにじゅうきゅうえん
  　　　　　(ichimanyonhyakunijuukyuuen)

Notes on Grammer 21

2. Hours of day : 〜時(ji) "o'clock"

1時	いちじ	(ichiji)
2時	にじ	(niji)
3時	さんじ	(sanji)
4時	**よじ**	(yoji)
5時	ごじ	(goji)
6時	ろくじ	(rokuji)
7時	**しちじ**	(shichiji)
8時	はちじ	(hachiji)
9時	**くじ**	(kuji)
10時	じゅうじ	(juuji)
11時	じゅういちじ	(juuichiji)
12時	じゅうにじ	(juuniji)

question word：何時　なんじ(nanji)

3. Minutes : 〜分(fun)

1分	**いっぷん**	(ippun)
2分	にふん	(nifun)
3分	さん**ぷ**ん	(sanpun)
4分	よん**ぷ**ん	(yonpun)
5分	ごふん	(gofun)
6分	**ろっぷん**	(roppun)
7分	ななふん	(nanafun)
8分	**はっぷん**	(happun)
	はちふん	(hachifun)
9分	きゅうふん	(kyuufun)
10分	**じっぷん**	(jippun)
	(じゅっぷん	(juppun))
20分	に**じっぷ**ん	(nijippun)
	(に**じゅっぷ**ん	(nijuppun))
30分	さん**じっぷ**ん	(sanjippun)
	(さん**じゅっぷ**ん	(sanjuppun))
	はん	(han)
40分	よん**じっぷ**ん	(yonjippun)
	(よん**じゅっぷ**ん	(yonjuppun))
50分	ご**じっぷ**ん	(gojippun)
	(ご**じゅっぷ**ん	(gojuppun))

question word：何分　なんぷん(nanpun)

Examples

1：00	1時	いちじ(ichiji)
2：03	2時3分	にじさんぷん(niji sanpun)
4：30	4時30分	よじさんじっぷん/よじはん(yoji sanjippun/ yojihan)
9：56	9時56分	くじごじゅうろっぷん(kuji gojuuroppun)

For further information on Japanese numbers, refer to Appendix "Numbers"of this book.

Notes on Discourse

I はい (Hai)

はい (hai) means "yes" as you see in Dialogue 1-1. はい (hai) has some other usages such as you can see in A and B.

A Response

はい (hai) is used to respond to calling a name.

  A：ルインさん。(Ruin san.)
   Lwin.
  B：はい。(Hai.)
   Yes. / Here. / Present.

B "Here you are."

はい (hai) is also used when handing over something as you see in Dialogue 1-3.

  A：200円いただきます。(Nihyakuen itadakimasu.)
   Two hundred yen, please.
  B：はい。(Hai.)
   Here you are.

II そうですか (Soo desu ka) ↘

そうですか (soo desu ka) is a reaction by the listener to indicate that new information conveyed by the speaker has been received. Though the sentence ends in か which is the particle for question sentences, here it is not a question sentence. It means "I see." It is pronounced with a falling intonation.

  A：だれが行きますか。(Dare ga ikimasu ka.)
   Who will go?
  B：ルインさんが行きます。(Ruin san ga ikimasu.)

Lwin will go.
A：そうですか。(Soo desu ka.)
　　I see.

Drill

練習1　Nが／は　Nを　　　Vます　　(imperfective affirmative form)
　　　　Nが／は　placeへ　行きます　(imperfective affirmative form)

〈STRUCTURE〉

a.

例)（example）
　　アリスさんは　本を　読みます。

1. 漢字
2. 新聞
3. 雑誌

b.

例) ルインさんは　日本語を　勉強します。

1. ひらがな
2. かたかな
3. 文法

c.

例) ルインさんは　テープを　聞きます。

1. ラジオ
2. CD
3. 音楽

d.

例) アリスさんは　サラダを　食べます。

1. 魚フライ定食
2. サンドイッチ
3. カレーライス

e.

例) ルインさんは　食堂へ　行きます。

1. 研究室(けんきゅうしつ)
2. 図書館(としょかん)
3. 留学生会館(りゅうがくせいかいかん)

練習2　　Vません　　（imperfective negative form）

〈STRUCTURE〉

例1）アリスさんは　本(ほん)を　　　　読(よ)みません。
例2）アリスさんは　食堂(しょくどう)へ　行(い)きません。

1. 日本語(にほんご)　　勉強(べんきょう)します
2. テープ　　　　　　聞(き)きます
3. サラダ　　　　　　食(た)べます
4. 新聞(しんぶん)　　読(よ)みます
5. 図書館(としょかん)　行(い)きます
6. 文法(ぶんぽう)　　勉強(べんきょう)します
7. ラジオ　　　　　　聞(き)きます
8. 魚(さかな)フライ定食(ていしょく)　食(た)べます

練習3　　Nは　Nを／へ　Vますか　（yes-no question）
　　　　　　はい、Vます／いいえ、Vません

〈STRUCTURE〉

例1）A：アリスさんは　サラダを　食(た)べますか。
　　　B：はい、食(た)べます。
例2）A：アリスさんは　サラダを　食(た)べますか。
　　　B：いいえ、食(た)べません。

1. ラジオ　　　　聞(き)きます
2. 図書館(としょかん)　行(い)きます
3. かたかな　　　勉強(べんきょう)します
4. 雑誌(ざっし)　読(よ)みます
5. CD　　　　　　聞(き)きます
6. 研究室(けんきゅうしつ)　行(い)きます

| 練習 4 | Question word（1） 何/どこ   (question with a question word)

〈STRUCTURE〉

a. 何

例) A：アリスさんは　何を　食べますか。
　　 B：サラダを　食べます。

1. 聞きます　　　CD
2. 読みます　　　新聞
3. 食べます　　　サンドイッチ
4. 勉強します　　ひらがなと漢字

b. どこ

例) A：アリスさんは　どこへ　行きますか。
　　 B：食堂へ　行きます。

1. 留学生会館
2. 図書館
3. 研究室

| 練習 5 |　　きのう　Vました　　　(perfective affirmative form)

〈STRUCTURE〉

例) ルインさんは　きのう　本を　　　読みました。

1. 　　　　　　　　文法　　　　　勉強します
2. 　　　　　　　　CD　　　　　　聞きます
3. 　　　　　　　　カレーライス　食べます
4. 　　　　　　　　図書館　　　　行きます
5. 　　　　　　　　新聞　　　　　読みます
6. 　　　　　　　　研究室　　　　行きます

| 練習 6 |　　きのう　Vませんでした　　(perfective negative form)

〈STRUCTURE〉

例1) アリスさんは　きのう　本を　読みませんでした。

(Use the words in | 練習 5 | above.)

例2) A：ルインさんは　きのう　本を　読みましたか。

B：はい、読(よ)みました。／いいえ、読(よ)みませんでした。

1. 文法(ぶんぽう)　　　　勉強(べんきょう)します
2. ラジオ　　　　聞(き)きます
3. カレーライス　　　　食(た)べます
4. 留学生会館(りゅうがくせいかいかん)　　　　行(い)きます
5. 新聞(しんぶん)　　　　読(よ)みます
6. ひらがな　　　　勉強(べんきょう)します
7. 食堂(しょくどう)　　　　行(い)きます

練習7　A mixture of imperfective & perfective forms

〈STRUCTURE〉
例）A：アリスさんは　あした　テープを　聞(き)きますか。
　　B：はい、聞(き)きます。／いいえ、聞(き)きません。

1. あした　　日本語(にほんご)　　勉強(べんきょう)します
2. きのう　　サラダ　　食(た)べます
3. きょう　　図書館(としょかん)　　行(い)きます
4. きのう　　本(ほん)　　読(よ)みます
5. あした　　研究室(けんきゅうしつ)　　行(い)きます
6. きょう　　音楽(おんがく)　　聞(き)きます

練習8　Question word（2）　だれ／何(なに)をする (question with a question word)

〈STRUCTURE〉
(Listen to the following five sentences and answer the questions below.)

> アリスさんはカレーライスを食(た)べました。
> バンバンさんは図書館(としょかん)へ行(い)きました。
> カーリンさんは本(ほん)を読(よ)みました。
> ルインさんは音楽(おんがく)を聞(き)きました。
> ナロンさんは日本語(にほんご)を勉強(べんきょう)しました。

a. だれ

例）A：だれが　カレーライスを　食(た)べましたか。
　　B：アリスさんが　食(た)べました。

1. 本（ほん）　　読（よ）みます
2. 音楽（おんがく）　聞（き）きます
3. 日本語（にほんご）　勉強（べんきょう）します
4. 図書館（としょかん）　行（い）きます

b. 何（なに）をする

例）A：アリスさんは　きのう　何を　しましたか。
　　B：カレーライスを　食（た）べました。

1. ナロンさん　　3. ルインさん
2. バンバンさん　4. カーリンさん

〈USAGE〉

(Talk about yourselves using the following dialogue.)

例）A：Bさん、きのう何（なに）をしましたか。
　　B：日本語を勉強（べんきょう）しました。
　　A：ああ、そうですか。

練習9　　　place で Vます　　（place of action）

〈STRUCTURE〉

例）ルインさんは日本語を勉強します。（大学（だいがく））
　　→　ルインさんは大学で日本語を勉強します。
1. ルインさんは本を読みます。（図書館）
2. アリスさんはごはんを食べます。（食堂（しょくどう））
3. アリスさんはテレビを見（み）ます。（留学生会館（りゅうがくせいかいかん））
4. ルインさんはコーヒーを飲（の）みます。（食堂）

〈USAGE〉

例）A：Bさんはどこで日本語を勉強しますか。
　　B：大学で勉強します。
　　A：あ、そうですか。

練習10　　Nも／Nは

〈STRUCTURE〉

a. も

b. は

例1）
アリスさんは魚フライ定食を食べます。
サラダも食べます。

1. ひらがな　勉強します　漢字
2. 新聞　　　読みます　　雑誌

例1）
アリスさんは魚フライ定食を食べます。
カレーライスは食べません。

1. ひらがな　勉強します　かたかな
2. 新聞　　　読みます　　本

例2）
ルインさんは食堂へ行きます。
研究室へも行きます。

1. 図書館　研究室

例2）
ルインさんは食堂へ行きます。
図書館へは行きません。

1. 研究室　図書館

例3）
アリスさんは魚フライ定食を食べます。
ルインさんも食べます。

1. 食堂へ行きます　カーリンさん

例3）
アリスさんは魚フライ定食を食べます。
ナロンさんは食べません。

1. 食堂へ行きます　バンバンさん

〈USAGE〉

例1） A：Bさんは魚フライ定食を食べますか。
　　　B：はい、食べます。
　　　A：サラダも食べますか。
　　　B：はい、サラダも食べます。／いいえ、サラダは食べません。

1. 新聞　　　読みます　　雑誌
2. テープ　　聞きます　　ラジオ
3. 図書館　　行きます　　研究室

例2） A：Bさんは魚フライ定食を食べますか。
　　　B：はい、食べます。
　　　A：Cさんも食べますか。
　　　C：はい、わたしも食べます。／いいえ、わたしは食べません。

1. 文法　　　勉強します
2. 新聞　　　読みます
3. 食堂　　　行きます

Aural Comprehension

I Listen to the conversations and answer the following questions.

(A)　On the way to the classroom

　　1．アリスさんはテープを聞きましたか。

　　2．アリスさんは何を読みましたか。

(B)　At lunch time

　　1．アリスさんは食堂へ行きますか。

　　2．ナロンさんは食堂へ行きますか。

(C)　In the co-op cafeteria　（いくら：how much）

　　1．カレーライスはいくらですか。

(D)　In the co-op cafeteria

　　1．ルインさんは何を食べますか。

　　2．いくらですか。

　　3．アリスさんは何を食べますか。

II　（数字）Listen to the conversations and write down the numbers with the counters.

　　Example　＿＿70えん＿＿

　　1．＿＿＿＿＿＿＿　2．＿＿＿＿＿＿＿　3．＿＿＿＿＿＿＿　4．＿＿＿＿＿＿＿

III One of the people in each conversation is you.

　　Listen to what the other person says and write down the answer to your question.

　　Your question：何を食べましたか。

　　Example　＿＿さかなをたべました。＿＿

　　1．＿＿＿＿＿＿＿＿＿　2．＿＿＿＿＿＿＿＿＿　3．＿＿＿＿＿＿＿＿＿

Reading Comprehension

きのうルインさんは図書館へ行きました。日本語を勉強しました。教科書を読みました。テープも聞きました。

アリスさんは研究室へ行きました。研究室で新聞を読みました。日本語は勉強しませんでした。

質問(questions)
1. ルインさんはどこへ行きましたか。
2. ルインさんはテープを聞きましたか。
3. アリスさんは研究室で何をしましたか。
4. アリスさんは研究室で日本語を勉強しましたか。

カーリンさんは食堂へ行きます。佐藤さんも行きます。カーリンさんはハンバーガーを食べます。コーヒーを飲みます。佐藤さんはうどんを食べます。コーヒーは飲みません。

- ハンバーガー　hamburger
- うどん　Japanese noodle

質問
1. カーリンさんはどこで食べますか。
2. カーリンさんはうどんを食べますか。
3. カーリンさんは何を飲みますか。
4. 佐藤さんはコーヒーを飲みますか。

Kanji Practice

New Kanji

1.	一	いち one ひとつ		9.	九	きゅう く nine ここのつ
(1)	一			(2)	ノ 九	
2.	二	に two ふたつ		10.	十	じゅう ten とお
(2)	一 二			(2)	一 十	
3.	三	さん three みっつ		11.	百	ひゃく hundred
(3)	一 二 三			(6)	一 ア 百 百 百	
4.	四	し よ よん よっつ four		12.	千	せん thousand
(5)	丨 冂 四 四			(3)	一 二 千	
5.	五	ご five いつつ		13.	万	まん ten thousand
(4)	一 丆 五 五			(3)	一 フ 万	
6.	六	ろく six むっつ		14.	円	えん yen
(4)	亠 六 六			(4)	丨 冂 円 円	
7.	七	しち seven なな ななつ		15.	年	ねん year とし
(2)	一 七			(6)	ノ 二 ケ 仁 生 年	
8.	八	はち eight やっつ		( ) : Kanji stroke count Bold letters : "on" readings Underlined letters : "kun" readings		
(2)	ノ 八					

Essential Words

1. 一年 (いち ねん) one year
2. 四年 (よ ねん) four years
3. 十年 (じゅう ねん) ten years
4. 十円 (じゅう えん) ten yen
5. 百円 (ひゃく えん) one hundred yen
6. 千円 (せん えん) one thousand yen
7. 三千円 (さん ぜん えん) three thousand yen
8. 一万円 (いち まん えん) ten thousand yen
9. 十万円 (じゅう まん えん) one hundred thousand yen
10. 百万円 (ひゃく まん えん) one million yen

Words

1. 一つ (ひと) one
2. 二つ (ふた) two
3. 三つ (みっ) three
4. 四つ (よっ) four
5. 五つ (いつ) five
6. 六つ (むっ) six
7. 七つ (なな) seven
8. 八つ (やっ) eight
9. 九つ (ここの) nine
10. 十 (とお) ten

Reading Practice

1. 四十
2. 九十
3. 三百
4. 五百
5. 六百
6. 八百円
7. 九百円
8. 八千円
9. 一万五千円
10. 四万九千円
11. 七万四千円
12. 九万七千円
13. 四十万円
14. 七年
15. 九年

Lesson 2

Dialogue しょうかい

2-1 In front of the Ryuugakusee Center

Satoo is a senior student in Lwin's laboratory.

佐藤　　：　ルインさん。
ルイン：　はい。
佐藤　　：　あの人はだれですか。
ルイン：　どの人ですか。
佐藤　　：　あの女の人です。
ルイン：　ああ、アリスさんです。
佐藤　　：　お友達ですか。
ルイン：　ええ。しょうかいします。

2-2 Introducing each other

ルイン： アリスさん、こちらは佐藤さんです。
佐藤： はじめまして。佐藤です。
アリス： はじめまして。アリスです。どうぞよろしく。
佐藤： こちらこそ、どうぞよろしく。お国はどちらですか。
アリス： カナダです。
佐藤： カナダですか。いつ日本に来ましたか。
アリス： 2週間前に来ました。
佐藤： そうですか。ご専門は何ですか。
アリス： 生物学です。佐藤さんのご専門は。
佐藤： 電子工学です。
アリス： そうですか。

佐藤： 今から授業ですか。
アリス： ええ。1時に始まります。
佐藤： そうですか。じゃ、また。
アリス： 失礼します。
ルイン： 失礼します。

2-3 Introducing oneself

ナロン： ナロンと申します。タイから来ました。
法学研究科の修士1年です。専門は国際法です。どうぞよろしくお願いします。

Vocabulary List

⟨ ⟩: dictionary form
˥ : accent fall (for words only)

Dialogue

2-1

しょうかい		introduction
さ˥とう	佐藤	[personal name]
あの		that [used before a noun]
ひと	人	person
～です		to be [See Notes on Grammar]
ど˥の		which [used before a noun]
おんな˥	女	woman
の		of, 's [Group 1 particle for modification]
おともだち	お友達	your friend [shows respect to the listener]
ともだち	友達	friend
しょうかいしま˥す（～が～を～に）⟨しょうかいする⟩		to introduce

2-2

こちら		this [polite form of これ]
はじめまして。		How do you do?
どうぞよろしく。		Nice to see you.
こちらこ˥そ		I should say (that)…
おくに	お国	your country
くに	国	country
ど˥ちら		where [polite form of どこ、どれ]
か˥なだ	カナダ	Canada
い˥つ		when
にほ˥ん	日本	Japan
に		to [Group 1 particle for place of arrival]
きま˥す⟨く˥る⟩ （～が～へ）	来ます⟨来る⟩	to come

～しゅうかん	～週間	weeks [used as an counter]
ま￣え	前	ago, before
に		on, at [Group 1 particle for time]
ごせんもん	ご専門	your major subject of study
せんもん	専門	major subject of study
な￣ん	何	what
せいぶつ￣がく	生物学	biology
でんしこ￣うがく	電子工学	electronic engineering
い￣ま	今	now
から		from [Group 1 particle for source]
じゅ￣ぎょう	授業	class
～じ	～時	... o'clock
はじまりま￣す　（～が）〈はじまる〉	始まります〈始まる〉	to begin
じゃ		well, then
また		again
じゃ、また。		See you again.
しつれいします。	失礼します。	Good-bye.

2-3

～ともうします。	～と申します。	My name is ....
た￣い	タイ	Thailand
ほうがくけんきゅうか	法学研究科	Graduate school of Law
しゅ￣うし	修士	master course
～ねん	～年	... grade
こくさいほう	国際法	international law
どうぞよろしくおねがいします。	どうぞよろしくお願いします。	Very nice to see you.

Drill

わだ	和田	[personal name]
やま￣かわ	山川	[personal name]
がくせい	学生	student
せんせ￣い	先生	teacher
いしゃ	医者	medical doctor
～じん	～人	[suffix of nationality]
～じゃありません		[negative form of です]
どいつ￣じん	ドイツ人	German

		Vocabulary List
かよ˥うび	火曜日	Tuesday
きんよ˥うび	金曜日	Friday
～でした		was, were [perfective form of です]
～じゃありませんでした		[negative form of でした]
かいしゃ˥いん	会社員	company employee
こうむ˥いん	公務員	government officer
なごやだ˥いがく	名古屋大学	Nagoya University
りゅうが˥くせい	留学生	international student
こうが˥くぶ	工学部	Faculty of Engineering
けいざいが˥くぶ	経済学部	Faculty of Economics
けんきゅ˥うせい	研究生	research student
だいがく˥いん	大学院	graduate school
いちね˥んせい	１年生	first grade
がくぶ	学部	faculty
これ		this
それ		it
あれ		that
ど˥れ		which
かばん		bag
じ˥しょ	辞書	dictionary
えんぴつ		pencil
しゃあぷぺ˥んしる	シャープペンシル	mechanical pencil
はい、そうです。		Yes, that's right.
いいえ、ちがいます。		No, it isn't.
ぼうるぺん	ボールペン	ball-point pen
けしごむ	けしゴム	eraser
の˥うと	ノート	notebook
この		this [used before a noun]
その		that [used before a noun]
おとこ˥	男	man
みゃ˥んまあ	ミャンマー	Myanmar
ど˥いつ	ドイツ	Germany
せんしゅう	先週	last week

Additional Vocabulary

にちようび	日曜日	Sunday
げつようび	月曜日	Monday
かようび	火曜日	Tuesday
すいようび	水曜日	Wednesday
もくようび	木曜日	Thursday
きんようび	金曜日	Friday
どようび	土曜日	Saturday

Related Vocabulary

University Terminology

がくぶ	学部	school, department
ぶんがくぶ	文学部	School of Letters
ほうがくぶ	法学部	School of Law
けいざいがくぶ	経済学部	School of Economics
きょういくがくぶ	教育学部	School of Education
りがくぶ	理学部	School of Science
こうがくぶ	工学部	School of Engineering
のうがくぶ	農学部	School of Agricultual
いがくぶ	医学部	School of Medicine
だいがくいん	大学院	graduate school
ほうがくけんきゅうか	法学研究科	Graduate School of Law
こうがくけんきゅうか	工学研究科	Graduate School of Engineering
りがくけんきゅうか	理学研究科	Graduate School of Science
こくさいかいはつけんきゅうか	国際開発研究科	Graduate School of International Development
せんもん	専門	major subject of study
けいざいがく	経済学	economics
ほうりつがく	法律学	law
ぶんがく	文学	literature
きょういくがく	教育学	pedagogy
ぶつりがく	物理学	physics
かがく	化学	chemistry

きかいこうがく	機械工学	mechanical engineering
じょうほうこうがく	情報工学	informatic engineering
りゅうがくせい	留学生	international student
だいがくせい	大学生	university student
がくぶせい	学部生	undergraduate student
だいがくいんせい	大学院生	graduate student
けんきゅうせい	研究生	research student
しゅうしかてい	修士課程	master course
はかせかてい	博士課程	doctor course
きょうじゅ	教授	professor
じょきょうじゅ	助教授	associate professor
こうし	講師	lecturer
じょしゅ	助手	assistant
かいしゃいん	会社員	company employee
こうむいん	公務員	government officer
いしゃ	医者	doctor
べんごし	弁護士	lawyer
きょうし	教師	teacher
ぎんこういん	銀行員	banker
けんきゅういん	研究員	researcher
えんじにあ	エンジニア	engineer

Notes on Grammar

I Noun sentences

A Sentence structure

The idea "Alice is a student." is expressed in Japanese as:

アリスさんは学生です。(Arisu san wa gakusee desu.)
Alice is a student.

In the above example, です(desu) is equivalent to the English "is." です(desu) is placed at the end of a sentence.

> Noun 1   は(wa)   Noun 2   です(desu)。

Examples
1. アリスさんはカナダ人です。(Arisu san wa Kanadajin desu.)
   Alice is a Canadian.
2. 和田さんは先生です。(Wada san wa sensee desu.)
   Ms. Wada is a teacher.
3. きょうは月曜日です。(Kyoo wa getsuyoobi desu.)
   Today is Monday.

B Conjugation of noun + です(desu)

です follows a noun and conjugates as follows.

† Table of the conjugation of です †

	Polite form	
	Affirmative form	Negative form
Imperfective form	です(desu)	じゃありません(ja arimasen)
Perfective form	でした(deshita)	じゃありませんでした(ja arimasen deshita)

> **Examples**
>
> 1. アリスさんはミャンマー人じゃありません。
>   (Arisu san wa Myanmaajin ja arimasen.)
>   Alice is not a Myanmarese.
> 2. ルインさんは先生でした。(Ruin san wa sensee deshita.)
>   Lwin was a teacher.
> 3. ルインさんは学生じゃありませんでした。
>   (Ruin san wa gakusee ja arimasen deshita.)
>   Lwin was not a student.

In formal situations では(dewa) is used instead of じゃ(ja). So ではありません(dewa arimasen) and ではありませんでした(dewa arimasen deshita) are used instead of じゃありません(ja arimasen) and じゃありませんでした(ja arimasen deshita).

C Question sentences and the way of answering

The way of making questions and the way of answering questions are the same as those of verb sentences. (See Lesson 1, Notes on Grammar IV.)

1. Yes-No questions

> **Examples**
>
> 1. A：アリスさんは学生ですか。(Arisu san wa gakusee desu ka.)
>   Is Alice a student?
>   B：はい、(アリスさんは)学生です。
>   (Hai, (Arisu san wa) gakusee desu.)
>   Yes, she is a student.
> 2. A：ルインさんは先生ですか。(Ruin san wa sensee desu ka.)
>   Is Lwin a teacher?
>   B：いいえ、(ルインさんは)先生じゃありません。
>   (Iie, (Ruin san wa) sensee ja arimasen.)
>   No, he is not a teacher.

There is another way of answering;

In answering positively, we say はい、そうです (Hai, soo desu).

In answering negatively, we say いいえ、ちがいます (Iie, chigaimasu).

So the above examples can also be said in the following way.

> **Examples**
>
> 1. A：アリスさんは学生ですか。(Arisu san wa gakusee desu ka.)
>   Is Alice a student?

B：はい、そうです。(Hai, soo desu.)
Yes, she is.

2. A：ルインさんは先生ですか。(Ruin san wa sensee desu ka.)
Is Lwin a teacher?
B：いいえ、ちがいます。(Iie, chigaimasu.)
No, he isn't.

Note that そうです (soo desu) and ちがいます (chigaimasu) can be used only to affirm or negate the noun which is focused in the question.

2. Questions with question words

When you want to know about Noun 2, the following type of questions are used.

Examples

1. A：アリスさんは何人ですか。(Arisu san wa nanijin desu ka.)
What nationality is Alice?
B：(アリスさんは) カナダ人です。
((Arisu san wa) Kanadajin desu.)
She is a Canadian.

2. A：きょうは何曜日ですか。(Kyoo wa nan'yoobi desu ka.)
What day of the week is it today?
B：(きょうは) 月曜日です。((Kyoo wa) getsuyoobi desu.)
It is Monday (today).

II Alternative questions

When there are two or more possibilities and you want to find out which one is correct, alternative questions are used. When you ask, you should say two or more predicates or question sentences with a rising intonation. When you answer, you should answer by choosing one predicate or sentence. The way of asking and answering these types of questions is as follows.

```
Question： __A__ か。↗  __B__ か。↗  (A ka. B ka.)
Answer：   __A__ 。(A.)              (A, B：predicate or sentence)
```

Examples

1. A：ルインさんは学生ですか。先生ですか。
(Ruin san wa gakusee desu ka. Sensee desu ka.)

Is Lwin a student, or a teacher?

B：（ルインさんは）学生です。((Ruin san wa) gakusee desu.)
He is a student.

2. A：魚を食べますか。サラダを食べますか。
(Sakana o tabemasu ka. Sarada o tabemasu ka.)
Are you going to eat fish, or salad?

B：サラダを食べます。(Sarada o tabemasu.)
I'm going to eat salad.

3. A：アリスさんが行きましたか。ルインさんが行きましたか。
(Arisu san ga ikimashita ka. Ruin san ga ikimashita ka.)
Did Alice go, or did Lwin go?

B：アリスさんが行きました。(Arisu san ga ikimashita.)
Alice did.

4. A：テレビを見ますか。音楽を聞きますか。
(Terebi o mimasu ka. Ongaku o kikimasu ka.)
Are you going to watch the television, or are you going to listen to some music?

B：テレビを見ます。(Terebi o mimasu.)
I'm going to watch the television.

III Demonstrative pronouns (1)

A これ(kore), それ(sore), あれ(are), どれ(dore)

When you want to refer to something which you don't know the name of, or when you want to avoid repetition of using the name of the thing you have already referred to, これ(kore), それ(sore) and あれ(are) are used.

```
これ(kore)
それ(sore)   } は(wa)   Noun   です(desu)。
あれ(are)
```

The difference of これ(kore), それ(sore) and あれ(are) depends on the distance from the thing to the speaker and the hearer. これ(kore) is used for referring to something near the speaker, それ(sore) for referring to something close to the hearer but far from the speaker, and あれ(are) is used for referring to something which is at a distance from both the speaker and the hearer.

あれ

speaker | hearer
これ　　それ

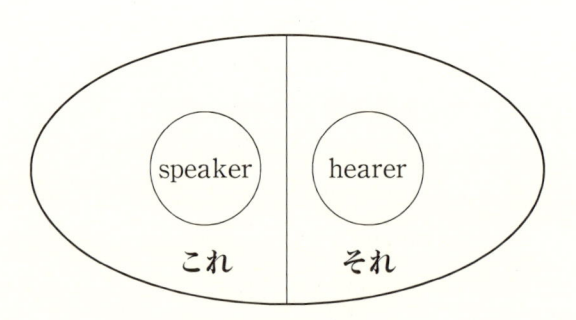

Examples

1. (A dictionary is near A, but far from B.)
   A：これは何_{なん}ですか。
   (Kore wa nan desu ka.)
   What is this?
   B：それは辞書_{じしょ}です。
   (Sore wa jisho desu.)
   It's a dictionary.

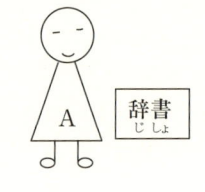

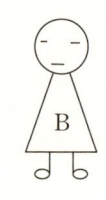

2. (A cassette tape is far from A, but near B.)
   A：それは何_{なん}ですか。
   (Sore wa nan desu ka.)
   What is that?
   B：これはテープです。
   (Kore wa teepu desu.)
   This is a cassette tape.

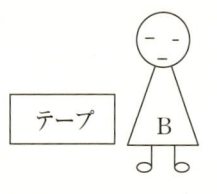

3. (A textbook is far from A and B.)
   A：あれは何_{なん}ですか。
   (Are wa nan desu ka.)
   What is that over there?
   B：あれは教科書_{きょうかしょ}です。
   (Are wa kyookasho desu.)
   That is a textbook.

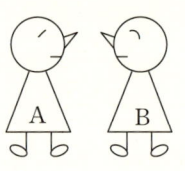

どれ(dore) "which one" is a question word inquiring about one of three or more things. In answering a question with どれ(dore), you should use これ(kore), それ

(sore) or あれ(are).

Examples

1. A：テープはどれですか。(Teepu wa dore desu ka.)
    Which one is the cassette tape?
    B：これです。(Kore desu.)
    This one is.
2. A：教科書はどれですか。(Kyookasho wa dore desu ka.)
    Which one is the textbook?
    B：あれです。(Are desu.)
    That one (over there).
3. A：図書館はどれですか。(Toshokan wa dore desu ka.)
    Which one is the library?
    B：あれです。(Are desu.)
    That one (over there).

B この(kono), その(sono), あの(ano), どの(dono)

これ(kore), それ(sore), あれ(are) and どれ(dore) change to この(kono), その(sono), あの(ano) and どの(dono) respectively before the noun they modify.

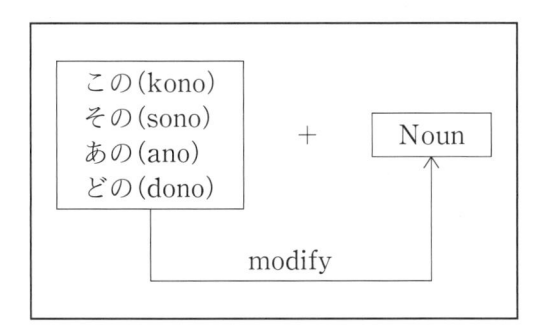

```
┌─────────────────────────────────────┐
│  この(kono)                          │
│  その(sono)    +    Noun             │
│  あの(ano)              ↑            │
│  どの(dono)             │            │
│         └──── modify ───┘            │
└─────────────────────────────────────┘
```

○ (Say)　　　：この本 (kono hon)　　this book
× (Do not say)：これ本 (kore hon)

Examples

1. A：それは何ですか。(Sore wa nan desu ka.)
    What is that?
    B：どれですか。(Dore desu ka.)
    Which one?
    A：その本です。(Sono hon desu.)
    That book.
    B：この本は教科書です。(Kono hon wa kyookasho desu.)
    This book is a textbook.

2. A：あの人はだれですか。(Ano hito wa dare desu ka.)
   Who is that person over there?
   B：あれはルインさんです。(Are wa Ruin san desu.)
   That is Lwin.
3. A：アリスさんはどの人ですか。(Arisu san wa dono hito desu ka.)
   Which person is Alice?
   B：あの人です。(Ano hito desu.)
   That person over there.

C こちら(kochira), そちら(sochira), あちら(achira), どちら(dochira)

こちら(kochira), そちら(sochira), あちら(achira) and どちら(dochira) are often used to refer to a person or a place when speaking more politely. For example こちら (kochira) takes the place of この人(kono hito), and どちら(dochira) takes the place of どこ(doko). The difference among こちら(kochira), そちら(sochira), あちら (achira) and どちら(dochira) is the same as that of これ(kore), それ(sore), あれ(are) and どれ(dore).

Examples
1. こちらはルインさんです。(Kochira wa Ruin san desu.)
   This person is Lwin. (Lit.)/This is Lwin.
2. お国はどちらですか。(Okuni wa dochira desu ka.)
   Where is your country? (Lit.)/Which country are you from?

IV Group 1 particles：の(no), から(kara), に(ni)

A の(no)：Noun 1 の Noun 2

When a noun modifies another noun, the modifying noun is followed by the particle の (no) which cannot be translated into one English word. The modifying noun must precede the modified noun. Note that all modifiers always precede the noun they modify.

```
┌─────────────────────────────────────────────┐
│   ┌──────────┐                ┌──────────┐  │
│   │ Noun 1   │  の (no)       │ Noun 2   │  │
│   └──────────┘                └──────────┘  │
│         └──────modify──────────────▲        │
│   (modifying noun)      (modified noun)     │
└─────────────────────────────────────────────┘
```

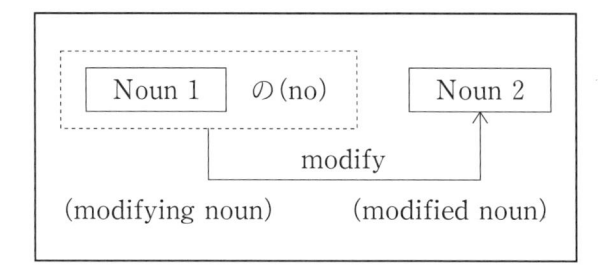

○(Say)　　　：ミャンマーのルインさん (Myanmaa no Ruin san)
×(Do not say)：ルインさんのミャンマー (Ruin san no Myanmaa)
　　　　　　　Lwin from Myanmar

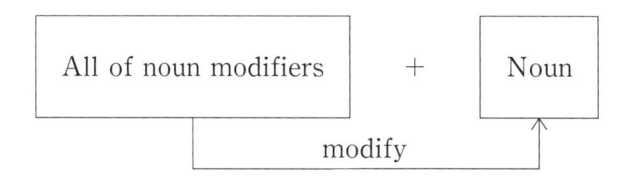

```
┌────────────────────┐        ┌────────┐
│ All of noun modifiers │  +   │ Noun   │
└────────────────────┘        └────────┘
        └──────modify────────────▲
```

Examples

1. ルインさんの本 (Ruin san no hon)
   Lwin's book
2. 日本語の先生 (Nihongo no sensee)
   a teacher of Japanese language
3. 名古屋大学の学生 (Nagoyadaigaku no gakusee)
   a student of Nagoya University
4. 名古屋大学の食堂 (Nagoyadaigaku no shokudoo)
   the cafeteria in Nagoya University
5. カナダのアリスさん (Kanada no Arisu san)
   Alice from Canada

The above combinations are used in the sentences as follows.

Examples

1. これはルインさんの本です。(Kore wa Ruin san no hon desu.)
   This is Lwin's book.
2. 日本語の先生に会いました。(Nihongo no sensee ni aimashita.)
   Someone* met a teacher of Japanese language.
3. カーリンさんは名古屋大学の学生です。
   　　　　　(Kaarin san wa Nagoyadaigaku no gakusee desu.)
   Karin is a student of Nagoya University.
4. 名古屋大学の食堂へ行きました。
   　　　　　(Nagoyadaigaku no shokudoo e ikimashita.)
   Someone* went to the cafeteria in Nagoya University.

5. カナダのアリスさんは学生です。
(Kanada no Arisu san wa gakusee desu.)
Alice from Canada is a student.

(*"Someone" may be the speaker.)

B から (kara)

から (kara) means "from" or "since." It follows a noun of place or a noun of time.

```
Place  }
Time   }  +  から (kara)
```

Examples
1. アリスさんはカナダから来ました。
(Arisu san wa Kanada kara kimashita.)
Alice comes from Canada.
2. ルインさんは大学から帰りました。
(Ruin san wa daigaku kara kaerimashita.)
(帰る：return, come or go back)
Lwin came home from the university.
3. 3時から勉強します。(Sanji kara benkyoo shimasu.)
Someone* will study from three o'clock.
4. あしたからテープを聞きます。(Ashita kara teepu o kikimasu.)
Someone* will listen to the tape starting tomorrow.

(*"Someone" may be the speaker.)

C に (ni)

1. Time

に (ni) indicates time. It follows a noun of specific time. There are some nouns of time which are never followed by に (ni), such as きのう (kinoo), きょう (kyoo), あした (ashita), which indicate relative time, and which were introduced in Lesson 1, Notes on Grammar VII. 先週 (senshuu : last week) also indicates relative time.

```
Specific time  +  に (ni)
Relative time  +  nil
```

> **Examples**
>
> 1. ルインさんは8時に大学へ来ます。
>   (Ruin san wa hachiji ni daigaku e kimasu.)
>   Lwin comes to the university at eight.
> 2. 授業は1時に始まります。(Jugyoo wa ichiji ni hajimarimasu.)
>   The class begins at one.
> 3. ルインさんは先週、日本へ来ました。
>   (Ruin san wa senshuu Nihon e kimashita.)
>   Lwin came to Japan last week.

2. Place of arrival

に (ni) also indicates the place of arrival.

> **Examples**
>
> 1. ルインさんは食堂に行きます。(Ruin san wa shokudoo ni ikimasu.)
>   Lwin will go to the cafeteria.
> 2. ルインさんは先週、日本に来ました。
>   (Ruin san wa senshuu Nihon ni kimashita.)
>   Lwin came to Japan last week.

に (ni) here is often used instead of group 1 particle へ (e) that indicates direction, which was introduced in Lesson 1.

V   Question word : いつ (itsu)

いつ (itsu) is used to ask time and means "when."

> **Examples**
>
> 1. A：いつ日本に来ましたか。(Itsu Nihon ni kimashita ka.)
>   When did you come to Japan?
>   B：先週来ました。(Senshuu kimashita.)
>   I came here last week.
> 2. A：いつ大学へ行きますか。(Itsu daigaku e ikimasu ka.)
>   When will you go to the university?
>   B：あした行きます。(Ashita ikimasu.)
>   I'll go there tomorrow.
> 3. A：いつ大学へ行きますか。(Itsu daigaku e ikimasu ka.)
>   When will you go to the university?
>   B：8時に行きます。(Hachiji ni ikimasu.)
>   I'll go there at eight o'clock.

VI Prefixes: お(o)- and ご(go)-

お(o)- and ご(go)- are prefixes to show politeness. In general, お(o)- is attached to words of native Japanese origin and ご(go)- to words of Sino-Japanese origin. (For further information see Lesson 16, Notes on Grammar I.)

Examples
1. お友達ですか。(Otomodachi desu ka.)
   (Is that person) your friend?
2. お国はどちらですか。(Okuni wa dochira desu ka.)
   Where are you from?
3. ご専門は何ですか。(Gosenmon wa nan desu ka.)
   What is your field of speciality?/What do you major in?
4. A: 何を飲みましたか。(Nani o nomimashita ka.)
   What did you drink?
   B: お水を飲みました。(Omizu o nomimashita.)   (水: water)
   I drank water.

Notes on Discourse

I カナダですか (Kanada desu ka) ↘

Read the following conversation from Dialogue 2-2.

    A：アリスさん、お国はどちらですか。(Arisu san, okuni wa dochira desu ka.)
       Alice, what country are you from ?
    B：カナダです。(Kanada desu.)
       Canada.
    A：カナダですか。(Kanada desu ka.)
       Canada. I see.

In the above example you can see the sentence カナダですか (Kanada desu ka). It is not a question sentence like the expression そうですか (soo desu ka) explained in Lesson 1, Notes on Discourse. The word in the answer カナダ (Kanada) is repeated in the sentence 〜ですか (desu ka) with a falling intonation, meaning "It's …. I see."

II じゃ、また (Ja, mata)

じゃ (ja) means "then" and is used to conclude a conversation. また (mata) means "again," and the combination of じゃ、また (ja, mata) is an expression for saying farewell.

Look at the following conversation shown in Dialogue 2-2.

    佐藤 ：今から授業ですか。(Ima kara jugyoo desu ka.)
        Do you have a class now ?
    アリス：ええ。1時に始まります。(Ee. Ichiji ni hajimarimasu.)
        Yes. The class begins at 1 o'clock.
    佐藤 ：そうですか。じゃ、また。(Soo desu ka. Ja, mata.)
        I see. Then, see you again.
    アリス：失礼します。(Shitsuree shimasu.)

See you.

There are also expressions such as the following: じゃ、またあした (ja, mata ashita) "See you tomorrow," じゃ、また来週 (ja, mata raishuu) "See you next week," and so on.

In the above conversation, Mr. Satoo, a senior student said じゃ、また (ja, mata) to Alice. If you use じゃ、また (ja, mata) as "good-bye," it sounds rather informal. When you use this expression to a superior, or senior, you should add words like this:

じゃ、また来週、お願いします。(Ja, mata raishuu onegaishimasu.)
Alright, then, next week. Thank you.

じゃ、また……失礼します。(Ja, mata ... shitsuree shimasu.)
Alright, then, ... Good-bye.

III 失礼します (Shitsuree shimasu)

A Leaving

失礼します (shitsuree shimasu) means "good-bye." It is used to a superior. In the above conversation (in II) Alice said this expression to Satoo, a senior student, instead of じゃ、また (ja, mata) or さようなら (sayoonara). さようなら (sayoonara) means "good-bye," but it is not used to a superior or in a formal situation.

B Entering

失礼します (shitsuree shimasu) is used not only when someone is leaving but also when entering a superior's room. You will see the example in Dialogue 9-1, Lesson 9, etc.

Drill

練習1　　N は N です　　(imperfective affirmative form)

〈STRUCTURE〉

例）ルインさんは　学生です。

1. 和田さん　　先生
2. 山川さん　　医者
3. アリスさん　カナダ人
4. 佐藤さん　　学生

　　　　　　　　　　　　　　ルイン　　　　　和田　　　　　山川
　　　　　　　　　　　　　　学生　　　　　　先生　　　　　医者

練習2　　N じゃありません　　(imperfective negative form)

〈STRUCTURE〉

a.

例）ルインさんは　先生じゃありません。

1. 和田さん　　医者
2. 山川さん　　学生
3. アリスさん　ドイツ人
4. 佐藤さん　　先生

b.

例1）A：ルインさんは　学生ですか。
　　　B：はい、学生です。
例2）A：ルインさんは　先生ですか。
　　　B：いいえ、先生じゃありません。

1. 和田さん　　先生
2. 山川さん　　学生
3. アリスさん　カナダ人
4. 佐藤さん　　医者
5. きょう　　　火曜日
6. きょう　　　金曜日

月曜日：Monday
火曜日：Tuesday
水曜日：Wednesday
木曜日：Thursday
金曜日：Friday
土曜日：Saturday
日曜日：Sunday

練習 3

Nでした (perfective affirmative form)
Nじゃありませんでした (perfective negative form)

〈STRUCTURE〉

a.

例) ルインさんは 国では 先生でした。学生じゃありませんでした。

1. バンバンさん　医者　　　学生
2. アリスさん　　学生　　　先生
3. カーリンさん　会社員　　学生

b.

例) A：ルインさんは 国では 先生でしたか。
　　B：はい、先生でした。／いいえ、先生じゃありませんでした。

1. バンバンさん　医者
2. アリスさん　　会社員
3. カーリンさん　公務員

エンジニア：engineer
弁護士：attorney-at-law, lawyer
教師：teacher
　高校：senior high school
　中学校：junior high school
　小学校：elementary school

練習 4

NのN

〈STRUCTURE〉

a.

例) 佐藤さんは　名古屋大学の　学生です。

1. ルインさん　　名古屋大学　　留学生
2. ルインさん　　工学部　　　　学生
3. カーリンさん　経済学部　　　研究生
4. ナロンさん　　大学院　　　　1年生
5. 和田さん　　　日本語　　　　先生
6. 和田さん　　　ルインさん　　先生

農学部：Faculty of Agriculture
理学部：Faculty of Science
医学部：Faculty of Medicine
法学部：Faculty of Law
文学部：Faculty of Letters
教育学部：Faculty of Education
修士課程：master course
博士課程：doctor course

---

b.

例) A：佐藤さんは　どこの　学生ですか。
　　B：名古屋大学の　学生です。

1. 和田さん　　何　　　　先生
2. 和田さん　　だれ　　　先生
3. ルインさん　何学部　　学生

〈話しましょう〉 (Let's talk about ourselves.)

例)（わたしは）ルインです。工学部の学生です。

練習5　　これ／それ／あれ／どれ

〈STRUCTURE〉
a.
例) A：これは　テープです。

1. これ　　教科書
2. それ　　新聞
3. それ　　CD
4. あれ　　かばん
5. あれ　　雑誌
6. あれ　　テレビ

b.
例) A：それは　CD ですか。
　　B：はい、（これは）CD です。／いいえ、（これは）CD じゃありません。

1. これ　　テープ
2. これ　　雑誌
3. それ　　CD
4. それ　　教科書
5. あれ　　テレビ
6. あれ　　辞書

c.
例) A：それは　何ですか。
　　B：（これは）新聞です。

1. それ　　CD
2. あれ　　雑誌
3. あれ　　かばん
4. これ　　日本語のテープ
5. これ　　日本語の教科書
6. それ　　専門の本

d. Question word　どれ
例) A：テープは　どれですか。
　　B：それです。

1.　CD　　　　　　　　これ
2.　雑誌(ざっし)　　　　あれ
3.　新聞(しんぶん)　　　これ
4.　教科書(きょうかしょ)　それ
5.　えんぴつ　　　　　　それ
6.　シャープペンシル　　あれ

〈USAGE〉

例）A：これはルインさんの教科書(きょうかしょ)ですか。
　　B：はい、そうです。／B：いいえ、ちがいます。
　　　　　　　　　　　　A：じゃ、だれの教科書(きょうかしょ)ですか。
　　　　　　　　　　　　B：アリスさんの教科書(きょうかしょ)です。
　　　　　　　　　　　　A：そうですか。

1.　あれ　　アリスさん　　　かばん
2.　これ　　ルインさん　　　ボールペン
3.　それ　　ナロンさん　　　けしゴム
4.　あれ　　カーリンさん　　ノート

| 練習6 | この／その／あの／どの＋N |

〈STRUCTURE〉

a.

例）この本(ほん)は　　日本語(にほんご)の本(ほん)です。

1.　このテープ　　　　日本語(にほんご)のテープ
2.　そのCD　　　　　　カーリンさんのCD
3.　あのかばん　　　　アリスさんのかばん
4.　あの人(ひと)　　　ナロンさん
5.　あの男(おとこ)の人(ひと)　佐藤(さとう)さん
6.　あの女(おんな)の人(ひと)　カーリンさん

b.　Question word　　どの

例）A：ルインさんは　どの人(ひと)ですか。
　　B：この人(ひと)です。

1.　アリスさん　　　　その人(ひと)
2.　カーリンさん　　　あの人(ひと)
3.　ナロンさん　　　　その人(ひと)

4. 佐藤さん　　　　あの人
5. 和田先生　　　　あの人

練習7　　place から　　（from）

〈STRUCTURE〉

例）ルインさんは　ミャンマーから　来ました。

1. アリスさん　　　カナダ
2. カーリンさん　　ドイツ
3. ナロンさん　　　タイ

〈USAGE〉

例）A：Bさんはどこから来ましたか。
　　B：ミャンマーから来ました。
　　A：ああ、そうですか。

練習8　　time に

〈STRUCTURE〉

a.
例1）山川さんは　先週　大学に　来ました。
例2）山川さんは　9時に　大学に　来ました。

1. 　　　　　きのう
2. 　　　　　きょう
3. 　　　　　10時
4. 　　　　　1時

b. Question word　いつ／何時

例1）A：いつ　大学に　来ましたか。
　　　B：先週　来ました。
例2）A：何時に　大学に　来ましたか。
　　　B：9時に　来ました。

(Use the words in a. above.)

〈USAGE〉

例）A：Bさん、いつ日本に来ましたか。
　　B：先週来ました。
　　A：あ、そうですか。

Aural Comprehension

I Listen to the conversations and answer the following questions.

(A) In front of the Ryuugakusee Center

1. ハンさんはアリスさんの友達ですか。

2. ハンさんは先生ですか。

(B) In front of the Ryuugakusee Center

1. カーリンさんの専門は何ですか。

2. カーリンさんはいつ日本に来ましたか。

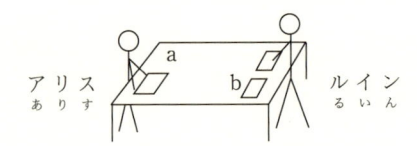

(C) In the classroom

1. アリスさんの教科書はどれですか。(a or b)

(D) In front of the Ryuugakusee Center   (次：next)

1. 次の日本語の授業は何時に始まりますか。

2. 日本語の先生は女の人ですか。

II （数字）Listen to the conversations and write down the numbers with the counters.

1. _____ 2. _____ 3. _____ 4. _____

III One of the people in each conversation is you.

Listen to what the other person says and write down the answer to your question.

Your question：どこの国の人ですか。

1. _____   2. _____   3. _____

Reading Comprehension

　ルインさんとアリスさんは２週間前に日本に来ました。ルインさんはミャンマーから来ました。専門は電子工学です。アリスさんはカナダから来ました。専門は生物学です。ルインさんとアリスさんは今、留学生センターの学生です。毎日、日本語を勉強します。

　佐藤さんはルインさんのせんぱいです。きょう、ルインさんはアリスさんを佐藤さんにしょうかいしました。

- 毎日　everyday
- せんぱい　senior student

質問

1. ルインさんはいつ日本に来ましたか。
2. ルインさんの国はどこですか。専門は何ですか。
3. アリスさんの国はどこですか。専門は何ですか。
4. ルインさんはだれにアリスさんをしょうかいしましたか。

　毎日、12時に食堂へ行きます。きのうはＡランチを食べました。Ａランチは350円です。メニューはごはんと魚と野菜とスープでした。スープは野菜のスープじゃありませんでした。卵のスープでした。

- メニュー　menu
- 野菜　vegetable
- スープ　soup
- 卵　egg

質問

1. 毎日、何時に食堂へ行きますか。
2. Ａランチはいくら(how much)ですか。
3. スープは野菜のスープでしたか。

Kanji Practice

New Kanji

16.	人	**じん** **にん** <u>ひと</u>	man human being	24.	日	**にち** <u>ひ</u>	day sun
(2)	ノ 人			(4)	丨 冂 日 日		
17.	山	**さん** <u>やま</u>	mountain	25.	月	**げつ がつ** <u>つき</u>	month moon
(3)	丨 山 山			(4)	ノ 刀 月 月		
18.	川	<u>かわ</u>	river	26.	火	**か** <u>ひ</u>	fire
(3)	ノ 川 川			(4)	丶 丷 少 火		
19.	田	<u>た</u>	rice field	27.	水	**すい** <u>みず</u>	water
(5)	丨 冂 冂 田 田			(4)	丨 가 가 水		
20.	門	**もん**	gate	28.	木	**もく** <u>き</u>	tree wood
(8)	丨 冂 冂 冂 門 門			(4)	一 十 才 木		
21.	女	**じょ** <u>おんな</u>	woman	29.	金	**きん** <u>かね</u>	gold money
(3)	く タ 女			(8)	ノ 八 今 今 余 金 金		
22.	子	**こ**	child	30.	土	**ど** <u>つち</u>	earth ground
(3)	丁 了 子			(3)	一 十 土		
23.	車	**しゃ** <u>くるま</u>	vehicle	( ) : Kanji stroke count Bold letters : "on" readings Underlined letters : "kun" readings			
(7)	一 戸 亘 車						

Essential Words

1. 人 (ひと) — person
2. カナダ人 (かなだじん) — a person from Canada
3. 山 (やま) — mountain
4. 川 (かわ) — river
5. 田 (た) — rice field
6. 門 (もん) — gate
7. 女の人 (おんなのひと) — woman
8. 女の子 (おんなのこ) — girl
9. 車 (くるま) — car
10. 日 (ひ) — sun
11. 一日 (いちにち) — a day
12. 月 (つき) — moon
13. 四月 (しがつ) — April
14. 火 (ひ) — fire
15. 水 (みず) — water
16. 木 (き) — tree
17. お金 (かね) — money
18. 土 (つち) — earth

Words

1. 100人 (にん) — 100 people
2. 女性 (じょせい) — woman
3. 子供 (こども) — child
4. 日曜日 (にちようび) — Sunday
5. 月曜日 (げつようび) — Monday
6. 火曜日 (かようび) — Tuesday
7. 水曜日 (すいようび) — Wednesday
8. 木曜日 (もくようび) — Thursday
9. 金曜日 (きんようび) — Friday
10. 土曜日 (どようび) — Saturday

Reading Practice

1. 女の人
2. 山
3. 川
4. 田
5. 門
6. 女の子
7. 車
8. 日
9. 月
10. 火
11. 水
12. 木
13. お金
14. 土

Lesson 3

Dialogue パーティーで

3-1 Asking what is going on lately

（かんぱい！　かんぱい！）

佐藤　　：　こんにちは。
アリス：　あ、こんにちは。
佐藤　　：　ひさしぶりですね。お元気ですか。
アリス：　ええ、おかげさまで。
佐藤　　：　このごろどうですか。
アリス：　毎日とてもいそがしいです。
佐藤　　：　日本語の勉強ですか。
アリス：　ええ。宿題と予習が大変なんです。
佐藤　　：　そうですか。
アリス：　でも、おもしろいです。

3-2 Asking about food

佐藤 ： これ、おいしいですよ。食べませんか。
アリス： それ、何ですか。
佐藤 ： 魚のフライです。
アリス： そうですか。
佐藤 ： 取りましょうか。
アリス： あ、すみません。いただきます。
佐藤 ： はい。どうぞ。
アリス： ありがとうございます。
佐藤 ： どうですか。
アリス： おいしいですね。
佐藤 ： アリスさん、魚は好きですか。
アリス： ええ、好きです。
　　　　 でも、おさしみはあまり……。
佐藤 ： さしみはだめですか。
アリス： ええ、生の魚はちょっと……。
佐藤 ： そうですか。

Vocabulary List

⟨ ⟩: dictionary form
˥ : accent fall (for words only)

Dialogue

3-1

ぱ˥あてぃい	パーティー	party
かんぱ˥い。		Cheers! [word of toast]
こんにちは。		Hello., Good afternoon.
ひさしぶりですね。		I haven't seen you for a long time.
おげんきですか。	お元気ですか。	How are you?
げ˥んき(な)	元気(な)	fine, healthy, energetic
おかげさまで。		I'm fine, thank you. [Lit. Thanks to you.]
このごろ		nowadays
ど˥う		how
ま˥いにち	毎日	everyday
とても		very
いそがし˥い		busy
べんきょう	勉強	study
しゅくだい	宿題	homework
よしゅう	予習	preparation for class
が		[Group 1 particle for subject]
たいへん(な)	大変(な)	hard, difficult
〜んです		[See Notes on Grammar.]
で˥も		but, however
おもしろ˥い		interesting

3-2

おいしい		delicious
よ		[Group 3 particle for emphasizing statement]
〜ませんか		Would you like to ...?
さかな	魚	fish
ふらい	フライ	fried (food)
とりま˥す⟨と˥る⟩ (〜が〜を)	取ります⟨取る⟩	to take

〜ましょうか		Shall I ... ? [See Notes on Grammar.]
すみません。		Thank you.
ありがとうございます。		Thank you.
ね		[Group 3 particle for agreement]
すき(な)	好き(な)	to like
(お)さしみ		raw fish [お：prefix to show politeness]
あまり		not very
だめ(な)		no good, unacceptable
なま	生	raw
ちょっと		a little [See Notes on Discourse.]

Drill

むずかしい	難しい	difficult
たかい	高い	expensive
じてんしゃ	自転車	bicycle
やすい	安い	inexpensive
おおきい	大きい	large
ちいさい	小さい	small
かめら	カメラ	camera
いい		good
ひま(な)		free, to have time
かんたん(な)	簡単(な)	easy, simple
しずか(な)	静か(な)	quiet
きれい(な)		beautiful, clean
いいめいる	Eメール	e-mail
べんり(な)	便利(な)	useful, convenient
しんせつ(な)	親切(な)	kind
にく	肉	meat
きらい(な)		to dislike
えいが	映画	movie
ばざあ	バザー	bazaar
かいます〈かう〉 (〜が〜を)	買います〈買う〉	to buy
ばす	バス	bus
どんな		what kind of
〜ましょう		Let's ... [See Notes on Grammar.]
かえります〈かえる〉(〜が〜へ)	帰ります〈帰る〉	to go back, to return

Notes on Grammar

I Adjective sentences

So far you have learned two types of Japanese sentences: sentences ending in a verb in its polite form (See Lesson 1) and sentences ending in a noun+です(desu) (See Lesson 2).

Now a third type, adjective sentences are introduced. There are two types of adjective sentences, -い(i) adjective sentences and -な(na) adjective sentences.

A -い(i) adjective sentences

1. Sentence structure

The basic sentence structure is shown as follows.

> Noun は(wa) -い(i)adjective です(desu)。

Examples
1. この本はおもしろいです。(Kono hon wa omoshiroi desu.)
   This book is interesting.
2. かたかなは難しいです。(Katakana wa muzukashii desu.)
   Katakana is difficult.
3. ルインさんはいそがしいです。(Ruin san wa isogashii desu.)
   Lwin is busy.

What is common in these three sentences above is that:
(1) All the sentences end in です(desu).
(2) All of them contain a word ending in -い(i) directly followed by です(desu).
(3) A noun+は(wa) always comes first and a word ending in -い(i)+です(desu) follows it.

A word ending in -い(i) will be called an -い(i) adjective in this textbook. A phrase ending in -い(i)+です(desu) is the polite form of an -い(i) adjective. The polite form of an -い(i) adjective is used at the end of a sentence.

Examples

1. 専門の本は高いです。(Senmon no hon wa takai desu.)
   Specialist books are expensive.
2. 日本語の勉強はおもしろいです。
   　　　　　　　　　(Nihongo no benkyoo wa omoshiroi desu.)
   Studying Japanese is interesting.

2. Conjugation

For the polite negative form, replace -い(i) by -く(ku) and add **ありません** (arimasen).

For the polite perfective form, replace -い(i) by -かった(katta) and add です(desu).

For the polite perfective negative form, replace -い(i) by -く(ku) and add **ありません でした**(arimasen deshita).

† Table of the conjugation of -い(i) adjective "いそがしいです" †

	Polite form	
	Affirmative form	Negative form
Imperfective form	いそがしいです (isogashii desu)	いそがしくありません (isogashiku arimasen)
Perfective form	いそがしかったです (isogashikatta desu)	いそがしくありませんでした (isogashiku arimasen deshita)

Examples

1. あしたルインさんはいそがしくありません。
   　　　　　　　(Ashita Ruin san wa isogashiku arimasen.)
   Lwin is not busy tomorrow.
2. きのうルインさんはいそがしかったです。
   　　　　　　　(Kinoo Ruin san wa isogashikatta desu.)
   Lwin was busy yesterday.
3. この本はおもしろくありませんでした。
   　　　　　　　(Kono hon wa omoshiroku arimasen deshita.)
   This book was not interesting.

There is one exception to this rule: **いいです**(ii desu) "be good." The negative form is **よくありません**(yoku arimasen). The perfective form is **よかったです**(yokatta desu), and **よくありませんでした**(yoku arimasen deshita) is the perfective negative form.

† Table of the conjugation of いいです †

	Polite form	
	Affirmative form	Negative form
Imperfective form	いいです (ii desu)	よくありません (yoku arimasen)
Perfective form	よかったです (yokatta desu)	よくありませんでした (yoku arimasen deshita)

Examples

1. この辞書はよくありません。(Kono jisho wa yoku arimasen.)
   This dictionary is not good.
2. きのうの映画はよかったです。(Kinoo no eega wa yokatta desu.)
   The movie which I watched yesterday was good.

3. Question sentences and the way of answering

The way of making questions and the way of answering questions are the same as those of verb sentences. (See Lesson 1, Notes on Grammer IV.)

Example

A：日本語の勉強はおもしろいですか。
(Nihongo no benkyoo wa omoshiroi desu ka.)
Is studying Japanese interesting?

B：はい、おもしろいです。(Hai, omoshiroi desu.)
Yes, it is.

4. -い(i) adjective as a noun modifier

The -い(i) adjective modifies a noun. It always precedes a noun which it modifies. For this purpose, the polite form is inadequate; you must use the -い(i) adjective without です(desu).

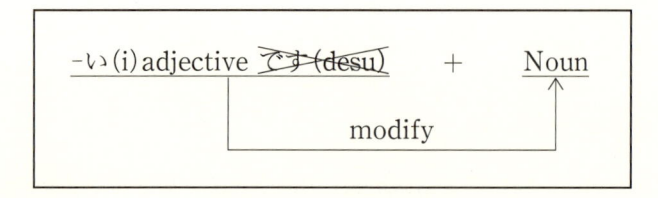

```
-い(i) adjective です(desu)    +    Noun
         └──────── modify ────────┘
```

Examples

1. これはおもしろい本です。(Kore wa omoshiroi hon desu.)
   This is an interesting book.
2. アリスさんはいい学生です。(Arisu san wa ii gakusee desu.)
   Alice is a good student.
3. おいしい魚を食べました。(Oishii sakana o tabemashita.)
   Someone* ate delicious fish.

(*"Someone" may be the speaker.)

B -な(na) adjective sentences

1. Sentence structure and conjugation

The basic sentence structure is as follows.

> Noun は(wa)　-な(na)adjective　です(desu)。

As shown in the Examples 1～4 below, 便利です (benri desu) has some functions that a noun has but also has some other functions just like an -い(i) adjective. In other words, 便利です (benri desu) comes at the end of a sentence.

The conjugation of -な(na) adjectives is the same as noun＋です(desu).

† Table of the conjugation of -な(na) adjective "便利です" †

	Polite form	
	Affirmative form	Negative form
Imperfective form	べんりです (benri desu)	べんりじゃありません (benri ja arimasen)
Perfective form	べんりでした (benri deshita)	べんりじゃありませんでした (benri ja arimasen deshita)

Examples

1. この辞書は便利です。(Kono jisho wa benri desu.)
   This dictionary is useful.
2. この辞書は便利じゃありません。(Kono jisho wa benri ja arimasen.)
   This dictionary isn't useful.
3. この辞書は便利でした。(Kono jisho wa benri deshita.)
   This dictionary was useful.
4. この辞書は便利じゃありませんでした。
   (Kono jisho wa benri ja arimasen deshita.)
   This dictionary wasn't useful.

2. Question sentences and the way of answering

The way of making questions and the way of answering questions are the same as those of verb sentences. (See Lesson 1, Notes on Grammar IV.)

Example

A：この辞書は便利ですか。(Kono jisho wa benri desu ka.)
Is this dictionary useful?

B：いいえ、便利じゃありません。(Iie, benri ja arimasen.)
No, it isn't useful.

3. -な(na) adjective as a noun modifier

The -な(na) adjective also modifies the noun it precedes. When -な(na) adjectives modify a noun, です(desu) is changed to な(na), as shown in Examples below. This kind of word will be called a -な(na) adjective in this textbook.

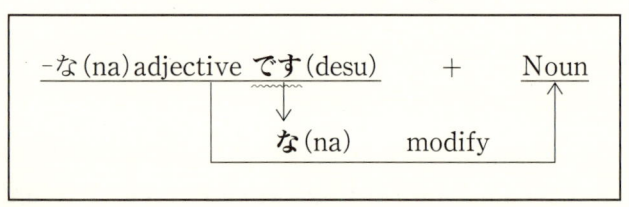

```
-な(na) adjective です(desu)    +    Noun
                 ↓                   ↑
                 な(na)    modify
```

Examples
1. ルインさんは静かな人です。(Ruin san wa shizuka na hito desu.)
   Lwin is a quiet person.
2. これは便利な辞書です。(Kore wa benri na jisho desu.)
   This is a useful dictionary.

4. 好き(suki) and きらい(kirai)

好きです(suki desu) "to like," and きらいです(kirai desu) "to dislike," act as -な(na) adjectives as follows. The first noun is the subject of a sentence and the second is the object.

```
Person は(wa)    Object が(ga)    好きです(suki desu)。
```

Examples
1. ルインさんは魚が好きです。(Ruin san wa sakana ga suki desu.)
   Lwin likes fish.
2. アリスさんは魚がきらいです。
                                (Arisu san wa sakana ga kirai desu.)
   Alice dislikes fish.
3. カーリンさんは魚が好きじゃありません。
                                (Kaarin san wa sakana ga suki ja arimasen.)
   Karin doesn't like fish.

II Invitation or suggestion

A V-ませんか(masen ka) and V-ましょう(mashoo)

Examples

1. 食堂へ行きます。(Shokudoo e ikimasu.)
   I will go to the cafeteria.
2. 食堂へ行きますか。(Shokudoo e ikimasu ka.)
   Are you going to the cafeteria?
3. 食堂へ行きませんか。(Shokudoo e ikimasen ka.)
   Would you like to go to the cafeteria?

Example 2 is a question form of Example 1. Example 3 seems to be a negative question form of Example 1, but Example 3 is used to make a suggestion or an invitation. In a suggestion or an invitation verbs should be in the imperfective negative form -ませんか(masen ka).

1. invitation

When you accept a speaker's invitation, -ましょう(mashoo) can be used to show agreement.

Example

A：食堂へ行きませんか。(Shokudoo e ikimasen ka.)
   Would you like to go to the cafeteria?
B：ええ、行きましょう。(Ee, ikimashoo.)
   Yes, let's.

2. suggestion

The other usage of -ませんか(masen ka) is to make a suggestion. When you accept a speaker's suggestion, the expression of your thanks such as **ありがとうございます** (arigatoo gozaimasu), etc. can be used.

Example

A：この薬を飲みませんか。(Kono kusuri o nomimasen ka.)
   　　　　　　　　　　　　　　　　　　　　　　　（薬：medicine)
   How about taking this medicine?
B：ありがとうございます。(Arigatoo gozaimasu.)
   Thank you.

B V-ましょうか(mashoo ka)

V-ましょうか(mashoo ka) can be used for an offer or invitation. When you accept a speaker's offer, the expressions of your thanks, like ありがとうございます(arigatoo gozaimasu), etc., can be used.

Examples
1. A：サラダを取りましょうか。(Sarada o torimashoo ka.)
   Shall I get you a salad?
   B：ありがとうございます。(Arigatoo gozaimasu.)
   Thank you.
2. A：窓を開けましょうか。(Mado o akemashoo ka.)
   Shall I open a window?
   　　　　　　　　　　　　　　　(窓を開ける：to open a window)
   B：ええ、お願いします。(Ee, onegai shimasu.)
   Yes, thank you.

III Extended predicate：んです(n desu) (1)

Examples
1. A：毎日いそがしいですか。(Mainichi isogashii desu ka.)
   Are you busy everyday?
   B：ええ、宿題が大変なんです。
   　　　　　　　　　　　　(Ee, shukudai ga taihenna n desu.)
   Yes, homework is hard.
2. A：それは何ですか。(Sore wa nan desu ka.)
   What is that?
   B：日本語の本です。おもしろいんです。
   　　　　　　　　　　　(Nihongo no hon desu. Omoshiroi n desu.)
   It's a Japanese book. (I am absorbed in reading it, because) It is interesting.

In the conversation in Example 1, B said 大変なんです(taihenna n desu) instead of 大変です(taihen desu). B answers A's question and gives more explanations for it.
The conversation in Example 2 starts with A's recognition that B is unusually absorbed in a book and A is interested in what kind of book B is reading. A asks "What is that book about?"
B answers A's question and after that B notices why A asked such a question, so B gives an explanation for that by saying "It is because the book is interesting."

In both examples, it is inadequate to say 大変です (taihen desu) or おもしろいです (omoshiroi desu) instead of 大変なんです (taihenna n desu) or おもしろいんです (omoshiroi n desu). The basic meaning of a sentence does not change by the addition of んです (n desu) to it. However, the presence of んです (n desu) adds certain overtones to the statement, because it indicates some explanation, either of what was said or done, or of what will be said or done. The connection of んです (n desu) is as follows. (See Lesson 8, Notes on Grammar II.)

	Sentence with extended predicate
この本はおもしろいです。 →	この本はおもしろいんです。
(Kono hon wa omoshiroi desu.)	(Kono hon wa omoshiroi n desu.)
This book is interesting.	
宿題が大変です。 →	宿題が大変なんです。
(Shukudai ga taihen desu.)	(Shukudai ga taihenna n desu.)
Homework is hard.	
あの人は学生です。 →	あの人は学生なんです。
(Ano hito wa gakusee desu.)	(Ano hito wa gakusee na n desu.)
That person is a student.	

IV Group 3 particles: ね(ne) and よ(yo)

ね(ne) and よ(yo) belong to the Group 3 particles and come at the end of a sentence. ね(ne) is used with a sentence to ask the hearer's agreement or to show the speaker's agreement, with a falling intonation. ね(ne) is used with a rising intonation to make a confirmation. (See Lesson 6, Dialogue.)

On the other hand, よ(yo) is used to state the speaker's own judgement or recognition emphatically. よ(yo) is pronounced with a slightly rising intonation.

Examples
1. A: この本を読みましたか。(Kono hon o yomimashita ka.)
   Did you read this book?
   B: はい。(Hai.)
   Yes.
   A: おもしろいですね。(Omoshiroi desu ne.)
   It's interesting, isn't it?
   B: ええ、そうですね。(Ee, soo desu ne.)
   Yes, it is.

2. A：この本を読みましたか。(Kono hon o yomimashita ka.)
   Did you read this book?
   B：いいえ。(Iie.)
   No.
   A：おもしろいですよ。(Omoshiroi desu yo.)
   It's really interesting.
   B：そうですか。(Soo desu ka.)
   I see.

V Adverbs：とても(totemo), 少し(sukoshi), ちょっと(chotto), あまり(amari)

A とても(totemo), 少し(sukoshi), ちょっと(chotto)

Adverbs modify a verb, an adjective or an adverb which they precede. とても (totemo) means "very much," 少し (sukoshi), ちょっと (chotto) means "a little." These adverbs show the degree of an action or state which a verb or adjective expresses.

Examples
1. この宿題は少し大変です。
   (Kono shukudai wa sukoshi taihen desu.)
   This homework is a little difficult.
2. この漢字はちょっと難しいです。
   (Kono kanji wa chotto muzukashii desu.)
   This kanji is a little bit difficult.
3. 毎日とてもいそがしいです。(Mainichi totemo isogashii desu.)
   I'm very busy everyday.

B あまり(amari)

あまり (amari) is always followed by a negative predicate. It means "not very" or "not so."

Examples
1. 魚はあまり好きじゃありません。
   (Sakana wa amari suki ja arimasen.)
   I don't like fish very much.
2. これはあまりよくありません。(Kore wa amari yoku arimasen.)
   This is not very good.

VI Conjunction：でも(demo)

でも(demo) means "but." It comes between two sentences.

> **Example**
> わたしは魚が好きです。でも、さしみは好きじゃありません。
> (Watashi wa sakana ga suki desu. Demo, sashimi wa suki ja arimasen.)
> I like fish, but I don't like raw fish.

VII Question words：どう(doo) and どんな(donna)

A どう(doo)

どう(doo) means "how." It is used to ask about the conditions of a thing or a person.

> **Examples**
> 1. A：日本語の勉強はどうですか。
>   (Nihongo no benkyoo wa doo desu ka.)
>   How is studying Japanese?
>   B：おもしろいです。(Omoshiroi desu.)
>   It's interesting.
> 2. A：大学の食堂はどうですか。
>   (Daigaku no shokudoo wa doo desu ka.)
>   How is the cafeteria in your university?
>   B：おいしいです。(Oishii desu.)
>   They serve good food.

B どんな(donna)

どんな(donna) means "what kind of." It precedes the noun it modifies.

> **Examples**
> 1. A：どんな本ですか。(Donna hon desu ka.)
>   What kind of book is it?
>   B：おもしろい本です。(Omoshiroi hon desu.)
>   It's an interesting book.
> 2. A：どんな人ですか。(Donna hito desu ka.)
>   What kind of person is she?
>   B：静かな人です。(Shizukana hito desu.)
>   She is a quiet person.

VIII Omission of the particles : は(wa), が(ga), を(o)

Look at the following sentences.

       a．これはいくらですか。(Kore wa ikura desu ka.)
          How much is this?
       b．これ、いくらですか。(Kore, ikura desu ka.)

Compared with sentence a. sentence b. lacks the particle は(wa). The difference is that while a. is uttered in an official way, b. is used in a familiar manner. Dropping the particle は(wa) makes a sentence colloquial. This is also the case with the omission of the particles が(ga) and を(o). The next sentence appears in Dialogue 1-3, line 1 of Lesson 1.

       魚フライ定食、お願いします。
                                  (Sakanafuraiteeshoku onegaishimasu.)
          Fried fish set, please.

The particle を(o) must be added to 魚フライ定食 (sakanafuraiteeshoku), when speaking formally.

Examples

    1．これ(は)、おいしいですよ。(Kore (wa), oishii desu yo.)
       This is delicious, you know.
    2．漢字(を)、勉強しましたか。(Kanji (o) benkyoo shimashita ka.)
       Did you study kanji?

Notes on Discourse

I ちょっと(Chotto)

A "a little"
As shown in Notes on Grammar VI of this lesson, ちょっと(chotto) is an adverb meaning "a little."

   1. A：サラダを食べましたか。(Sarada o tabemashita ka.)
       Did you eat salad?
      B：はい、ちょっと食べました。(Hai, chotto tabemashita.)
       Yes, I had a little.

B Softening one's words
ちょっと(chotto) can be considered as a signal to soften one's words or thoughts, and to give them a tone of reserve.

   1. この本はちょっとおもしろくありません。
                              (Kono hon wa chotto omoshiroku arimasen.)
      This book is not so interesting.
   2. A：映画、見ませんか。(Eega, mimasen ka.)
       Would you like to watch the movie?
      B：あ、きょうはちょっといそがしいんです。
                              (A, kyoo wa chotto isogashii n desu.)
       I'm a little busy today.

C Negative reply
ちょっと(chotto) is also used to give a negative reply. As an indirect expression, it is used in the sentence pattern of [topic noun＋particle は(wa)] followed by ちょっと(chotto), without referring to the predicate.

   1. A：さしみはだめですか。(Sashimi wa dame desu ka.)
       Don't you eat "sashimi"?

　　　　B：ええ、生の魚はちょっと……。(Ee, nama no sakana wa chotto....)
　　　　No, I don't eat raw fish.
2.　　A：あしたはどうですか。(Ashita wa doo desu ka.)
　　　　How about tomorrow?
　　　　B：あしたはちょっと……。(Ashita wa chotto....)
　　　　Tomorrow is not so good.

Drill

練習1　Nは　　Aです　　　(imperfective affirmative form)
　　　　　Nは　Nが　Aです　　(imperfective affirmative form)

〈STRUCTURE〉

a.

例）日本語は　　　　　　難しいです。

1. 漢字　　　　　　　　おもしろい
2. 魚フライ定食　　　　おいしい
3. アリスさん　　　　　いそがしい
4. 専門の本　　　　　　高い
5. 自転車　　　　　　　安い
6. ルインさんのかばん　大きい
7. アリスさんのかばん　小さい
8. 日本のカメラ　　　　いい

b.

例）ルインさんは　　元気です。

1. ルインさん　　　ひま
2. 宿題　　　　　　大変
3. ひらがな　　　　簡単
4. 図書館　　　　　静か
5. 食堂　　　　　　きれい
6. Eメール　　　　便利
7. カーリンさん　　親切

c.

例）日本語は　　漢字が　　難しいです。

1. 日本語　　ひらがな　おもしろい
2. 日本語　　文法　　　大変
3. ルインさん　魚　　　好き
4. ルインさん　肉　　　きらい

⟨USAGE⟩

例) A：日本語は 難しいですか。
　　B：はい、難しいです。
　　A：何が 難しいですか。
　　B：文法が 難しいです。

練習2　　いＡ くありません　　　(imperfective negative form)
　　　　　なＡ じゃありません　　(imperfective negative form)

⟨STRUCTURE⟩

a.

例) 日本語は 難しくありません。

(Use the words in 練習1 a.)

b.

例) ルインさんは 元気じゃありません。

(Use the words in 練習1 b.)

c.

例) A：日本語は 難しいですか。
　　B：はい、難しいです。／いいえ、難しくありません。

1. 漢字　　　　　　　おもしろい
2. ルインさん　　　　ひま
3. アリスさん　　　　いそがしい
4. ルインさん　　　　元気
5. 魚フライ定食　　　おいしい
6. ルインさん　コーヒー　好き

d. Question word　どう

例) A：日本語は どうですか。
　　B：おもしろいです。／おもしろくありません。

1. 文法　　簡単
2. 漢字　　難しい
3. 宿題　　大変

| 練習 3 | い A かったです | (perfective affirmative form) |
| | な A でした | (perfective affirmative form) |

〈STRUCTURE〉

a.

例) 宿題は　　　　難しかったです。

1. アリスさん　　　いそがしい
2. 魚フライ定食　　おいしい
3. 専門の本　　　　高い
4. 映画　　　　　　おもしろい
5. かばん　　　　　安い
6. パーティー　　　いい

b.

例) ルインさんは　元気でした。

1. ルインさん　　ひま
2. 宿題　　　　　大変
3. 図書館　　　　静か

| 練習 4 | い A くありませんでした | (perfective negative form) |
| | な A じゃありませんでした | (perfective negative form) |

〈STRUCTURE〉

a.

例) 宿題は　難しくありませんでした。

(Use the words in 練習3 a. above.)

b.

例) ルインさんは　元気じゃありませんでした。

(Use the words in 練習3 b. above.)

c.

例) A：ルインさんは　元気でしたか。
　　B：はい、元気でした。／いいえ、元気じゃありませんでした。

1. 魚フライ定食　　おいしい
2. 宿題　　　　　　大変
3. 専門の本　　　　高い

4. アリスさん　　　いそがしい
5. 図書館　　　　静か
   （としょかん）　（しず）
6. パーティー　　　いい

〈USAGE〉

①

例）A：きのう魚フライ定食を食べました。
　　　　　（さかな）（ていしょく）（た）
　　B：おいしかったですか。
　　A：はい、おいしかったです。／いいえ、おいしくありませんでした。

1. 漢字を勉強しました。　　　　大変
   （かんじ）（べんきょう）　　（たいへん）
2. バザーでかばんを買いました。　安い
   　　　　　　　　　（か）　　（やす）

②

例）A：きのう映画を見ました。
　　　　　（えいが）（み）
　　B：どうでしたか。
　　A：とてもおもしろかったです。

1. パーティーへ行きました。　　いい
2. 日本語を勉強しました。　　　ちょっと大変
   （にほんご）（べんきょう）　　　　（たいへん）

練習5　　あまり ～ ません

〈STRUCTURE〉

例）A：ひらがなは難しいですか。
　　　　　　　　　（むずか）
　　B：いいえ、あまり難しくありません。
　　　　　　　　　　（むずか）

1. きょうはいそがしいです。
2. 魚は好きです。
   （さかな）（す）
3. バスは便利です。
   　　　（べんり）
4. 小さい辞書はいいです。
   　　　　（じしょ）
5. 先週はいそがしかったです。
   （せんしゅう）
6. 予習は大変でした。
   （よしゅう）（たいへん）

練習6　　A／どんな＋N

〈STRUCTURE〉

a.

例）これは本です。（おもしろいです。）→　これはおもしろい本です。
　　　　（ほん）　　　　　　　　　　　　　　　　　　　　（ほん）

1. これは本です。(高いです。)
2. これは宿題です。(難しいです。)
3. アリスさんは人です。(いいです。)

b.
例) ルインさんは学生です。(元気です。) → ルインさんは元気な学生です。

1. これは辞書です。(便利です。)
2. ナロンさんは学生です。(静かです。)
3. アリスさんは人です。(きれいです。)

c. Question word　どんな
例) A：アリスさんは　どんな人ですか。
　　B：きれいな人です。

1. カーリンさん　　　　人　　　親切
2. ルインさん　　　　　学生　　元気
3. ルインさんの辞書　　辞書　　小さい
4. ルインさんのかばん　かばん　大きい

練習7　　Vませんか／Vましょう

〈STRUCTURE〉
a. invitation
例) A：食堂へ行きませんか。
　　B：ええ、行きましょう。

1. コーヒーを飲みます。
2. CDを聞きます。
3. 会館へ帰ります。
4. 映画を見ます。

b. suggestion
例) A：このサラダ、おいしいですよ。食べませんか。
　　B：はい。ありがとうございます。

1. コーヒー　　おいしい　　飲みます
2. 本　　　　　おもしろい　読みます

Aural Comprehension

I Listen to the conversations and answer the following questions.

(A)　After eating lunch　　（お昼ごはん：lunch）

1．女の人は何を食べましたか。

2．女の人は魚が好きですか。

(B)　On campus : Alice meets Ms. Nakata by accident.

1．アリスさんはこのごろどうですか。

2．何が大変ですか。

(C)　In the International students dormitory

1．映画はおもしろかったですか。

2．アリスさんはビデオを見ますか。

(D)　About food　　（どうして：why　ベジタリアン：vegetarian　牛乳：milk　たまご：egg）

1．ジョンさんはどうしてさしみを食べませんか。

2．ジョンさんはたまごを食べますか。

II （数字）Listen to the conversations and write down the numbers with the counters.

　　1．_____　2．_____　3．_____　4．_____

III One of the people in each conversation is you.

　　Listen to what the other person says and write down the answer to your question.

　　Your question：これは魚ですか。肉(meat)ですか。（Is this fish or meat ?）

　　1．_____　2．_____　3．_____

Reading Comprehension

バンバンさんは3週間前に日本に来ました。先週、日本語の授業が始まりました。授業はおもしろいです。でも、宿題と予習が大変です。毎日とてもいそがしいです。部屋で、教科書を読みます。テープも聞きます。きのう、留学生会館のパーティーに行きました。パーティーでおいしい食べ物を食べました。魚のフライも食べました。でも、さしみは食べませんでした。生の魚はあまり好きじゃあありません。

- 部屋　room
- 食べ物　food

質問

1. バンバンさんはいつ日本に来ましたか。
2. 日本語の授業はいつ始まりましたか。
3. バンバンさんはこのごろどうですか。
4. バンバンさんは何が大変ですか。
5. バンバンさんはパーティーでさしみを食べましたか。
6. バンバンさんは生の魚が好きですか。

Kanji Practice

New Kanji

No.	Kanji	Reading	Meaning	No.	Kanji	Reading	Meaning
31.	口	**こう** / くち	mouth	39.	友	とも	friend
(3)	丨 冂 口			(4)	一 ナ 方 友		
32.	目	**もく** / め	eye, suffix for ordinals	40.	大	**だい** / おおきい	big, large
(5)	丨 冂 円 目 目			(3)	一 ナ 大		
33.	耳	みみ	ear	41.	小	**しょう** / ちいさい	little, small
(6)	一 丆 丆 乊 耳 耳			(3)	亅 小 小		
34.	手	て	hand	42.	本	**ほん** / もと	book, origin
(4)	一 二 三 手			(5)	一 十 才 木 本		
35.	足	あし / たりる / たす	foot, leg; to be enough; to add up; to add to	43.	明	あかるい	bright
(7)	丶 冂 口 旦 早 足 足			(8)	丨 冂 月 日 明 明 明 明		
36.	先	**せん** / さき	ahead, priority	44.	男	**だん** / おとこ	man, human male
(6)	丿 亠 卄 生 先 先			(7)	丨 冂 田 田 田 男 男		
37.	生	**せい** / いきる / うまれる、なま	life, to be alive; to be born; raw	45.	好	すき(な)	to like, favorite
(5)	丿 一 牛 生 生			(6)	乀 夂 女 奴 奵 好		
38.	学	**がく**	to study				
(8)	丶 丷 ⺍ ⺍ 学 学 学 学						

( ) : Kanji stroke count
Bold letters : "on" readings
Underlined letters : "kun" readings

Essential Words

1. 口 (くち) — mouth
2. 目 (め) — eye
3. 耳 (みみ) — ear
4. 手 (て) — hand
5. 足 (あし) — foot
6. 先生 (せんせい) — teacher
7. 学生 (がくせい) — student
8. 友達 (ともだち) — friend
9. 大きい (おお) — big
10. 大学 (だいがく) — university
11. 大学生 (だいがくせい) — university student
12. 小さい (ちい) — small
13. 本 (ほん) — book
14. 日本 (にほん) — Japan
15. 日本人 (にほんじん) — Japanese person
16. 明るい (あか) — bright
17. 男の人 (おとこ ひと) — man
18. 好き(な) (す) — to like, favorite

Words

1. 人口 (じんこう) — population
2. 二つ目 (ふた め) — second
3. 足りる (た) — to be enough
4. 足す (た) — to add up, to add to
5. 先に (さき) — ahead
6. 小学生 (しょうがくせい) — elementary student
7. 生きる (い) — to live
8. 生まれる (う) — to be born
9. 生 (なま) — raw
10. 男性 (だんせい) — man

Reading Practice

1. 小さい口
2. 大きい目
3. 小さい耳
4. 大きい手
5. 小さい足
6. 大きい本
7. 男の子
8. 日本人の学生
9. 日本人の友達 (だち)
10. 好きな本

Lesson 4

Dialogue いろいろな建物(たてもの)

4-1 On campus

アリス(ありす)： 広(ひろ)いですね。
ルイン(るいん)： そうですね。
アリス： 図書館(としょかん)の右(みぎ)に高(たか)い建物(たてもの)がありますね。
ルイン： あの白(しろ)いのですか。
アリス： ええ。あれは何(なん)ですか。
ルイン： ああ、あれは工学部(こうがくぶ)の１号館(ごうかん)です。
アリス： そうですか。

Dialogue いろいろな建物

4-2 Asking where the classroom is

Alice asks a student that passes by where the classroom is.

アリス：　　すみません。
男の人：　　はい。
アリス：　　あのう、21番教室はどこですか。
男の人：　　あ、21番教室は2階です。
アリス：　　2階のどの辺ですか。
男の人：　　ええと、階段の左に20番教室があります。
アリス：　　はい。
男の人：　　21番はそのおくです。
アリス：　　はい。どうもありがとうございました。
男の人：　　いいえ。

4-3 Looking for Lwin at the laboratory

Thinking Lwin is in his laboratory, Alice has come looking for him.

アリス：　　すみません。
学生：　　　はい。
アリス：　　こちらは本田研究室ですか。
学生：　　　いいえ、ちがいます。本田研究室は向こうです。
アリス：　　あ、そうですか。どうもすみません。

◇　　　　◇　　　　◇

アリス：　　すみません。こちら、本田研究室ですか。

学生　：　はい、そうです。

アリス：　あのう、ルイン(るいん)さん、いますか。

学生　：　ルイン(るいん)さんですか。あ、ルイン(るいん)さんは食堂(しょくどう)へ行(い)きました。

アリス：　あ、そうですか。どうも。

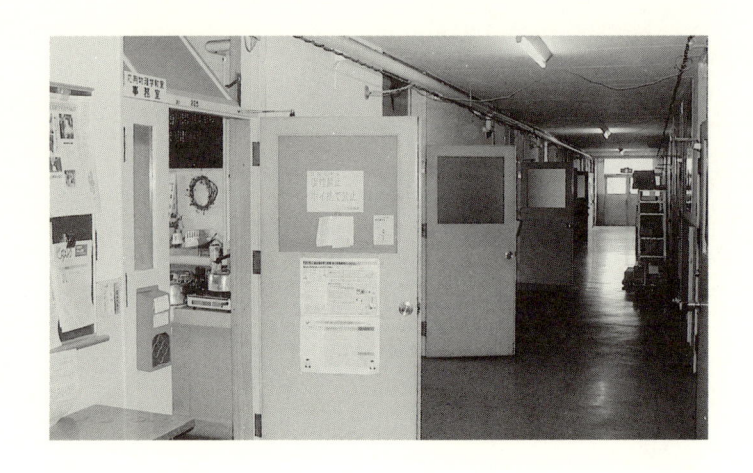

4-Supplement   デパートの売り場で

At the food section

ルイン： すみません。
店員 ： はい。
ルイン： これ、いくらですか。
店員 ： 160円です。
ルイン： じゃ、これ、2つください。
店員 ： はい。

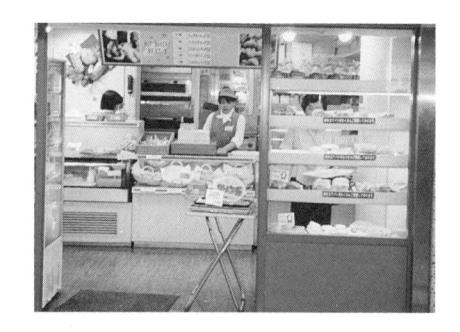

At the shirt section

店員 ： いらっしゃいませ。
ルイン： すみません。これのL、ありますか。
店員 ： ああ、グレーのLは今、ございませんが。
ルイン： そうですか。ほかの色はありますか。
店員 ： はい。赤と青はございますが。
ルイン： そうですか。うーん。
　　　　 じゃ……。どうも。

Vocabulary List

⟨ ⟩ : dictionary form
┐ : accent fall (for words only)

Dialogue

4-1

いろいろ(な)		various
たて┐もの	建物	building
ひろ┐い	広い	spacious, big
そうですね。		Yes, it is.
みぎ	右	right
に		in, at [particle for existence place]
たか┐い	高い	high, tall
あрима┐す⟨あ┐る⟩ (〜に〜が)		There is ... [used for non-living things]
しろ┐い	白い	white
の		one [particle for noun substitution]
ああ、		oh
〜ごうかん	〜号館	building number ... [counter]

4-2

すみません。		Excuse me.
あのう		Um ...
〜ばん	〜番	number ... [counter]
きょうしつ	教室	classroom
〜かい	〜階	...th floor [counter]
どのへん	どの辺	where about
〜へん	〜辺	around, near by, in the vicinity
ええと		Let me see ...
かいだん	階段	stairs
ひだり	左	left
お┐く		behind, beyond
どうもありがとうございました。		Thank you very much.
いいえ。		No problem.

4-3

ほんだ	本田	[personal name]

むこう		over there, that away
どうもすみません。		I'm sorry.
いま｜す〈いる〉　　（～に～が）		There is ... [used for living things]
どうも。		Thank you.

4-Supplement

でぱ｜あと	デパート	department store
うりば	売り場	section of a dept. store
い｜くら		how much
ください。		I'll take ....
ふたつ｜	2つ	two
いらっしゃいませ。		Can I help you?
え｜る	L	large size
ぐれ｜い	グレー	gray
ございま｜す		[polite form of あります]
ほか		other
いろ｜	色	color
あ｜か	赤	red
あ｜お	青	blue
う一ん。		Well, let me see.

Drill

つくえ	机	desk
いす		chair
とけい	時計	clock, watch
でんわ	電話	telephone
こんぴゅ｜うたあ	コンピューター	computer
ここ		here
そこ		there
あそこ		there
こんぴゅうたある｜うむ	コンピュータールーム	computer room
うえ	上	on, above
した	下	under, below
ま｜え	前	in front of
うしろ	後ろ	behind
あいだ	間	between
となり		next to
な｜か	中	inside

そば		near
そと	外	outside
いぬ	犬	dog
ねこ		cat
へや	部屋	room
えあこん	エアコン	air conditioner
れいぞうこ	冷蔵庫	refrigerator
あぱあと	アパート	apartment
き	木	tree
ゆうびんきょく	郵便局	post office
ほけんかんりしつ	保健管理室	health control center
りゅうがくせいせんたあ	留学生センター	Education Center for International Students
せいきょう	生協	co-op
きた	北	north
みなみ	南	south
にし	西	west
ひがし	東	east
といれ	トイレ	toilet, restroom
えれべいたあ	エレベーター	elevator
えすかれいたあ	エスカレーター	escalator
くつ		shoes
しゃつ	シャツ	shirt
かさ		umbrella
くろい	黒い	black
あかい	赤い	red
あおい	青い	blue
けさ		this morning
こうちゃ	紅茶	(black) tea
～ふん/ぷん	～分	minute(s)
～がつ	～月	month
～にち	～日	day
たんじょうび	誕生日	birthday

Notes on Grammar

I Location of a thing or a person

A Structure of existential sentences

All things or all persons occupy a definite place. The basic English pattern "There is something/someone somewhere." is expressed in the following patterns in Japanese.

> Place　に(ni)　Non-living thing　が(ga)　あります(arimasu)。

> Place　に(ni)　Living thing　が(ga)　います(imasu)。

The verb あります(arimasu) is used when the noun preceding が(ga), the subject of a sentence, is a non-living or non-moving thing.

The verb います(imasu) is used with living things which can move by themselves, such as human beings and animals.

Examples

1. 大学に食堂があります。(Daigaku ni shokudoo ga arimasu.)
   There is a cafeteria at the university.
2. 教室にテレビがあります。(Kyooshitsu ni terebi ga arimasu.)
   There is a TV in the classroom.
3. 食堂にルインさんがいます。(Shokudoo ni Ruin san ga imasu.)
   Lwin is in the cafeteria.
4. 東京に友達がいます。(Tookyoo ni tomodachi ga imasu.)
   I have a friend in Tokyo.

In this pattern the place or the location is signaled by the particle に(ni). に(ni) indicates the place where a thing or a person is located, while で(de), which has already been introduced in Lesson 1, Notes on Grammar III, indicates the place where an action takes place. In addition, the particle へ(e) which was also introduced in Lesson 1, Notes on Grammer III, indicates the direction in which an actor goes or comes.

> **Examples**
>
> 1. 図書館に本があります。(Toshokan ni hon ga arimasu.)
>   There are books in the library.
> 2. 図書館で本を読みます。(Toshokan de hon o yomimasu.)
>   Someone* reads books in the library.
> 3. ルインさんは図書館へ行きます。(Ruin san wa toshokan e ikimasu.)
>   Lwin goes to the library.
>
> (*"Someone" may be the speaker.)

B Nouns of place

The following are some nouns of place used in a phrase indicating a location.

(1) 大学 (daigaku)   university
     食堂 (shokudoo)   cafeteria
     教室 (kyooshitsu)   classroom
     1階 (ikkai)   the first floor

(2) ここ (koko)   here
     そこ (soko)   there or the hearer's area
     あそこ (asoko)   over there
     どこ (doko)   where

The difference among ここ(koko), そこ(soko), あそこ(asoko) and どこ(doko) in (2) is the same as that of これ(kore), それ(sore), あれ(are) and どれ(dore).

(3) 机の上   (tsukue no ue)   on the desk
        下   (shita)   under the desk
     建物の前   (tatemono no mae)   in front of the building
        後ろ   (ushiro)   behind the building
        中   (naka)   inside the building
        外   (soto)   outside the building
        おく   (oku)   at the far end of the building
        となり (tonari)   next to the building
        横   (yoko)   on the side of the building
        そば   (soba)   by the building
        近く   (chikaku)   near the building
        右   (migi)   on the right of the building
        左   (hidari)   on the left of the building
        東   (higashi)   on the east side of the building

	西 にし	(	nishi)	on the west side of the building
	南 みなみ	(	minami)	on the south side of the building
	北 きた	(	kita)	on the north side of the building
ＡとＢの間 あいだ	(A to B	no aida)		between A and B

(4)　ルインさんのところ (Ruin san no tokoro)　　place where Lwin is, Lwin's place
　　　友達のところ (tomodachi no tokoro)　　place where a friend is, a friend's place
　　　ともだち

(4) shows that ルインさん (Ruin san) is the name of a person, while ルインさんのところ (Ruin san no tokoro) is a noun of place. When you want to say "I went to Lwin's,"
say (○)　：ルインさんのところへ行きました。(Ruin san no tokoro e ikimashita.)
　　　　　　　　　　　　　　い
don't say (×)：ルインさんへ行きました。(Ruin san e ikimashita.)
　　　　　　　　　　　い

Examples

1. 1階にトイレがあります。(Ikkai ni toire ga arimasu.)
   いっかい
   There is a rest room on the first floor.

2. あそこに高い建物があります。
   　　　　たか　たてもの
   　　　　　　　　(Asoko ni takai tatemono ga arimasu.)
   There is a tall building over there.

3. 机の上に本があります。(Tsukue no ue ni hon ga arimasu.)
   つくえ　うえ　ほん
   There is a book on the desk.

4. 工学部の前に図書館があります。
   こうがくぶ　まえ　としょかん
   　　　　　　　　(Koogakubu no mae ni toshokan ga arimasu.)
   There is a library in front of the Faculty of Engineering.

   cf. 工学部の前でアリスさんに会いました。
   　　こうがくぶ　まえ　　　　　　あ
   　　　　　　　　(Koogakubu no mae de Arisu san ni aimashita.)
   I met Alice in front of the Faculty of Engineering.

C Sentence structure describing where things are

When what exists is the topic of a sentence, the following sentence patterns are used.

| Non-living thing | は (wa) | Place | に (ni) | あります (arimasu)。|

| Living thing | は (wa) | Place | に (ni) | います (imasu)。|

Examples

1. ルインさんは食堂にいます。(Ruin san wa shokudoo ni imasu.)
   しょくどう
   Lwin is in the cafeteria.

2. 図書館は工学部の前にあります。
   (Toshokan wa koogakubu no mae ni arimasu.)
   The library is in front of the Faculty of Engineering.
3. カーリンさんはどこにいますか。
   (Kaarin san wa doko ni imasu ka.)
   Where is Karin?
4. A：かばんはどこにありますか。(Kaban wa doko ni arimasu ka.)
   Where is the bag?
   B：机の下にあります。(Tsukue no shita ni arimasu.)
   It's under the desk.

D Humble form of あります(arimasu)：ございます(gozaimasu)

ございます(gozaimasu) means the same as あります(arimasu). This form is called a humble form and used when it is necessary for the speaker to humble himself/herself in order to show respect, or deference to the hearer. For example, sales clerks who are working for a department store use ございます(gozaimasu) instead of あります(arimasu) when they speak to customers.

Examples

1. Customer：このシャツのLサイズはありますか。
   (Kono shatsu no eru-saizu wa arimasu ka.)
   Is there an L-size shirt of this one?
   Clerk　　：はい、ございます。(Hai, gozaimasu.)
   Yes, there is.
2. Customer：くつ売り場はどこにありますか。
   (Kutsu uriba wa doko ni arimasu ka.)
   Where is the shoe department?
   Clerk　　：2階にございます。(Nikai ni gozaimasu.)
   It is on the second floor.

II Substitution：の(no) as a substitute for a noun

Example

A：これはだれのかばんですか。(Kore wa dare no kaban desu ka.)
Whose bag is this?
B：わたしのです。(Watashi no desu.)
It's mine.

A：赤いのは。(Akai no wa.)
How about the red one?

B：アリスさんのです。(Arisu san no desu.)
It's Alice's.

In a modifier+noun, like noun+の(no)+noun, -い(i)adjective+noun, etc., a modified noun can be replaced by の(no), when the referent is obvious between the speaker and the hearer. And omit one の(no) in the case of noun + の(no)+の(no). Take ルインさんの本(Ruin san no hon) for example. When 本(hon) is replaced by の, you may expect ルインさんのの(Ruin san no no). However, the correct form is ルインさんの(Ruin san no).

-い(i)adjective + Noun	赤いかばん (akai kaban)	→ 赤いの (akai no)
-な(na)adjective + Noun	便利な辞書 (benrina jisho)	→ 便利なの (benrina no)
Noun + の(no) + Noun	ルインさんの本 (Ruin san no hon)	→ ルインさんの (Ruin san no)

Examples

1. A：これはアリスさんの本ですか。
   (Kore wa Arisu san no hon desu ka.)
   Is this Alice's book?

   B：いいえ、アリスさんのじゃありません。ルインさんのです。
   (Iie, Arisu san no ja arimasen. Ruin san no desu.)
   No, it's not Alice's. It's Lwin's.

2. A：あそこに高い建物がありますね。
   (Asoko ni takai tatemono ga arimasu ne.)
   You can see a tall building over there, can't you?

   B：あの白いのですか。(Ano shiroi no desu ka.)
   Are you talking about that white one?

III Substitution：です(desu) as a substitute for a verb

Examples

1. A：何を食べますか。(Nani o tabemasu ka.)

　　　　　　　What do you eat?
　　　　B：サラダです。(Sarada desu.)
　　　　　　I eat salad.
　2.　A：どこへ行きますか。(Doko e ikimasu ka.)
　　　　　　Where are you going?
　　　　B：図書館です。(Toshokan desu.)
　　　　　　I'm going to the library.
　3.　A：カーリンさんはどこにいますか。
　　　　　　　　　　　　(Kaarin san wa doko ni imasu ka.)
　　　　　　Where is Karin?
　　　　B：食堂です。(Shokudoo desu.)
　　　　　　She's in the cafeteria.

In each of the examples above, です(desu) serves as a substitute for the verb used in the previous sentence, 食べます(tabemasu) "to eat," 行きます(ikimasu) "to go" or います(imasu) "to be." です(desu) is used to avoid repeating the verb mentioned previously. です(desu) can replace not only the imperfective form of a verb but also the perfective form of a verb.

です(desu) cannot be used alone. It follows a noun. The Group 1 particles, が(ga), を(o), へ(e) and に(ni) are omitted before です(desu), while から(kara), etc. can be kept.

Examples　1.　A：辞書はどこにありますか。(Jisho wa doko ni arimasu ka.)
　　　　　　　　Where is the dictionary?
　　　　　B：机の上です。(Tsukue no ue desu.)
　　　　　　　It's on the desk.
　2.　A：ルインさんはどこから来ましたか。
　　　　　　　　　　　　(Ruin san wa doko kara kimashita ka.)
　　　　　　Where did Lwin come from?
　　　　B：ミャンマーからです。(Myanmaa kara desu.)
　　　　　　He came from Myanmar.
　3.　アリス　：ルインさんは何を食べますか。
　　　　　　　　　　　　(Arisu: Ruin san wa nani o tabemasu ka.)
　　　　　　　　What will you eat?
　　　ルイン　：わたしは魚です。(Ruin: Watashi wa sakana desu.)
　　　　　　　　I'll eat fish.
　　　アリス　：カーリンさんは。(Arisu: Kaarin san wa.)

How about you, Karin?

カーリン：肉です。(Kaarin: Niku desu.)
I'll eat meat.

The sentence わたしは魚です (Watashi wa sakana desu) may sound strange. But this です (desu) does not mean the equality of two nouns.

IV Demonstrative pronouns (2): それ (sore) and その (sono)

それ (sore) and その (sono) were introduced in Lesson 2, Notes on Grammar III. They can also be used to refer to what was just mentioned.

Examples
1. A：日本語の勉強はどうですか。
   (Nihongo no benkyoo wa doo desu ka.)
   How is your study of Japanese going?
   B：毎日宿題があります。(Mainichi shukudai ga arimasu.)
   I have homework everyday.
   A：それは大変ですね。(Sore wa taihen desu ne.)
   That's hard, isn't it?
2. A：トイレはどこですか。(Toire wa doko desu ka.)
   Where is the rest room?
   B：階段の右に20番教室があります。
   (Kaidan no migi ni nijuuban kyooshitsu ga arimasu.)
   Room 20 is on the right of the stairs.
   A：はい。(Hai.)
   I see.
   B：トイレはその前です。(Toire wa sono mae desu.)
   The rest room is in front of it.

それ (sore) in the above Example 1 stands for 毎日宿題があります (Mainichi shukudai ga arimasu). その (sono) in the above Example 2 stands for 20番教室の (nijuuban kyooshitsu no).

V Question words: いくら(ikura) and いくつ(ikutsu)

A いくら(ikura)

いくら(ikura) means "how much." It is used for talking about money.

Example
A: あれはいくらですか。(Are wa ikura desu ka.)
How much is that?
B: 3800円です。(Sanzenhappyakuen desu.)
It costs 3800 yen.

B いくつ(ikutsu)

いくつ(ikutsu) means "how many" or "how old." It is used to ask the number of things or the age of a person.

Examples
1. A: テープはいくつ買いましたか。
(Teepu wa ikutsu kaimashita ka.)
How many cassette tapes did you buy?
B: 3つです。(Mittsu desu.) (3つ: three, a numeral of Type B, See the Notes on Grammar VII of this lesson.)
I bought three.
2. A: ルインさんはいくつですか。(Ruin san wa ikutsu desu ka.)
How old is Lwin?
B: 25さいです。(Nijuugosai desu.)   (さい: 〜years old)
He is 25 years old.

VI Conjunctions: じゃ(ja) and では(dewa)

じゃ(ja) means "if so" or "then."
では(dewa) is a formal form of じゃ(ja).

Examples
1. A: これはいくらですか。(Kore wa ikura desu ka.)
How much is this?
B: 500円です。(Gohyakuen desu.)
It's 500 yen.

    A：じゃ、これをください。(Ja, kore o kudasai.)
      If so, I'll take this.
 2. 先生：じゃ、また、あした。(Sensee: Ja, mata, ashita.)
      O.K. See you again tommorow.
    学生：はい。では、失礼します。
              (Gakusee: Hai. Dewa, shitsuree shimasu.)
      O.K. Good-bye.

VII Numerals and some numbers (2)

Numerals of Type A and some counters like 円(en) for money, 時(ji) for the hour of the day, and 分(fun) for the minute, were introduced in Lesson 1, Notes on Grammar IX. Here, Numerals of Type B, which are of Japanese origin, are introduced.

A Numerals of Type B

1つ	ひとつ(hitotsu)		11	じゅういち(juuichi)
2つ	ふたつ(futatsu)		12	じゅうに(juuni)
3つ	みっつ(mittsu)		13	じゅうさん(juusan)
4つ	よっつ(yottsu)		:	
5つ	いつつ(itsutsu)			
6つ	むっつ(muttsu)			
7つ	ななつ(nanatsu)			
8つ	やっつ(yattsu)			
9つ	ここのつ(kokonotsu)			
10	とお(too)			

question word：いくつ(ikutsu)

Numerals of Type B go only as far as 10; beyond 10, Type A numerals are used.

B Some other Japanese numbers

1. **Name of the month：~月(gatsu)**

1月	いちがつ(ichigatsu)
2月	にがつ(nigatsu)
3月	さんがつ(sangatsu)
4月	しがつ(shigatsu)

5月　ごがつ(gogatsu)
6月　ろくがつ(rokugatsu)
7月　**しち**がつ(shichigatsu)
8月　はちがつ(hachigatsu)
9月　**く**がつ(kugatsu)
10月　じゅうがつ(juugatsu)
11月　じゅういちがつ(juuichigatsu)
12月　じゅうにがつ(juunigatsu)
question word：何月　なんがつ(nangatsu)

2. Day of the month：～日 (nichi/ka)

1日	**ついたち**(tsuitachi)	11日	じゅういちにち(juuichinichi)
2日	**ふつか**(futsuka)	12日	じゅうににち(juuninichi)
3日	**みっか**(mikka)	14日	じゅう**よっか**(juuyokka)
4日	**よっか**(yokka)	17日	じゅう**しち**にち(juushichinichi)
5日	**いつか**(itsuka)	19日	じゅう**く**にち(juukunichi)
6日	**むいか**(muika)	20日	**はつか**(hatsuka)
7日	**なのか**(nanoka)	24日	にじゅう**よっか**(nijuuyokka)
8日	**ようか**(yooka)	27日	にじゅう**しち**にち(nijuushichinichi)
9日	**ここのか**(kokonoka)	29日	にじゅう**く**にち(nijuukunichi)
10日	**とおか**(tooka)	30日	さんじゅうにち(sanjuunichi)

question word：何日　なんにち(nannichi)

3. Person(s)：～人(nin)

1人　**ひとり**(hitori)
2人　**ふたり**(futari)
3人　さんにん(sannin)
4人　**よ**にん(yonin)
5人　ごにん(gonin)
6人　ろくにん(rokunin)
7人　ななにん(nananin)／しちにん(shichinin)
8人　はちにん(hachinin)
9人　きゅうにん(kyuunin)
10人　じゅうにん(juunin)
question word：何人　なんにん(nannin)

Notes on Discourse

I そうですね (Soo desu ne)

Read the following conversation from Dialogue 4-1, Lesson 4.

    A：広いですね。(Hiroi desu ne.)
       It's spacious, isn't it ?
    B：そうですね。(Soo desu ne.)
       Yes, it is, isn't it.

As shown in Notes on Grammar for Lesson 3, ね(ne) is a Group 3 particle for agreement. そうですね(soo desu ne) is used to agree with what A said. If the speaker wants to show his/her impression strongly, ね(ne) is pronounced with a prolonged intonation.

This discourse pattern is often used as a greeting or a conversation starter. B can simply repeat what A said.

    A：暑いですね。(Atsui desu ne.)
       It's hot, isn't it ?
    B：そうですね。(Soo desu ne.)
       Yes, it is, isn't it.

    A：寒いですね。(Samui desu ne.)
       It's cold, isn't it ?
    B：ええ、寒いですね。(Ee, samui desu ne.)
       Yes, it is, isn't it.

II すみません (Sumimasen)

A "I am sorry."

すみません(sumimasen) is basically used for an apology, meaning "I am sorry" as you see in Dialogue 4-3.

 A：こちらは本田研究室ですか。(Kochira wa Honda kenkyuushitsu desu ka.)
  Is this Prof. Honda's laboratory?
 B：いいえ、ちがいます。(Iie, chigaimasu.)
  No, it isn't.
 A：あ、そうですか。どうもすみません。(A, soo desu ka. Doomo sumimasen.)
  Oh, I see. I'm sorry.

B "Excuse me."

すみません (sumimasen) is also used to attract attention, meaning "Excuse me" as you see in Dialogue 4-2.

 A：すみません。(Sumimasen.)
  Excuse me.
 B：はい。(Hai.)
  Yes.
 A：あのう、21番教室はどこですか。(Anoo, 21ban kyooshitsu wa doko desu ka.)
  Where is classroom 21?

C "Thank you."

すみません (sumimasen) is used to express gratitude when one thinks it causes a person some trouble as you can see in Dialogue 3-2.

 A：取りましょうか。(Torimashoo ka.)
  Shall I get some for you?
 B：あ、すみません。いただきます。(A, sumimasen. Itadakimasu.)
  Oh, thank you. I'll have some.

III あのう (Anoo)

あのう (anoo) is used as a signal to start a conversation, and is also used as a sign to hesitate to say something because one thinks that what one wants to say may bother the hearer.

あのう (anoo) in Dialogue 4-2 was uttered, because Alice felt her question might bother the man. It should be pronounced in a low, flat tone.

アリス：すみません。(Sumimasen.)
　　　Excuse me.
男の人：はい。(Hai.)
　　　Yes.
アリス：あのう、21番教室はどこですか。
　　　　　　　　(Anoo, 21ban kyooshitsu wa doko desu ka.)
　　　Um..., where is classroom 21?

IV ええと (Eeto)

Read the following conversation from Dialogue 4-2.

アリス：2階のどの辺ですか。(Nikai no dono hen desu ka.)
　　　Whereabouts on floor 2 is it?
男の人：ええと、階段の左に20番教室があります。
　　　　　　　(Eeto, kaidan no hidari ni 20ban kyooshitsu ga arimasu.)
　　　Um..., classroom 20 is to the left of the stairs.
アリス：はい。(Hai.)
　　　O.K.
男の人：21番はそのおくです。(21ban wa sono oku desu.)
　　　Classroom 21 is just down there.

ええと (eeto) is used as a phrase to indicate that the speaker is still thinking and as a sign to indicate that the speaker is trying to recollect something.
In Dialogue 4-2 the man needs some time to find the answer to Alice's question and says ええと (eeto) meaning "Let me see" and then gives an answer.

A：すみません。今、何時ですか。(Sumimasen. Ima nanji desu ka.)
　　Excuse me, what time is it now?
B：ええと、2時15分です。(Eeto, 2ji 15fun desu.)
　　Let me see, it's 2:15.

Drill

練習1 place に N が あります／います

〈STRUCTURE〉

a.

例1） 教室（きょうしつ）に ___机（つくえ）___ が あります。
例2） 教室（きょうしつ）に ___ルインさん___ が います。

1. テレビ
2. いす
3. 時計（とけい）
4. アリスさん
5. カーリンさん

b.

例1-1） A：教室（きょうしつ）に ___机（つくえ）___ が ありますか。
　　　　B：はい、あります。
　1-2） A：教室（きょうしつ）に ___電話（でんわ）___ が ありますか。
　　　　B：いいえ、ありません。
例2-1） A：教室（きょうしつ）に ___ルインさん___ が いますか。
　　　　B：はい、います。
　2-2） A：教室（きょうしつ）に ___ナロンさん___ が いますか。
　　　　B：いいえ、いません。

1. テレビ
2. コンピューター
3. アリスさん
4. 和田先生（わだせんせい）
5. 時計（とけい）

c. Question with a question word　　ここ／そこ／あそこ

　　教室　　　　コンピュータールーム　　　研究室　　　　　食堂

例1）　A：教室に 何が ありますか。
　　　　B：テレビが あります。
例2）　A：教室に だれが いますか。
　　　　B：ルインさんが います。

1. コンピュータールーム　　　ナロンさん
2. 研究室　　　　　　　　　　電話
3. 研究室　　　　　　　　　　和田先生
4. 食堂　　　　　　　　　　　アリスさんとカーリンさん
5. 食堂　　　　　　　　　　　時計
6. ここ　　　　　　　　　　　教科書
7. そこ　　　　　　　　　　　CD
8. あそこ　　　　　　　　　　テレビ

練習2　　Nの上／下／前／後ろ……NとNの間　　(location)

〈STRUCTURE〉
a.
例1）　　机　の　　　　　上に　　本が あります。
例2）　アリスさんの　　　となりに　ルインさんが います。

1. 机　　　　　　　　下　　　　かばん
2. かばん　　　　　　中　　　　辞書
3. カーリンさん　　　前　　　　アリスさん
4. アリスさん　　　　後ろ　　　カーリンさん
5. アリスさん　　　　左　　　　ナロンさん
6. アリスさん　　　　右　　　　ルインさん

7. ルインさん　　　　　　そば　　　テレビ
8. 教室(きょうしつ)　　　　　　外(そと)　　　犬とねこ(いぬ)
9. ルインさんとナロンさん　　間(あいだ)　　アリスさん

b.
例1) A：__机(つくえ)__ の __上(うえ)__ に 何(なに)が ありますか。
　　　B：__本(ほん)__ が あります。
例2) A：__アリスさんの__ __となりに__ だれが いますか。
　　　B：__ルインさんが__ います。

1. 机(つくえ)　　　　　下(した)　　　かばん
2. かばん　　　　　　中(なか)　　　辞書(じしょ)
3. カーリンさん　　　前(まえ)　　　アリスさん
4. アリスさん　　　　右(みぎ)　　　ルインさん
5. ルインさん　　　　そば　　　　テレビ

〈USAGE〉
例) A：Bさんの部屋(へや)にエアコンがありますか。
　　　B：はい、あります。／　B：いいえ、ありません。
　　　A：あ、いいですね。　　A：あ、そうですか。

1. Bさんの部屋(へや)　　　　冷蔵庫(れいぞうこ)
2. 留学生会館(りゅうがくせいかいかん)　　コンピュータールーム
3. Bさんのアパート　　　　留学生(りゅうがくせい)

| 練習3 | Nは placeに あります／います |

〈STRUCTURE〉

a.

例) 本は　　　　　　机の　　　　　上に　あります。

1. かばん　　　　　机　　　　　　下
2. 辞書　　　　　　かばん　　　　中
3. ルインさん　　　アリスさん　　となり
4. カーリンさん　　アリスさん　　後ろ
5. アリスさん　　　ナロンさん　　右
6. テレビ　　　　　ルインさん　　そば
7. ねこ　　　　　　教室　　　　　外

b.

例) A：ルインさんは どこに いますか。
　　B：アリスさんの となりに います。

1. アリスさん　　　カーリンさん　　　前
2. ナロンさん　　　アリスさん　　　　左
3. 本　　　　　　　机　　　　　　　　上
4. 犬　　　　　　　木　　　　　　　　下
5. 郵便局　　　　　図書館　　　　　　東
6. 工学部　　　　　図書館　　　　　　北
7. 生協　　　　　　図書館　　　　　　南
8. 生協　　　　　　留学生センター　　西
9. 保健管理室　　　郵便局　　　　　　東

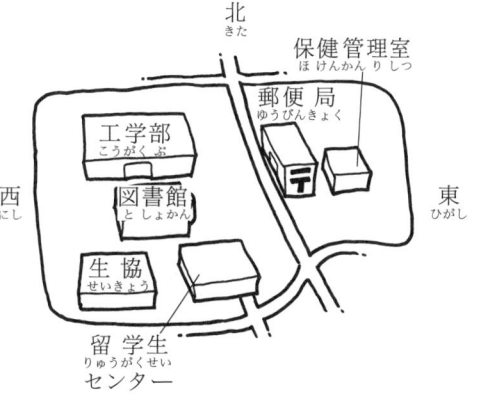

〈USAGE〉

① (デパートで)

例) A：すみません、トイレはどこにありますか。

　　B：エレベーターのとなりにあります。

　　A：どうもありがとうございました。

　　B：いいえ。

1. かばん売り場

2. くつ売り場
3. シャツ売り場
4. かさ売り場
5. エスカレーター

②
例) A：Bさんの部屋はどこにありますか。
　　B：会館の3階にあります。
　　A：あ、そうですか。

1. 研究室
2. アパート

練習4　　〜の　　(as a substitute for a noun)

〈STRUCTURE〉

（いろいろなかばんがあります。）

例1) 黒いかばんは5000円です。→　黒いのは5000円です。
例2) このかばんはアリスさんのかばんです。→　このかばんはアリスさんのです。

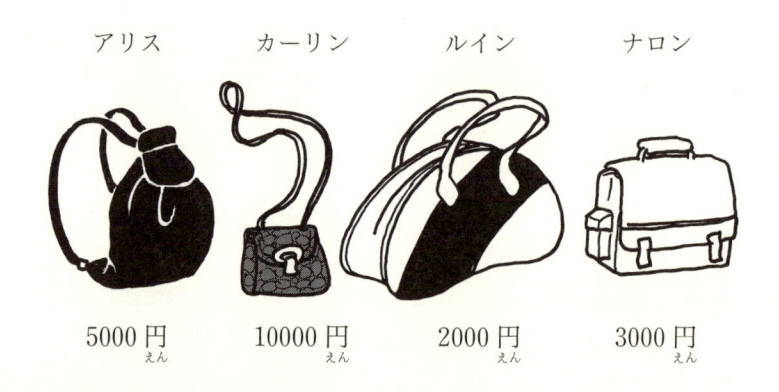

アリス　　カーリン　　ルイン　　ナロン
5000円　　10000円　　2000円　　3000円

1. 小さいかばんは10000円です。
2. このかばんはカーリンさんのかばんです。
3. 黒いかばんはアリスさんのかばんです。
4. 大きいかばんはだれのかばんですか。
5. ナロンさんのかばんは3000円のかばんですか。
6. 白いかばんはルインさんのかばんじゃありません。

〈USAGE〉

(教室で)

例) A：この<u>かばん</u>はだれのですか。
　　B：<u>カーリンさん</u>のです。
　　A：その<u>黒い</u>のは。
　　B：<u>わたし</u>のです。
　　A：ああ。

```
N+の／いA
黄色の／黄色い：yellow
茶色の／茶色い：brown
緑色の　　　　：green
```

1. 青いボールペン　　赤い
2. 小さいノート　　　大きい

練習5　　です　　(as a substitute for a verb)

〈STRUCTURE〉

例) 工学部はどこにありますか。(郵便局の前)
　　　→　A：工学部はどこにありますか。
　　　　　B：郵便局の前です。

1. 雑誌はどこにありますか。(机の上)
2. アリスさんは何を食べますか。(魚フライ定食)
3. アリスさんはどこにいますか。(食堂)
4. ルインさんはどこへ行きましたか。(研究室)
5. いつ日本へ来ましたか。(先週)
6. けさ何を飲みましたか。(コーヒー)

〈USAGE〉

(食堂で)

例) A：Bさん、何を食べますか。
　　B：<u>魚フライ定食</u>です。Aさんは。
　　A：わたしは<u>カレーライス</u>です。
　　B：あ、そうですか。

1. 飲みます　　コーヒー　　紅茶

練習6　　…時…分

〈STRUCTURE〉

例) A：今、何時ですか。
　　B：<u>9時5分</u>です。

1. 10   50
2. 4   4
3. 1   17
4. 7   26

〈USAGE〉

例）A：あのう、ちょっとすみません。今、何時ですか。
　　B：ええと、9時 40 分です。
　　A：あ、そうですか。どうもありがとうございました。
　　B：いいえ。

| 練習7 | …月…日 |

〈STRUCTURE〉

例）A：きょうは（何月）何日ですか。
　　B：9月 16 日です。

1. 4   24
2. 7   1
3. 5   3
4. 11   20

〈USAGE〉

例）A：Bさん、誕生日はいつですか。
　　B：4月2日です。
　　A：あ、そうですか。
　　B：Aさんの誕生日は。
　　A：9月 17 日です。
　　B：ああ。

Aural Comprehension

I Listen to the conversations and answer the following questions.

  (A) On the campus

   1. 郵便局の後ろに何がありますか。
   2. 工学部はどこにありますか。

  (B) On the campus

   1. 工学部の本田先生の研究室はどこですか。

  (C) Number game : Write the numbers in the appropriate boxes.

   1. ①、②、③、④はどこにありますか。

  (D) Satoo visits Lwin's room in the International student dormitory to study together.

   (コピー機：copy machine コンビニ：convenience store 道：street)

   1. コンビニはどの建物ですか。

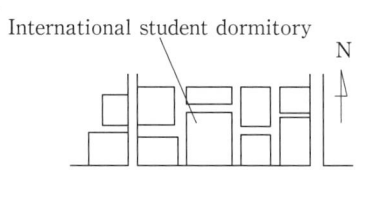

II (数字) Listen to the conversations and write down the numbers with the counters.

   1. _____ 2. _____ 3. _____ 4. _____

III One of the people in each conversation is you.

   Listen to what the other person says and write down the answer to your question.

   Your question：どこにありますか。 (1. 新聞 2. かぎ：key) 3. シャープペンシル：mechanical pencil)

   1. _____ 2. _____ 3. _____

Reading Comprehension

この建物の中にいろいろな教室があります。1階に事務室と11番教室と12番教室があります。コンピュータールームもあります。コンピュータールームは入り口の左にあります。2階に21番教室と22番教室と23番教室があります。21番教室は階段のとなりにあります。22番教室はそのとなりです。23番教室はその前です。

- いろいろな　various
- 事務室　office
- 入り口　entrance

Write the <u>number</u> of each room and the words 'computer room' in the appropriate rooms on the illustration below.

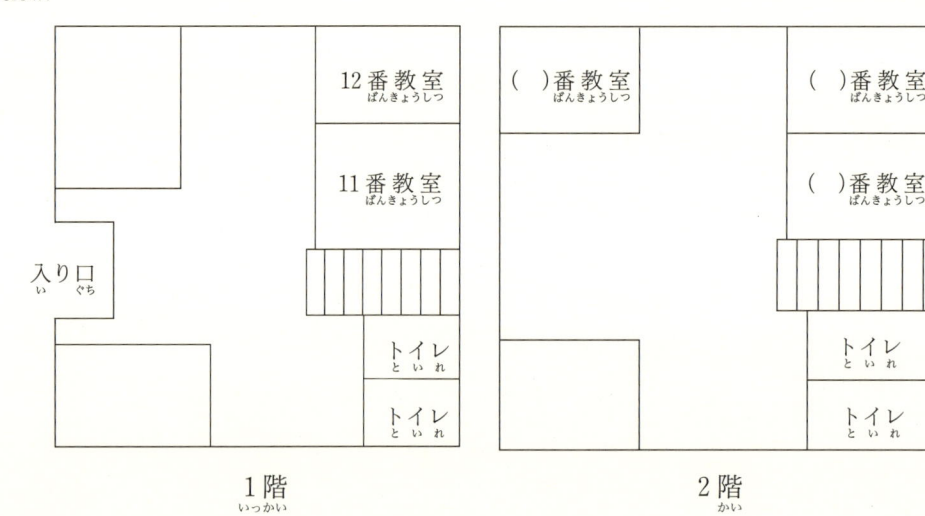

質問

1. 建物の1階には何がありますか。
2. コンピュータールームは1階のどこにありますか。
3. 21番教室は2階のどこにありますか。
4. 22番教室のとなりに何がありますか。
5. 23番教室は2階のどこにありますか。

Kanji Practice

New Kanji

46.	上	**じょう** うえ	upper	54.	北	**ほく** きた	north
(3)	丨 丨 上			(5)	一 十 ᅣ 北 北		
47.	中	**ちゅう** なか	middle, inside throughout	55.	工	**こう**	manufacturing construction
(4)	丶 口 口 中			(3)	一 T 工		
48.	下	**か** した	lower	56.	部	**ぶ**	part section
(3)	一 丁 下			(11)	丶 亠 ㇾ 立 产 音 音 音 部 部		
49.	右	みぎ	right	57.	名	**めい** な	name
(5)	ノ ナ 右			(6)	ノ ク タ タ 名 名		
50.	左	ひだり	left	58.	白	しろい しろ	white
(5)	一 ナ 左			(5)	ノ 亻 白 白 白		
51.	東	**とう** ひがし	east	59.	青	あおい あお	blue
(8)	一 日 申 東 東			(8)	一 十 キ 主 青 青		
52.	西	**せい** にし	west	60.	何	なに (なん)	what which how many
(6)	一 广 币 西 西 西			(7)	ノ 亻 仁 仃 仃 何 何		
53.	南	みなみ	south				
(9)	一 十 冂 内 内 南 南						

( ) : Kanji stroke count
Bold letters : "on" readings
Underlined letters : "kun" readings

Essential Words

1. 上 (うえ) upper
2. 中 (なか) inside
3. 下 (した) lower
4. 右 (みぎ) right
5. 左 (ひだり) left
6. 東 (ひがし) east
7. 西 (にし) west
8. 南 (みなみ) south
9. 北 (きた) north
10. 工学部 (こうがくぶ) faculty of engineering
11. 学部 (がくぶ) faculty
12. 名大 (めいだい) short form for Nagoya University
13. 白い (しろい) white
14. 青い (あおい) blue
15. 何 (なに) what

Words

1. 一日中 (いちにちじゅう) all day long
2. 東口 (ひがしぐち) east gate
3. 東京 (とうきょう) Tokyo
4. 西口 (にしぐち) west gate
5. 南門 (みなみもん) south gate
6. 北門 (きたもん) north gate
7. 工学 (こうがく) engineering
8. 何曜日 (なんようび) what day of the week
9. 何日 (なんにち) how many days, what date
10. 白 (しろ) white
11. 青 (あお) blue

Reading Practice

1. 机の上 (つくえ)
2. かばんの中
3. 机の下 (つくえ)
4. 左
5. 右
6. 東
7. 西
8. 南
9. 北
10. 学部
11. 工学部
12. 白いくつ
13. 青いかばん
14. 何がありますか
15. 何ですか

Lesson 5

Dialogue　地下鉄に乗る

5-1　On the way to Motoyama Station

Lwin and Yamashita, a Japanese student, are going to Nagoya Castle together.

ルイン： 山下さん。
山下　： はい。
ルイン： 名古屋城までどうやって行きますか。
山下　： ええと、本山から地下鉄に乗ります。
ルイン： はい。
山下　： そして市役所で降ります。
ルイン： あ、そうですか。
山下　： ええ。
ルイン： どのぐらいかかりますか。
山下　： そうですねえ。30分ぐらいです。
ルイン： あ、そうですか。どこかで乗りかえますか。
山下　： ええ、栄で乗りかえます。
ルイン： あ、そうですか。
山下　： ええ。

5-2 Asking about the bus to Nagoya Port from the bus terminal

Alice and Bambang are going to Nagoya Port together.

アリス　　：　バンバンさん。
バンバン　：　はい。
アリス　　：　名古屋港は何番のバスですか。
バンバン　：　さあ……。
　　　　　　　だれかに聞きましょうか。
アリス　　：　そうですね。

◇　　　　◇　　　　◇

バンバン　：　すみません。
　　　　　　　あのう、ちょっとうかがいますが。
女の人　　：　はい。
バンバン　：　名古屋港行きは何番ですか。
女の人　　：　ええと……22番です。
バンバン　：　あ、22番ですか。
女の人　　：　はい。
バンバン　：　あのう、名古屋港までいくらですか。
女の人　　：　200円です。
バンバン　：　あ、そうですか。
女の人　　：　ええ。でも、名古屋港は地下鉄が便利ですよ。
バンバン　：　あ、そうですか。どうもありがとうございました。

Vocabulary List

〈 〉: dictionary form
┐: accent fall (for words only)

Dialogue

5-1

ちかてつ		地下鉄	subway
のりま┐す〈のる〉	（〜が〜に）	乗ります〈乗る〉	to get on, to take, to ride
やま┐した		山下	[personal name]
なごや┐じょう		名古屋城	Nagoya Castle
まで			to, as far as [Group 1 particle for goal]
ど┐うやって			how
もとやま		本山	[name of a place]
そして			and then
しゃ┐くしょ		市役所	City Hall
おりま┐す〈おり┐る〉	（〜が〜を）	降ります〈降りる〉	to get off
どのぐらい			how long, how much
かかりま┐す〈かか┐る〉	（〜が）		it takes, it costs
そうですねえ。			Well [expression of thinking]
〜ぐらい			about ...
ど┐こか			somewhere
のりかえま┐す〈のりかえ┐る〉	（〜が〜を〜に）	乗りかえます〈乗りかえる〉	to change (trains/buses)
さかえ		栄	[name of a place]

5-2

なごや┐こう		名古屋港	Nagoya Port
さあ…。			I have no idea.
だ┐れか			somebody
ききま┐す〈きく〉	（〜が〜に〜を）	聞きます〈聞く〉	to ask
ちょっとうかがいますが。			Excuse me, may I ask a question?
が			[Group 4 particle for introductory remarks]
〜ゆき		〜行き	for ...

Drill

で		by, with, in [Group 1 particle for means]
はし		chopsticks
にゅうす	ニュース	news
うぉうくまん	ウォークマン	Walkman
なまえ	名前	name
かきます〈かく〉 (〜が〜を)	書きます〈書く〉	to write
と		with [Group 1 particle]
はなします〈はなす〉 (〜が〜を)	話します〈話す〉	to speak, to tell, to talk
てがみ	手紙	letter
ないふ	ナイフ	knife
ふぉうく	フォーク	fork
すぷうん	スプーン	spoon
て	手	hand
たくしい	タクシー	taxi
くるま	車	car
でんしゃ	電車	train
あるいて	歩いて	on foot
なごやえき	名古屋駅	Nagoya Station
ひこうき	飛行機	airplane
めいだいまえ	名大前	[name of a bus stop]
〜じかん	〜時間	... hour(s)
とうきょう	東京	[name of a place]
しんかんせん	新幹線	the Shinkansen
くうこう	空港	airport
ぎんこう	銀行	bank
を		through, along, from [Group 1 particle]
でます〈でる〉 (〜が〜を)	出ます〈出る〉	to leave
うち		house
はん	半	and half
とおります〈とおる〉 (〜が〜を)	通ります〈通る〉	to go through, to pass through
なにか	何か	something
ぱん	パン	bread
あいます〈あう〉 (〜が〜に)	会います〈会う〉	to meet
なにも	何も	not anything
すうぱあ	スーパー	supermarket

Notes on Grammar

I Question words ＋ か(ka) or も(mo)

A Question words ＋ か(ka)

In the conversation below 何か(nani ka) means "something" or "anything" and 何(nani) means "what."

Examples

1. A：けさ、何か食べましたか。(Kesa nani ka tabemashita ka.)
   Did you eat anything this morning?
   B：はい。(Hai.)
   Yes, I did.

2. A：何を食べましたか。(Nani o tabemashita ka.)
   What did you eat?
   B：パンを食べました。(Pan o tabemashita.)
   I ate some bread.

In Example 1, A wants to know whether B ate something this morning or not, so A uses 何か(nani ka) instead of 何を(nani o). B needs not refer to the thing he ate in his answer. In Example 2, A wants to know what B ate, and so A uses 何を(nani o). When question words such as 何(nani), だれ(dare), どこ(doko), etc. are followed by the particle か(ka), their meanings change.

Question word		Question word＋か	
何(nani)	what	何か(nani ka)	something or anything
だれ(dare)	who	だれか(dare ka)	someone or anyone
どこ(doko)	where	どこか(doko ka)	somewhere or anywhere
いつ(itsu)	when	いつか(itsuka)	some time or some day

Question words with か(ka) can be used in affirmative sentences or in interrogative sentences. The particle か(ka) replaces particles が(ga) and を(o), but か(ka) is followed by other Group 1 particles.

> **Examples**
>
> 1. だれか来ました。(Dare ka kimashita.)
>   Someone came.
> 2. 何か飲みますか。(Nani ka nomimasu ka.)
>   Do you drink something?
> 3. どこかでコーヒーを飲みましたか。
>   (Doko ka de koohii o nomimashita ka.)
>   Did you drink coffee anywhere?
> 4. だれかに聞きましょうか。(Dare ka ni kikimashoo ka.)
>   Shall we ask someone?

B Question words ＋ も (mo)

Question words like 何 (nani) "what," だれ (dare) "who," どこ (doko) "where," etc. can also be followed by the particle も (mo).

> **Examples**
>
> 1. だれも来ませんでした。(Dare mo kimasen deshita.)
>   Nobody came here.
> 2. 何も読みませんでした。(Nani mo yomimasen deshita.)
>   I didn't read anything.

A question word＋も (mo) before a negative predicate means "nothing," "nobody," "nowhere," etc. Some question words＋も (mo) before an affirmative predicate have an all-inclusive meaning such as いつも (itsumo) "always."

† Table of the meaning of question words＋も (mo) construction †

Question word		＋も (mo)	＋Negative pred.	＋Affirmative pred.
何 (nani)	what	何も (nani mo)	nothing	——
だれ (dare)	who	だれも (dare mo)	nobody	——
どこ (doko)	where	どこも (doko mo)	nowhere	everywhere
いつ (itsu)	when	いつも (itsu mo)	never	always
どれ (dore)	which	どれも (dore mo)	none	everything
どちら (dochira)	which	どちらも (dochira mo)	neither one	both

Remember that the particle も (mo) replaces particles が (ga) and を (o), but follows other Group 1 particles, whereas the particle か (ka) precedes other Group 1 particles. (See Lesson 1, Notes on Grammar VI.)

Examples

1. A：だれか来ましたか。(Dare ka kimashita ka.)
   Did anyone come here?
   B：いいえ、だれも来ませんでした。
   　　　　　　　　　　(Iie, dare mo kimasen deshita.)
   No, nobody came.
2. A：どこかへ行きましたか。(Doko ka e ikimashita ka.)
   Did you go anywhere?
   B：いいえ、どこへも行きませんでした。
   　　　　　　　　　　(Iie, doko e mo ikimasen deshita.)
   No, I didn't go anywhere.
3. ルインさんはいつも部屋にいません。
   　　　　　　　(Ruin san wa itsu mo heya ni imasen.)
   Lwin is never in his room.
4. ルインさんはいつも部屋にいます。
   　　　　　　　(Ruin san wa itsu mo heya ni imasu.)
   Lwin is always in his room.
5. どちらも好きじゃありません。(Dochira mo suki ja arimasen.)
   I like neither one of them.
6. どちらも好きです。(Dochira mo suki desu.)
   I like both of them.

II Group 1 particles：で(de), を(o), まで(made)

A で(de)

で(de) also means "by," "by means of," "with" or "in." It is different from で(de) indicating the place of an action. (See Lesson 1, Notes on Grammar III.)

Examples

1. バスで大学へ行きます。(Basu de daigaku e ikimasu.)
   I go to the university by bus.
2. はしで魚を食べます。(Hashi de sakana o tabemasu.)
   I eat fish with chopsticks.
3. 日本語で話しましょう。(Nihongo de hanashimashoo.)
   Let's speak in Japanese.

B を(o)

In this lesson you will learn two more meanings of the particle を(o).

1. "through" or "along"

Examples
1. このバスは名古屋大学を通りますか。
   (Kono basu wa Nagoyadaigaku o toorimasu ka.)
   Does this bus go by way of Nagoya University?
2. この道を通りましょう。(Kono michi o toorimashoo.) (道：street)
   Let's go along this street.

2. "from"

Examples
1. 駅でバスを降りました。(Eki de basu o orimashita.)
   I got off the bus at the station.
2. 毎日8時にうちを出ます。(Mainichi hachiji ni uchi o demasu.)
   I leave home at eight everyday.

C まで(made)

まで(made) means "as far as," "to" and "until." A noun of place or time precedes まで(made).

Examples
1. きのう、東京まで行きました。(Kinoo Tookyoo made ikimashita.)
   I went as far as Tokyo yesterday.
2. 大学からうちまで20分ぐらいかかります。
   (Daigaku kara uchi made nijippun gurai kakarimasu.)
   It takes about 20 minutes from the university to home.
3. 来年の3月まで日本にいます。
   (Rainen no sangatsu made Nihon ni imasu.)
   I'll stay in Japan till next March.
4. 3時まで図書館にいました。(Sanji made toshokan ni imashita.)
   I was in the library until three o'clock.

III Conjunctive particle (Group 4 particle): が(ga)

が(ga) means "but," and connects an introductory remark and the main part of a conversation. Before you start the main part of a conversation on the phone, you may tell your name to the listener by saying, "This is A speaking, but...." Before you ask a stranger for directions on the street, you may say "Excuse me, but...." "This is A speaking.," and "Excuse me.," etc. are called introductory remarks. They are necessary to make a conversation flow smoothly.

Examples
1. すみませんが……。(Sumimasen ga....)
   Excuse me, but....
2. ちょっとうかがいますが……。(Chotto ukagaimasu ga....)
   Excuse me, but may I ask you a question?
3. もしもし、こちらはルインですが……。
   (Moshimoshi, kochira wa Ruin desu ga....)
   Hello, this is Lwin speaking, but....

As you have already noticed, all the sentences above are followed by が(ga). が(ga) is added to the end of an introductory remark and the main part of a coversation follows it. The particles which have a similar function to が(ga) will be called Group 4 particles. The basic function of Group 4 particles is to connect two sentences.

IV Question word : どうやって(doo yatte)

どうやって(doo yatte) means "how" or "in what way."

Examples
1. A：大学までどうやって来ますか。
   (Daigaku made doo yatte kimasu ka.)
   How do you come to the university?
   B：バスで来ます。(Basu de kimasu.)
   I come here by bus.
2. A：栄までどうやって行きますか。
   (Sakae made doo yatte ikimasu ka.)
   How can I get to Sakae?
   B：本山までバスで行きます。(Motoyama made basu de ikimasu.)
   Go to Motoyama by bus.
   本山から栄まで地下鉄で行きます。
   (Motoyama kara Sakae made chikatetsu de ikimasu.)
   From Motoyama to Sakae, go by subway.

こうやって(koo yatte) "this way," そうやって(soo yatte) "that way" and ああやって (aa yatte) "that way" act in the same way as どうやって(doo yatte). The difference among them is the same as that among これ(kore), それ(sore), あれ(are) and どれ(dore).

The question word 何+で(nan/nani + de) is used when you ask what vehicles or tools are used instead of どうやって(doo yatte).

Examples
1. A：名古屋駅から栄まで何で行きますか。
　　　(Nagoyaeki kara Sakae made nan de ikimasu ka.)
　　How can I get to Sakae from Nagoya station?
　B：地下鉄で行きます。(Chikatetsu de ikimasu.)
　　You go by subway.
2. A：何でごはんを食べますか。(Nan de gohan o tabemasu ka.)
　　What do you eat with?
　B：はしで食べます。(Hashi de tabemasu.)
　　I eat with chopsticks.

V Words for approximate amounts：ぐらい(gurai)／くらい(kurai)

ぐらい(gurai) or くらい(kurai) means "about." They follow quantity words. どのぐらい(dono gurai)／どのくらい(dono kurai) and どれぐらい(dore gurai)／どれくらい(dore kurai) mean "about how much." いくつぐらい(ikutsu gurai)／いくつくらい(ikutsu kurai) means "about how many."

Example
A：大学からうちまで、どのぐらいかかりますか。
　　(Daigaku kara uchi made dono gurai kakarimasu ka.)
　About how long does it take from the university to home?
B：20分ぐらいかかります。(Nijippun gurai kakarimasu.)
　It takes about 20 minutes.

VI Conjunction：そして(soshite)

そして(soshite) means "and" or "then." It comes between two sentences or two clauses, and shows the temporal sequence of two events.

Examples
1. 駅までバスで行きます。そして、地下鉄に乗ります。
　(Eki made basu de ikimasu. Soshite chikatetsu ni norimasu.)

Someone* goes to the station by bus and then takes the subway.
2. きのうデパートへ行きました。そして、かばんを買いました。
   (Kinoo depaato e ikimashita. Soshite kaban o kaimashita.)
   I went to a department store yesterday and bought a bag.

(*"Someone" may be the speaker.)

Notes on Discourse

I そうですねえ (Soo desu nee)

そうですね (soo desu ne) was introduced in Notes on discourse, Lesson 4 as an expression of agreement. そうですね (soo desu ne) is used in the situation of not only agreement but when the speaker is thinking. The English equivalent is "Let me see." or "Well...." It is pronounced with a prolonged intonation. In Dialogue 5-1 Alice asks Yamashita, a Japanese friend, how long it takes to Nagoya Castle. Yamashita cannot answer at once and takes some time to think with the expression そうですねえ (soo desu nee).

> アリス：どのぐらいかかりますか。(Donogurai kakarimasu ka.)
> How long does it take ?
> 山下：そうですねえ。30分ぐらいです。(Soo desu nee. Sanjippun gurai desu.)
> Well..., it takes about 30 minutes.

II ちょっとうかがいますが (Chotto ukagaimasu ga)

Read the following conversation Dialogue 5-2, Lesson 5.

> A：すみません。(Sumimasen.)
> Excuse me.
> あのう、ちょっとうかがいますが。(Anoo, chotto ukagaimasu ga.)
> May I ask you something ?
> B：はい。(Hai.)
> Yes.
> A：名古屋港行きは何番ですか。(Nagoyakoo-yuki wa nanban desu ka.)
> What number bus goes to Nagoya Port ?

ちょっとうかがいますが (chotto ukagaimasu ga) is a polite expression that means "May I ask you something ?" It is usually used to strangers.

Drill

練習1　Nで　(means)

〈STRUCTURE〉

例) はしで　ごはんを食べます。

1. テレビ　　　　ニュースを見ます
2. ウォークマン　テープを聞きます
3. えんぴつ　　　名前を書きます
4. 日本語　　　　先生と話します
5. 日本語　　　　手紙を書きます

〈USAGE〉

例) A：Bさんの国では、何でごはんを食べますか。
　　B：はしで食べます。
　　A：ああ、そうですか。

1. スプーン　　2. ナイフとフォーク　　3. 手

練習2　placeから　placeまで　Nで　行きます

〈STRUCTURE〉

a.
例) ここから　栄　まで　バスで　行きます。

1. 地下鉄　　3. タクシー　　5. 電車
2. 自転車　　4. 車　　　　　6. 歩いて　(no particle)

b.
例) A：ここから　栄　まで　{どうやって / 何で}　行きますか。
　　B：バスで　行きます。

1. ここ　　本山　　　　　自転車
2. ここ　　名古屋駅　　　地下鉄
3. ここ　　留学生会館　　バス

4. ここ　　郵便局(ゆうびんきょく)　　歩(ある)いて
5. 名古屋(なごや)　　Bさんの国(くに)　　飛行機(ひこうき)

〈USAGE〉

例) A：Bさんは留学生会館(りゅうがくせいかいかん)ですか。
　　B：はい。
　　A：大学(だいがく)までどうやって来(き)ますか。
　　B：自転車(じてんしゃ)で来(き)ます。
　　A：ああ、そうですか。

練習3　　time　かかります

〈STRUCTURE〉

例) A：名大前(めいだいまえ)から　本山(もとやま)まで　(バスで)　{どのぐらい / 何分(なんぷん)}　かかりますか。

　　B：10分(じっぷん)　かかります。

1. 本山(もとやま)　　栄(さかえ)　　(地下鉄(ちかてつ))　　10分(じっぷん)
2. 本山(もとやま)　　名古屋駅(なごやえき)　　(地下鉄(ちかてつ))　　15分(ふん)
3. ここ　　留学生会館(りゅうがくせいかいかん)　　(自転車(じてんしゃ))　　20分(にじっぷん)
4. ここ　　名古屋港(なごやこう)　　(車(くるま))　　40分(よんじっぷん)
5. ここ　　郵便局(ゆうびんきょく)　　(歩(ある)いて)　　10分(じっぷん)
6. タイ　　日本(にほん)　　(飛行機(ひこうき))　　6時間(じかん)　(何時間(なんじかん))
7. 東京(とうきょう)　　名古屋(なごや)　　(新幹線(しんかんせん))　　2時間(じかん)　(何時間(なんじかん))

〈USAGE〉

例) A：Bさん、会館(かいかん)から留学生(りゅうがくせい)センターまで　どのぐらい／何分(なんぷん)　かかりますか。
　　B：そうですね。バスで20分(にじっぷん)ぐらいかかります。
　　A：そうですか。

1. 大学(だいがく)　　空港(くうこう)

練習4　　timeから　timeまで

〈USAGE〉

例) A：すみません
　　B：はい。
　　A：郵便局(ゆうびんきょく)は何時(なんじ)から何時(なんじ)までですか。
　　B：9時(くじ)から5時(ごじ)までです。

A：そうですか。どうもありがとうございました。

1. 図書館（としょかん）　2. 保健管理室（ほけんかんりしつ）　3. 生協（せいきょう）　4. 銀行（ぎんこう）

練習5　Nに V／Nを V

a. Nに乗ります／Nを降ります

〈STRUCTURE〉

例1) 名大前で バスに 乗ります。
例2) 名大前で バスを 降ります。

1. 桜山（さくらやま）　　地下鉄（ちかてつ）　　　　　　　　　　（桜山：name of a place）
2. 栄（さかえ）　　　　タクシー
3. 本山（もとやま）　　バス

b. Nを出ます

〈STRUCTURE〉

例) 8時に 会館を 出ます。

1. 7時　　　うち
2. 3時　　　留学生センター
3. 5時　　　研究室
4. 9時半　　名古屋駅

c. Nを通ります

〈STRUCTURE〉

例) このバスは 名大前を 通ります。

1. この地下鉄　　本山
2. 東山線　　　　栄　　　　　　　　　　　　　　（東山線：Higashiyama line）
3. 桜通線　　　　桜山　　　　　　　　　　　　　（桜通線：Sakuradoori line）

〈USAGE〉

例) A：あのう、すみません。
　　　このバスは名大前を通りますか。
　　B：はい、通ります。／いいえ、通りません。
　　A：あ、そうですか。ありがとうございました。

1. この地下鉄　　桜山
2. 東山線　　　　栄
3. 桜通線　　　　名古屋駅

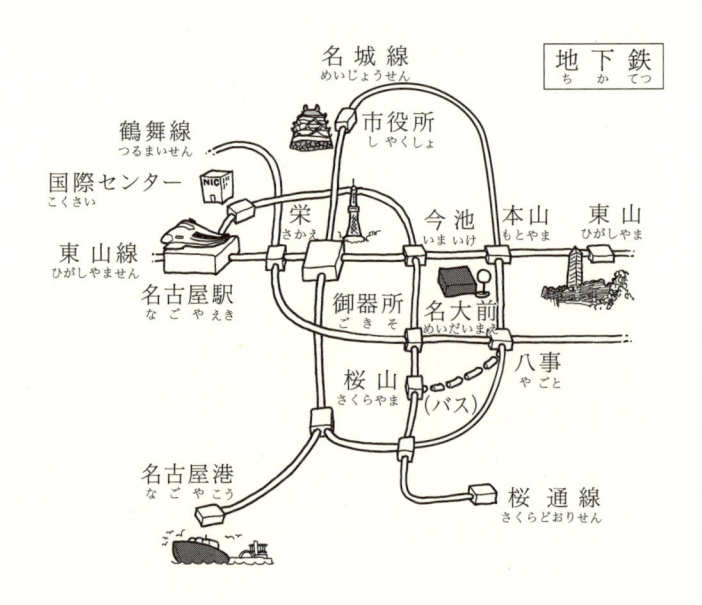

地下鉄
ちかてつ

名城線
めいじょうせん

鶴舞線
つるまいせん

市役所
しやくしょ

国際センター
こくさい

栄
さかえ

今池
いまいけ

本山
もとやま

東山
ひがしやま

東山線
ひがしやません

名古屋駅
なごやえき

御器所
ごきそ

名大前
めいだいまえ

桜山
さくらやま

（バス）

八事
やごと

名古屋港
なごやこう

桜通線
さくらどおりせん

練習6　　そして

〈STRUCTURE〉

例) 大学へ行きました。日本語を勉強しました。
　　　だいがく　い　　　にほんご　べんきょう
　　→　大学へ行きました。そして、日本語を勉強しました。
　　　　だいがく　い　　　　　　　にほんご　べんきょう

1. 食堂へ行きました。ごはんを食べました。
   しょくどう　い　　　　　　　　　　　た
2. 研究室へ行きました。本田先生に会いました。
   けんきゅうしつ　い　　ほんだせんせい　あ
3. 図書館へ行きました。本を読みました。
   としょかん　い　　　ほん　よ
4. バスで本山へ行きました。地下鉄に乗りました。
   　　　もとやま　い　　　ちかてつ　の
5. 栄へ行きました。かばんを買いました。
   さかえ　い　　　　　　　　　　　か
6. 桜山で地下鉄を降りました。うちへ帰りました。
   さくらやま　ちかてつ　お　　　　　　　かえ

〈話しましょう〉（練習2～6）

(Let's talk about the places to which you have been.)

例) きのう、栄へ行きました。
　　　　　さかえ　い
　　3時に大学を出ました。
　　じ　だいがく　で
　　本山までバスで行きました。
　　もとやま　　　　い
　　そして、本山で地下鉄に乗りました。
　　　　　　もとやま　ちかてつ　の
　　栄で地下鉄を降りました。
　　さかえ　ちかてつ　お
　　大学から栄まで40分かかりました。
　　だいがく　さかえ　よんじっぷん

名古屋港：Nagoya Port
なごやこう
名古屋城：Nagoya Castle
なごやじょう
東山公園：Higashiyama Park
ひがしやまこうえん
テレビ塔：TV Tower
　　　とう
名古屋国際センター：
なごやこくさい
　　Nagoya International Center, etc.

練習7　　Question word＋か／Question word＋も〜ません

〈STRUCTURE〉

例1）けさパンを食べました。（何）　→　A：けさ　何か　食べましたか。
　　　　　　　　　　　　　　　　　　　B：はい、食べました。
　　　　　　　　　　　　　　　　　　　A：何を　食べましたか。
　　　　　　　　　　　　　　　　　　　B：パンを　食べました。

例2）きのう栄へ行きました。（どこ）　→　A：きのう　どこかへ　行きましたか。
　　　　　　　　　　　　　　　　　　　B：はい、行きました。
　　　　　　　　　　　　　　　　　　　A：どこへ　行きましたか。
　　　　　　　　　　　　　　　　　　　B：栄へ　行きました。

1. テレビの上に本があります。（何）
2. となりの部屋にルインさんがいます。（だれ）
3. 木の下にねこがいます。（何）
4. きのうルインさんが来ました。（だれ）
5. きのうテレビを買いました。（何）
6. きのうアリスさんに会いました。（だれ）
7. 電話は1階にあります。（どこ）
8. 友達と日本語で話しました。（だれ）

例3）けさパンを食べました。（何）　→　A：けさ　何か　食べましたか。
　　　　　　　　　　　　　　　　　　　B：いいえ、何も　食べませんでした。
例4）きのう栄へ行きました。（どこ）　→　A：きのう　どこかへ　行きましたか。
　　　　　　　　　　　　　　　　　　　B：いいえ、どこへも　行きませんでした。

(Use the words in 例1) and 例2) above.)

〈USAGE〉

例）A：きのうどこかへ行きましたか。
　　B：はい、デパートへ行きました。／　B：いいえ、どこへも行きませんでした。
　　A：そうですか。　　　　　　　　　　　A：そうですか。
　　　　何か買いましたか。
　　B：はい、かばんを買いました。／いいえ、何も買いませんでした。
　　　　安かったです。

1. 先週　　　スーパー
2. きのう　　バザー
3. きのう　　パーティー

Aural Comprehension

I Listen to the conversations and answer the following questions.

(A) At the bus stop

1. 女の人は栄へ何で行きますか。
2. 栄は何番のバスが通りますか。

(B) Asking a person who is at bus stop

1. 女の人は何番のバスで行きますか。

(C) About visiting an aquarium

(水族館：aquarium　たくさん：a lot　駅：station)

1. 水族館は、駅から何分ぐらいかかりますか。
2. 水族館はどうでしたか。

(D) Asking where Century Hall is

(センチュリーホール：(name of a hall)　コンサート：concert　家：house　近く：near place)

1. センチュリーホールはどこで降りますか。
2. 友達の家はどこにありますか。

II (数字) Listen to the conversations and write down the numbers with the counters.

1. _____ 2. _____ 3. _____ 4. _____

III One of the people in each conversation is you.

Listen to what the other person says and write down the answer to your question.

Your question：どこで降りますか。

1. _____ 2. _____ 3. _____

Reading Comprehension

カーリンさんの日記（diary）

4月8日

　きょう、山下さんと京都へ行きました。8時にアパートを出ました。そして駅で山下さんに会いました。9時3分の新幹線に乗りました。京都まで1時間かかりました。京都駅からバスで金閣寺へ行きました。金閣寺はとてもきれいでした。庭もきれいでした。そこで抹茶を飲みました。ちょっと苦かったです。

　それからレストランへ行きました。てんぷらを食べました。とてもおいしかったです。7時半にアパートに帰りました。楽しかったです。

- 京都　　　name of a place
- 庭　　　　garden
- それから　and then
- 楽しい　　pleasant
- 駅　　　　station
- 抹茶　　　powdered tea
- レストラン restaurant
- 金閣寺　　Golden Pavilion
- 苦い　　　bitter
- てんぷら　name of Japanese food

質問

1. カーリンさんはいつ京都へ行きましたか。
2. だれと行きましたか。
3. どうやって行きましたか。
4. 京都までどのぐらいかかりましたか。
5. どこで抹茶を飲みましたか。
6. 何時にアパートに帰りましたか。

Kanji Practice

New Kanji

61.	分	ふん　ぶん わかる	minute, portion to understand	69.	古	ふるい	old
(4)	ノ 八 分 分			(5)	一 十 十 古 古		
62.	時	じ	time hour	70.	赤	あかい　あか	red
(10)	丨 冂 日 日 旷 旷 時 時			(7)	一 十 土 ナ 亣 赤 赤		
63.	半	はん	half	71.	多	おおい	much many numerous
(5)	ヽ ゛ 二 半 半			(6)	ノ ク タ タ 多 多		
64.	今	こん いま	now	72.	元	げん	origin foundation
(4)	ノ 八 今 今			(4)	二 テ 元		
65.	高	こう たかい	high expensive	73.	気	き	spirit
(10)	ヽ 亠 宀 古 古 高 高 高			(6)	ノ ニ 气 気 気		
66.	安	あん やすい	peace cheap	74.	便	べん　びん	convenience mail
(6)	ヽ ゛ 宀 灾 安 安			(9)	ノ イ 亻 亻 仨 仨 佢 伊 便		
67.	広	ひろい	broad wide	75.	利	り	advantage
(5)	ヽ 亠 广 広 広			(7)	一 二 千 禾 禾 利 利		
68.	新	しん あたらしい	new				
(13)	亠 宀 立 立 辛 新 新 新						

( )：Kanji stroke count
Bold letters："on" readings
Underlined letters："kun" readings

Essential Words

1. 一分 (いっぷん) — one minute
2. 二分 (にふん) — two minutes
3. 四時 (よじ) — four o'clock
4. 七時半 (しちじはん) — half past seven
5. 今 (いま) — now
6. 今月 (こんげつ) — this month
7. 高い (たか) — high, expensive
8. 安い (やす) — peace, cheap
9. 広い (ひろ) — broad, wide
10. 新しい (あたら) — new
11. 古い (ふる) — old
12. 赤い (あか) — red
13. 多い (おお) — much, many
14. 元気な人 (げんきなひと) — energetic person
15. 便利な本 (べんりなほん) — convenient book

Words

1. 分かる (わ) — to understand
2. 十分(な) (じゅうぶん) — enough, sufficient
3. 半分 (はんぶん) — half
4. 今年 (ことし) — this year
5. 赤 (あか) — red
6. 郵便局 (ゆうびんきょく) — post office

Reading Practice

1. 今、九時半です。
2. これは新しいです。
3. この本は古いです。
4. あれは安くありません。
5. これは高かったです。
6. この大学は広いです。
7. 学生が多いです。
8. バスは便利じゃありません。
9. 赤いかばんはアリスさんのです。
10. ルインさんは元気な人です。

Lesson 6

Dialogue 図書館で

6-1 At the library counter

ルイン： すみません。

司書 ： はい。

ルイン： 雑誌のバックナンバーはどこにありますか。

司書 ： いつごろのですか。

ルイン： 去年のです。

司書 ： 地下1階です。

ルイン： あのう、地下1階のどの辺ですか。

司書 ： その階段を降りてください。左側に雑誌のコーナーがあります。

ルイン： あ、そうですか。どうも。

◇　　　◇

ルイン： すみません。
　　　　これ、借りたいんですが。

司書 ： あ、雑誌はだめなんです。

ルイン： あ、そうですか。

司書　：　あちらの機械でコピーしてください。
ルイン：　はい。

6-2　In front of the copy machine

ルイン：　あのう、すみません。
学生　：　はい。
ルイン：　コピー機の使い方を、ちょっと教えてくださいませんか。
学生　：　あ、いいですよ。コピーカードはありますか。
ルイン：　はい。
学生　：　まず、そこにカードを入れてください。
ルイン：　ここですね。
学生　：　ええ。あっ、反対ですよ。
ルイン：　あっ、こうですか。
学生　：　はい、そうです。それから、ここに本を置いてください。
ルイン：　はい。
学生　：　次に、紙のサイズを選んでください。
ルイン：　はい。
学生　：　最後に、このボタンを押してください。
ルイン：　はい……、あれっ。
学生　：　あっ、もう一度押してください。
ルイン：　はい。あっ、出ました、出ました。
　　　　　分かりました。どうもありがとうございました。助かりました。
学生　：　いいえ、どういたしまして。

Vocabulary List

⟨ ⟩: dictionary form
⌐: accent fall (for words only)

Dialogue

6-1

し⌐しょ		司書	librarian
バックナ⌐ンバー			back issue
いつごろ			around what time
きょ⌐ねん		去年	last year
ち⌐か		地下	underground
〜てください			Please ....
おりま⌐す⟨おり⌐る⟩	(〜が〜を)	降ります⟨降りる⟩	to go down (the stairs)
〜がわ		〜側	on the side of ...
コ⌐ーナー			corner
〜たい			to want to ...
かりま⌐す⟨かりる⟩	(〜が〜に〜を)	借ります⟨借りる⟩	to borrow, to rent
あちら			that way
きか⌐い		機械	machine
コ⌐ピーします ⟨コ⌐ピーする⟩	(〜が〜を)		to copy

6-2

コピ⌐ーき		コピー機	copy machine
つかいま⌐す⟨つかう⟩	(〜が〜を)	使います⟨使う⟩	to use
〜かた		〜方	method, way
おしえま⌐す⟨おしえる⟩	(〜が〜に〜を)	教えます⟨教える⟩	to teach
〜てくださいませんか			Will you ... for me?
いいですよ。			Sure.
コピーカ⌐ード			photocopying card
ま⌐ず			first of all
に			on, at [Group 1 particle for place]
カ⌐ード			card
いれま⌐す⟨いれる⟩	(〜が〜に〜を)	入れます⟨入れる⟩	to put in
はんたい		反対	the other way around
こ⌐う			this way, like this
それから			and then

おきま|す〈おく〉	（～が～に～を）	置きます〈置く〉	to put
つぎ|に		次に	next
かみ|		紙	paper
サ|イズ			size
えらびま|す〈えら|ぶ〉	（～が～を）	選びます〈選ぶ〉	to choose
さ|いごに		最後に	finally
ボタン			button
おしま|す〈おす〉	（～が～を）	押します〈押す〉	to push
あれっ。			Oh!?
もういちど		もう一度	once more
でま|す〈で|る〉	（～が）	出ます〈出る〉	to come out
わかりま|す〈わか|る〉	（～が）	分かります〈分かる〉	to understand
たすかりました。		助かりました。	Thanks for helping me.
どういたしまして。			You are welcome.

Drill

でんわば|んごう		電話番号	telephone number
ま|つ	（～が～を）	待つ	to wait
りょ|うり		料理	cooking
つく|る	（～が～を）	作る	to make
よぶ	（～が～を）	呼ぶ	to call
ジュ|ース			juice
いそ|ぐ	（～が）	急ぐ	to hurry
タイご		タイ語	Thai language
ほし|い			to want
ビ|デオ			video
でんしじ|しょ		電子辞書	electronic dictionary
か		課	lesson
プリント			handout
スケジュ|ール			schedule
いか|が			how [polite form of どう]
きょ|うと		京都	[name of a place]
でんわする		電話する	to make a phone call
ワープロ			word processor
おおさか		大阪	[name of a place]
サ|インする	（～が～に）		to sign
メールボ|ックス			mailbox
メ|モ			memorandum
さと|う		砂糖	sugar

Notes on Grammar

I Expressions of request or polite command

A V-てください

In this lesson you will learn two ways of expressing requests or polite commands. In IA and B you will learn sentences ending in a verb in the -て form＋ください(V-てください).

Examples
1. 名前を書いてください。
   Please write your name.
2. あした大学に来てください。
   Please come to the university tomorrow.
3. この本を読んでください。
   Please read this book.

The form of a verb ending in -て or -で is called the -て form of a verb. It functions as a connector of two predicates. It has a lot of usages. In this lesson, it shows a request or polite command, when followed by -ください.

B Formation rule of the -て form of verbs

The following shows how to make the -て form of a verb.

1. Group 1 verbs, or verbs ending in -eru or -iru

Change the final -る to -て.

† Table of the -て form of Group 1 verbs †

Dictionary form	-て form	-ます form (Polite form)
でる　　to leave たべる　to eat	でて たべて	でます たべます
いる　　to be, exist おりる　to get off	いて おりて	います おります

2. Group 2 verbs, or verbs ending in -u

(1) Verbs ending with -く or -ぐ : Change -く or -ぐ to -いて or -いで, respectively.

†Table of the -て form of Group 2 verbs (1)†

Dictionary form		-て form	-ます form (Polite form)
かく	to write	かいて	かきます
きく	to listen	きいて	ききます
およぐ	to swim	およいで	およぎます
ぬぐ	to take off	ぬいで	ぬぎます

There is one exception : The -て form of the verb いく "go" is いって, not いいて.

(2) Verbs ending with -す : Change -す to -して.

†Table of the -て form of Group 2 verbs (2)†

Dictionary form		-て form	-ます form (Polite form)
はなす	to speak	はなして	はなします
おす	to push	おして	おします
かす	to lend	かして	かします

(3) Verbs ending with -う, -つ, or -る : Change -う, -つ or -る to -って.

†Table of the -て form of Group 2 verbs (3)†

Dictionary form		-て form	-ます form (Polite form)
かう	to buy	かって	かいます
まつ	to wait	まって	まちます
のる	to get on	のって	のります
とおる	to go through	とおって	とおります

(4) Verbs ending with -ぶ, -む, or -ぬ : Change -ぶ, -む or -ぬ to -んで.

†Table of the -て form of Group 2 verbs (4)†

Dictionary form		-て form	-ます form (Polite form)
よむ	to read	よんで	よみます
のむ	to drink	のんで	のみます
しぬ	to die	しんで	しにます
よぶ	to call	よんで	よびます

3. Irregular verbs

† Table of the -て form of two Irregular verbs †

Dictionary form	-て form	-ます form (Polite form)
くる　to come する　to do	きて して	きます します

Examples

1. ちょっと待ってください。
   Please wait a moment.
2. 階段をおりてください。
   Please go downstairs.
3. あの機械でコピーしてください。
   Please make a photocopy using that machine.
4. カードを入れてください。
   Please put in your card.
5. あした3時に来てください。
   Please come here at 3 o'clock tomorrow.

C　V-てくださいませんか

If you replace ください with くださいませんか, you will sound more polite. The -て form of a verb＋くださいませんか (V-てくださいませんか) is used with deference to a superior or a stranger.

Examples

1. 日本語を教えてくださいませんか。
   Would you teach me Japanese?
2. すみません、そのボタンを押してくださいませんか。
   Excuse me, but would you push that button?

II　Expression of the speaker's and the hearer's desire

A　ほしいです

（わたしは）　Xが　ほしいです。	I want X.
（あなたは）　Xが　ほしいですか。	Do you want X?

In X が ほしいです, X indicates the things which the speaker wants in a declarative sentence. In a question sentence, X indicates the things which the person addressed wants. The particle が does not indicate the subject but the direct object of ほしいです. ほしいです behaves as an -い adjective. The imperfective negative form is ほしくありません, and the perfective affirmative form is ほしかったです.

† Table of the conjugation of ほしいです †

	Affirmative form	Negative form
Imperfective form	ほしいです	ほしくありません
Perfective form	ほしかったです	ほしくありませんでした

Examples

1. コンピューターがほしいです。
   I want a computer.
2. この本はほしくありません。
   I do not want this book.
3. このCDがほしかったです。
   I wanted this CD.
4. A：どんな辞書がほしいですか。
   What kind of dictionary do you want?
5. B：小さい辞書です。
   I want a small one.

B V(base)たいです

Examples

1. 京都へ行きたいです。
   I want to go to Kyoto.
2. 日本語で話したいです。
   I want to speak in Japanese.
3. このくつを買いたいです。
   I want to buy these shoes.

What are common in these three examples above are:
(1) All sentences end with です, so they are polite.
(2) です follows a word ending in -たい.
(3) The verb form preceding -たいです is "the -ます form minus -ます," which is called the verb base of a verb{V(base)}in this textbook.

† Table of the V(base)たいです†

Polite form		Verb base	Verb base ＋ -たいです
たべます	to eat	たべ	たべたいです
いきます	to go	いき	いきたいです
はなします	to speak	はなし	はなしたいです
きます	to come	き	きたいです
します	to do	し	したいです

The word -たいです indicates the speaker's or the hearer's desire and changes a verb into an -い adjective. -たいです behaves as ほしいです, as shown above.

The direct object of the verb base＋-たいです {V(base)たいです} is indicated by the particle を or が.

† Table of the conjugation of V-たいです†

	Polite form	
	Affirmative form	Negative form
Imperfective form	V-たいです	V-たくありません
Perfective form	V-たかったです	V-たくありませんでした

Examples

1. 日本語の本を/が読みたいです。
   I want to read a Japanese book.

2. 魚は食べたくありません。
   I don't want to eat fish.

3. タクシーには乗りたくありません。
   I don't want to take a taxi.

4. きのうデパートへ行きたかったです。
   I wanted to go to the department store yesterday.

5. A：日本で何を勉強したいですか。
   What do you want to study in Japan?
   B：国際法を勉強したいです。
   I want to study international law.

C Avoidance of a desirative sentence in a question

Japanese people tend to avoid the use of ほしいです or -たいです in a question sentence. Instead of X がほしいですか or X を/が V-たいですか, X は どう/いかが

ですか should be used. いかが is the polite counterpart of どう, and it is better to use it when talking to your superiors.

Example
A：先生、コーヒーはいかがですか。
Would you like some coffee?
B：ええ、いただきますよ。
Yes, please.

III Extended meaning of the verb あります

In Lesson 4, you learned the existential sentence X に Y が あります (X: place, Y: thing). In this lesson other usages will be introduced.

A Possession

The verb あります can be used to show the idea of possession. The noun X preceding に is the possessor.

Examples
1. 学生には時間があります。
   Students have (a lot of) time.
2. A：コピーカードはありますか。
   Do you have a photocopying card?
   B：いいえ、ありません。
   No, I don't.

B "to take place"

The verb あります also means "to take place" or "to be held" when あります is used for events such as parties and meetings. Note that the place X is followed by the particle で indicating the place of the action.

Examples
1. 留学生センターのロビーでパーティーがあります。
   A party will take place in the lobby in the Ryuugakusee Center.
2. 授業は21番教室であります。
   Classes are held in Room No. 21.

IV Suffix : かた

-かた means "way," "method," etc. It is used to change a sentence ending in a verb into a noun equivalent.

Examples
1. a. ルインさんが話す。
   Lwin speaks.
   b. ルインさんの話し方
   Lwin's way of speaking
2. a. 日本語を話す。
   (X) speaks Japanese.
   b. 日本語の話し方
   (X's) way of speaking Japanese
3. a. ルインさんが日本語を話す。
   Lwin speaks Japanese.
   b. ルインさんの日本語の話し方
   Lwin's way of speaking Japanese
4. a. ルインさんが日本語で話す。
   Lwin speaks in Japanese.
   b. ルインさんの日本語での話し方
   Lwin's way of speaking in Japanese

The verb base of a verb precedes **かた**.
Note that in Examples 1 through 3, が and を are replaced by の. However, in Example 4 the particle で is followed by の. In general, all Group 1 particles except が and を are followed by の.

Nounが	Nounで	Nounを	Verb
↓	↓	↓	
Nounの	Nounでの	Nounの	Verb(base)＋かた

Examples
1. 日本語の話し方を勉強したいです。
   I want to study how to speak Japanese.
2. コピーのし方が分かりません。

Notes on Grammar 153

I don't know how to make a photocopy of this.

The particle に when it indicates direction is never used in this construction. へ is used instead.

Example

a. 東京に行く。
   とうきょう い
   (X) goes to Tokyo.

b. 東京への行き方
   とうきょう い かた
   (X's) way of going to Tokyo

c. 東京への行き方を教えてください。
   とうきょう い かた おし
   Please tell me how to get to Tokyo.

V Verb modifiers：こう, そう, ああ, どう

こう means "this way," そう "that way" and ああ "that way." どう means "how." The differences between these are similar to これ, それ, あれ and どれ. They modify the verb they precede.

Examples

1. A：この漢字はどう書きますか。
      かんじ か
      How do you write this kanji?
   B：こう書きます。
      か
      We write it this way.

2. A：この機械はどう使いますか。
      きかい つか
      How do you use this machine?
   B：ここにカードを入れてください。
      い
      Please put your card in here.
   A：こうですか。
      Like this?

VI Words for temporal sequence：まず, それから, 最後に
さいご

When one describes or explains some actions which are supposed to be done in order in a certain period of time, these words are used in the order shown in the following example.

Example

A：まず、そこにカードを入れてください。
   い

　　　　　First, please put your card in there.
B：はい。
　　　　　Yes.
A：それから、ここに本を置いてください。
　　　　　Secondly, please put your book here.
B：はい。
　　　　　Yes.
A：最後に、このボタンを押してください。
　　　　　At the end, push this button, please.
B：はい。ありがとうございました。
　　　　　I see. Thank you very much.

VII Group 1 particle：に

に in そこにカードを入れてください in the seventh line, Dialogue 6-2, and in ここに本を置いてください in the eleventh line, Dialogue 6-2, indicates the place where something is to be put or written.

Examples
1. かばんを机の上に置いてください。
   Please put your bag on the desk.
2. この紙に名前を書いてください。
   Please write your name on this sheet.

Notes on Discourse

1 ～たいんですが

Read the following conversation in Dialogue 6-1 (at the library counter).

> ルイン：すみません。これ、借りたいんですが。
> Excuse me. I'd like to borrow this.
>
> 司書　：あ、雑誌はだめなんです。
> Oh, magazines cannot be borrowed.

In Notes on grammar in this lesson -**たいです** was introduced to express one's desire.

> いいカメラが買いたいです。(I want to buy a good camera.)

As you can see in the above conversation, -**たいんですが** is used to express the speaker's desire to ask some response from the other person(s). It is one way to ask permission from someone or to ask someone for help. It is often used at the beginning of the discourse.

(at the library counter)　A：図書館カードを作りたいんですが。
　　　　　　　　　　　　　I'd like to make a library card. (So what should I do ? Would you help me ?)
　　　　　　　　　　　B：はい。じゃ、お名前を書いてください。
　　　　　　　　　　　　　O.K. Then, please write down your name.

(in class)　　　　　　　A：ちょっとトイレに行きたいんですが。
　　　　　　　　　　　　　I'd like to go to the toilet. (May I ?)
　　　　　　　　　　　B：どうぞ。
　　　　　　　　　　　　　Please go ahead.

(at the office counter)　A：あのう、ホームステイの申しこみをしたいんですが。
　　　　　　　　　　　　　I'd like to apply for a home stay program. (Would you help me ?)
　　　　　　　　　　　B：はい。
　　　　　　　　　　　　　Yes.

II　ここですね ↗

As you see in Notes on Grammar, Lesson 3 the Group 3 particle ね with a rising intonation is used to confirm the information which the speaker has received. This type of ね is almost equal to the English tag question like "..., don't you ?," " isn't it ?," " right ?," and so on.

Look at the following conversation shown in Dialogue 6-2. A student is telling Lwin how to use the photo copying machine.

  学生　：まず、そこにカードを入れてください。
     Please put the card in there.
  ルイン：ここですね。
     Here right ?
  学生　：ええ。
     Yes.

In the above conversation Lwin said ここですね with a rising intonation to confirm the right place where he should put the card in.

Here is another example of this ね.

  A：専門は経済ですね。
    Your major subject is economics, isn't it ?
  B：はい、そうです。
    Yes, that's right.

Drill

練習 1　　Vてください

〈STRUCTURE〉

例）食堂で食べる　→　食堂で食べてください。

1. テレビを見る
2. 栄で降りる
3. 栄で乗りかえる
4. 電話番号を教える
5. このえんぴつを使う
6. 教科書を買う
7. ちょっと待つ
8. 辞書を取る
9. 料理を作る
10. 会館へ帰る
11. ナロンさんを呼ぶ
12. 教科書を読む
13. ジュースを飲む
14. 日本語で話す
15. ボタンを押す
16. テープを聞く
17. 名前を書く
18. 急ぐ
19. 食堂へ行く
20. 漢字を勉強する
21. アリスさんをしょうかいする
22. 1時に来る

〈USAGE〉

（友達に）

例）A：Bさん。

　　B：はい。

　　A：（ちょっと）この漢字を読んでください。

　　B：はい。

1. 電話番号を書く
2. タイ語を教える
3. その辞書を取る

（研究室で）

4. これをコピーする
5. このコンピューターを使う
6. 郵便局へ行く

練習2　Nが　ほしいです

〈STRUCTURE〉

例）コンピューター　→　A：Bさんは今、何がほしいですか。
　　　　　　　　　　　　B：（わたしは）コンピューターがほしいです。

1. テレビ
2. ビデオ
3. ウォークマン
4. 電子辞書（でんしじしょ）
5. 自転車（じてんしゃ）

〈USAGE〉

① (at school)

例）A：あのう、すみません。
　　B：はい。
　　A：テープがほしいんですが。
　　B：あ、テープですか。どうぞ。
　　A：どうもすみません。

1. 4課の宿題（しゅくだい）
2. きのうの授業（じゅぎょう）のプリント
3. スケジュールの紙（かみ）

② (at the shop, etc.)

例）A：いらっしゃいませ。
　　B：あのう、小（ちい）さいカメラがほしいんですが。
　　A：はい。これはいかがですか。
　　B：そうですね……。

1. 電子辞書（でんしじしょ）
2. 大（おお）きいくつ
3. 青（あお）いかさ

練習3　Nが　Vたいです

〈STRUCTURE〉

例）コーヒーを飲（の）む　→　A：Bさんは今、何がしたいですか。
　　　　　　　　　　　　　　B：コーヒーが飲（の）みたいです。

1. 新聞（しんぶん）を読（よ）む
2. 専門（せんもん）の辞書（じしょ）を買（か）う
3. 京都（きょうと）へ行（い）く
4. 国（くに）の友達（ともだち）に会（あ）う
5. 映画（えいが）を見（み）る
6. うちに帰（かえ）る

〈USAGE〉

（大学で）

例) A：すみません。
　　B：はい。
　　A：これをコピーしたいんですが。
　　B：はい。

1. コンピューターを使う　　3. トイレに行く
2. 本を借りる

練習4　　Vかた

〈STRUCTURE〉

例1) 漢字を読む　→　漢字の読み方が分かりません。
例2) 電話する　→　電話のし方が分かりません。
例3) 東京へ行く　→　東京への行き方が分かりません。

1. 漢字を書く　　　　5. 佐藤さんが話す
2. ワープロを使う　　6. 大阪へ行く
3. コピーをする　　　7. 日本語で手紙を書く
4. 日本語を勉強する

〈USAGE〉

例) A：すみません。
　　B：はい。
　　A：このコンピューターの使い方を教えてくださいませんか。
　　B：ええ、いいですよ。

1. この漢字を読む　　3. 日本語で手紙を書く
2. 京都へ行く

練習5　　Nに

〈STRUCTURE〉

例) ここ　　カードを入れる　→　ここにカードを入れてください。

1. ここ　　　　　　　本を置く
2. ここ　　　　　　　名前を書く
3. この紙　　　　　　サインする

4. メールボックス　　メモを入れる
5. そこ　　　　　　　かばんを置く
6. コーヒー　　　　　砂糖を入れる

〈USAGE〉

例）A：名前を書いてください。
　　B：あのう、どこに書きますか。
　　A：ここに書いてください。
　　B：はい。

1. 名前　　　　この紙
2. 電話番号　　このノート

Aural Comprehension

I Listen to the conversations and answer the following questions.

   (A)　At the reference counter in the library　　(ID カード：ID card)

   　　1．まず何を作りますか。

   　　2．男の人は図書館の人に何を出しましたか。

   (B)　At the library counter　　(ニューズウィーク：(name of a magazine)　上がる：to go up)

   　　1．ニューズウィークは何階にありますか。

   　　2．ニューズウィークはどこにありますか。

   (C)　At the library counter

   　　1．男の人は何冊本を借りますか。

   　　2．いつまで借りますか。

   (D)　Using the subway card vending machine

   　　1．女の人は何をしましたか。

   　　　　まず_____。それから_____。

   　　2．女の人はいくらのカードを買いましたか。

II　(数字) Listen to the conversations and write down the numbers with the counters.

   　　1．_____　2．_____　3．_____　4．_____

III　One of the people in each conversation is you.

   　　Listen to what the other person says and write down what you have to do.

   　　(写真：photo)

   　　Your action：あなた(ジョン)は何をしますか。

   　　1．_____　2．_____　3．_____

Reading Comprehension

メール

山下さん
　京都は楽しかったです。金閣寺はとてもきれいでしたね。写真はできましたか。見せてください。京都にはいろいろなお寺がありますね。また行きたいです。
　今週の金曜日に、わたしの部屋でパーティーをします。ルインさんとアリスさんと佐藤さんが来ます。国の料理を作ります。
山下さんも来てください。午後5時からです。よろしく。
カーリン

カーリンさんへ
　メール、ありがとう。京都の写真ができました。いい写真があります。見せますね。
　金曜日は5時半までいそがしいです。でも、パーティーへ行きます。
じゃ、金曜日に会いましょう。＼(^o^)／　　　　　　　　　　　　山下

- 楽しい　pleasant
- できる　to be made, to be ready
- また　again
- 金閣寺　Golden Pavilion
- 見せる　to show
- 今週　this week
- 写真　photo
- (お)寺　temple
- 午後　afternoon

質問

1. いつパーティーをしますか。
2. どこでしますか。
3. だれが行きますか。
4. だれが写真を見せますか。
5. 山下さんは5時にはカーリンさんの部屋にいますか。

Kanji Practice

New Kanji

76.	行	こう いく、おこなう	to go, to do to carry out	84.	会	かい あう	meeting to meet
(6)	ノ ノ 彳 行 行			(6)	ノ 人 会 会 会		
77.	使	つかう	to use	85.	見	けん みる	to see
(8)	ノ イ 仁 仁 仁 伊 使 使			(7)	丨 冂 目 目 見		
78.	言	いう	word to say	86.	買	かう	to buy
(7)	二 三 言 言 言			(12)	丶 冖 罒 罒 罒 胃 胃 買 買		
79.	話	わ はなす	conversation to speak	87.	書	しょ かく	to write
(13)	丶 言 言 言 訂 託 話			(10)	フ ユ ヨ 크 聿 聿 書 書 書		
80.	読	よむ	to read	88.	聞	ぶん きく	to hear to ask
(14)	二 三 言 言 訂 詁 詁 読 読			(14)	丨 ｢ ｢ 門 門 門 門 聞 聞		
81.	食	しょく たべる	food to eat	89.	来	らい くる	to come
(9)	ノ 人 人 今 今 今 食 食 食			(7)	一 厂 쿠 平 来 来		
82.	飲	のむ	to drink	90.	通	つう とおる	to go through
(12)	ノ 人 ク 今 食 食 食 飲 飲			(10)	マ ア 丙 甬 甬 涌 通 通		
83.	教	きょう おしえる	to teach	( ) : Kanji stroke count Bold letters : "on" readings Underlined letters : "kun" readings			
(11)	+ 土 耂 考 孝 孝 孝 教 教						

Essential Words

1. 行く（い）to go
2. 使う（つか）to use
3. 言う（い）to say
4. 話す（はな）to speak
5. 読む（よ）to read
6. 食べる（た）to eat
7. 飲む（の）to drink
8. 教える（おし）to teach
9. 会う（あ）to meet
10. 見る（み）to see
11. 買う（か）to buy
12. 書く（か）to write
13. 聞く（き）to listen
14. 来る（く）to come
15. 来年（らいねん）next year
16. 来月（らいげつ）next month
17. 通る（とお）to go through

Words

1. 行う（おこな）to do
2. 会話（する）（かいわ）conversation
3. 教会（きょうかい）church
4. 学会（がっかい）academic society
5. 見学（する）（けんがく）visit for study
6. 新聞（しんぶん）newspaper
7. 交通（こうつう）traffic

Reading Practice

1. 大学へ行きます。
2. コンピューターを使います。
3. 先生に言います。
4. 友達（だち）と話しました。
5. 本を読みます。
6. サラダを食べます。
7. コーヒーを飲みました。
8. 日本語（ご）を教えます。
9. 先生に会いました。
10. テレビを見ました。
11. ビデオを買います。
12. ひらがなを書きます。
13. テープを聞きました。
14. 大学に来ました。
15. このバスは本山（もとやま）を通ります。

Lesson 7

Dialogue 郵便局で

7-1 After class

ルイン： アリスさん。

アリス： はい。

ルイン： コーヒー、飲みに行きませんか。

アリス： いいですね。でも、ちょっとこれを出しに行きたいんです。郵便局は何時までですか。

ルイン： 5時までですよ。

アリス： そうですか。今4時半ですねえ。うーん。

ルイン： ああ、じゃ、先に郵便局に行って、それからきっさてんへ行きましょう。

アリス： いいですか。

ルイン： ええ、きょうはひまですから。

7-2 Sending a parcel by airmail

アリス　　　： これ、航空便でお願いします。
郵便局員： はい。
アリス　　　： 何日ぐらいで着きますか。
郵便局員： カナダは1週間ぐらいですね。
アリス　　　： ああ、1週間ですか。
郵便局員： 急ぎますか。
アリス　　　： ええ。
郵便局員： じゃ、EMSはいかがですか。
アリス　　　： それ、何ですか。
郵便局員： Express Mail Serviceの略です。少し高いですが、速くて、便利ですよ。
アリス　　　： そうですか。いくらですか。
郵便局員： 1680円です。
アリス　　　： じゃ、それでお願いします。
郵便局員： じゃ、この用紙に記入してください。
アリス　　　： はい。

(Alice fills in the form.)

これでいいですか。

郵便局員： あ、すみません。
ここにサインが要ります。

アリス： あ、はい。

◇　　　◇　　　◇

アリス： それから、はがき5枚と130円の切手10枚ください。
郵便局員： はい。ええと、全部で3230円です。
アリス： はい。あっ、財布を忘れました。ちょっとそこの機械でお金を出してきます。
郵便局員： はい。どうぞ。
アリス： すみません。

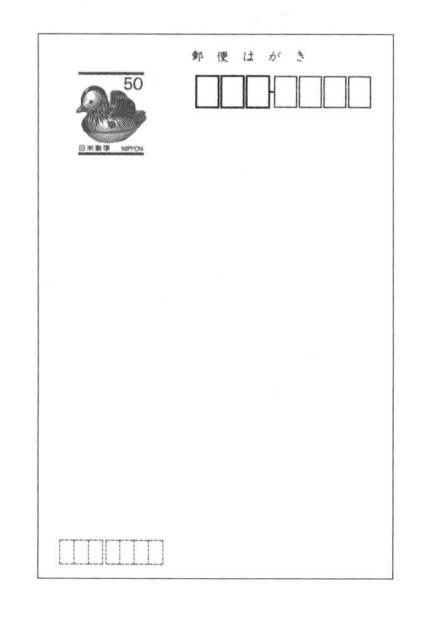

7-Supplement　事務室で
じむしつ

Naron needs to sign a form at the office every month to receive his scholarship. After signing, he applies for a field trip planned by the ryuugakusee office.

ナロン　　　：　すみません。

事務の人：　はい。
じむ ひと

ナロン　　　：　あのう、奨学金のサインをしたいんですが。
しょうがくきん

事務の人：　あ、はい。ここにお願いします。
ねが

ナロン　　　：　はい。(Naron signs the form.)

あ、それから、工場見学の申しこみをしたいんですが。
こうじょうけんがく　もう

事務の人：　はい。じゃ、この用紙に、お名前、住所、電話番号を記入して
ようし　　　　なまえ　じゅうしょ　でんわばんごう　きにゅう
ください。

ナロン　　　：　はい。(Naron fills in the form)

これでいいですか。

事務の人：　はい。けっこうです。

ナロン　　　：　お願いします。
ねが

Discourse Practice and Activity

Discourse Practice : Inviting

Let's think about what you would say in response to the following task and carry out a conversation.   Refer to **Dialogue 7-1**.

⟨Task⟩

Let's invite a friend to do something together. For example, going to see a movie or going out for lunch. Decide on the time and place as required.

On the other hand, think about what you would say if you were invited. Think about what to say to accept and/or refuse the invitation.

あなた：(アリス)さん。
友達(ともだち)：はい。
　　　　⋮

(Example)
1　ルイン：アリスさん。
　　アリス：はい。
　　ルイン：きっさてんへ行(い)きませんか。
　　アリス：いいですね。行(い)きましょう。
　　　　⋮

2　ルイン：アリスさん。
　　アリス：はい。
　　ルイン：きっさてんへ行(い)きませんか。
　　アリス：ああ、今から授業(じゅぎょう)なんです。
　　ルイン：そうですか。じゃあ、また。

Activity : Speech

Talk about a nice experience you had. For example, going on a trip or having a party, etc.

Let's listen to a speech made by friend, and ask him/her some questions.

(Example)
先週(せんしゅう)の日曜日(にちようび)、はじめて海(うみ)を見(み)ました。日本人(にほんじん)の友(とも)だちと車(くるま)で海(うみ)に行(い)きました。海(うみ)に足(あし)を入(い)れました。ちょっと冷(つめ)たかったです。海(うみ)の近(ちか)くのレストランで日本(にほん)の食(た)べ物(もの)を食(た)べました。6時(じ)にアパートへ帰(かえ)りました。楽(たの)しかったです。

(はじめて：for the first time　海(うみ)：sea　足(あし)：foot　冷(つめ)たい：cold　楽(たの)しい：pleasant)

Vocabulary List

⟨ ⟩ : dictionary form
┐ : accent fall (for words only)

Dialogue

7-1

に		[Group 1 particle for purpose of motion]
いいですね。		That's a good idea.
だしま┐す⟨だ┐す⟩　(〜が〜に〜を)	出します⟨出す⟩	to mail (letters)
さきに		first, before the rest
きっさてん		coffee shop
いいですか。		Is that O.K.?
から		because [Group 4 particle for reason clauses]

7-2

ゆうびんきょ┐くいん	郵便局員	post office clerk
こうくうびん	航空便	airmail
な┐んにち	何日	how many days
で		in [Group 1 particle for period of time]
つきま┐す⟨つ┐く⟩　(〜が〜に)	着きます⟨着く⟩	to arrive
イーエムエ┐ス	EMS	EMS (Express Mail Service)
りゃ┐く	略	abbreviation, acronym
が		but [Group 4 particle]
はや┐い	速い	fast
よ┐うし	用紙	form (to fill in)
きにゅうしま┐す　(〜が〜に〜を)　⟨きにゅうする⟩	記入します ⟨記入する⟩	to fill in
これでいいですか。		Is this O.K.?
サ┐イン		signature
いりま┐す⟨いる⟩　(〜に〜が)	要ります⟨要る⟩	to need
はがき		postcard

〜まい	〜枚	[counter for flat things]
きって	切手	postal stamp
ぜんぶ	全部	all
で		[Group 1 particle for a unit of things]
(お)かね	(お)金	money
さいふ	財布	wallet, purse
わすれます　(〜が〜を)〈わすれる〉	忘れます〈忘れる〉	to forget
だします〈だす〉　(〜が〜を)	出します〈出す〉	to withdraw (money)
〜てきます		to do something and come back
すみません。		I'm sorry.

7-Supplement

じむしつ	事務室	office
しょうがくきん	奨学金	scholarship
こうじょう	工場	factory, plant
けんがく	見学	study visit, field trip
もうしこみ(をする)	申しこみ(をする)	application (to apply)
じゅうしょ	住所	address
けっこうです。		That's fine.

Drill

あさ	朝	morning
おきます〈おきる〉(〜が)	起きます〈起きる〉	to get up
あびます(シャワーを)(〜が〜を)〈あびる〉	浴びます〈浴びる〉	to take a shower
あさごはん	朝ごはん	breakfast
ねます〈ねる〉　(〜が)		to go to bed, to sleep
いっしょに		together
(お)さけ	(お)酒	alcohol
ドル		dollar
かえる　(〜が〜を〜に)		to change
れんしゅうする　(〜が〜を)	練習する	to practice
おぼえます　(〜が〜を)〈おぼえる〉	覚えます〈覚える〉	to memorize
あたまがいい	頭がいい	smart

ハ[￢]ンサム(な)		handsome
ベ[￢]ッド		bed
インドネ[￢]シア		Indonesia
みず	水	water
ひるご[￢]はん	昼ごはん	lunch
やすみじ[￢]かん	休み時間	break (time)
いってらっしゃい。		[greeting to person leaving a place to come back]
コ[￢]ンサート		concert
プ[￢]ール		swimming pool
およ[￢]ぐ (〜が)	泳ぐ	to swim
ところ[￢]		place
あそぶ (〜が)	遊ぶ	to play
ふくしゅう	復習	review
て[￢]んき	天気	weather
こうえん	公園	park
ど[￢]うして		why
テ[￢]スト		test
てんぷら		[name of Japanese food]
(お)ず[￢]し		[name of Japanese food]
ピ[￢]クニック		picnic
りんご		apple
〜さつ	〜冊	[counter for books]
とりにく	とり肉	chicken
グ[￢]ラム		gram
ビデオテ[￢]ープ		video tape
〜ほん	〜本	[counter for tapes, long things]
レポ[￢]ート		report
みっか	3日	three days
ド[￢]クター		doctor ('s degree)
〜かげつ	〜か月	month(s) [counter]
〜ねん	〜年	year(s) [counter]
ふつか	2日	two days
しゃしん	写真	picture
できま[￢]す〈でき[￢]る〉(〜が)		to be ready, to be made

Notes on Grammar

I The -て form of -い adjectives, -な adjectives, and noun＋です

The -て form of a verb has been introduced in Lesson 6, Notes on Grammar I as V -てください. -い adjectives, -な adjectives, and noun＋です also have -て forms.

A Formation rule: -い adjectives

The -て form of -い adjectives can be obtained by deleting です and changing the final -い to -くて. But the -て form of いい "good" is よくて.

$$-い \rightarrow -くて$$

† Table of the -て form of -い adjectives †

-い adjective		-て form
むずかしい	difficult	むずかしくて
おもしろい	interesting	おもしろくて
やすい	cheap	やすくて
おおきい	big	おおきくて

B Formation rule: -な adjectives, and noun＋です

The -て form of -な adjectives, and noun＋です can be obtained by changing です to で.

$$\sim です \rightarrow \sim で$$

† Table of the -て form of -な adjectives, and noun＋です†

-な adjective, and noun＋です	-て form
げんきです　　fine	げんきで
ひまです　　　free	ひまで
ほんです　　　to be a book	ほんで
がくせいです　to be a student	がくせいで

II Function and usages of the -て form

A Function of the -て form

The -て form is used to connect two or more predicates.

Examples

1. EMS は速くて、便利です。
   EMS is fast and convenient.
2. ルインさんは名古屋大学の学生で、ミャンマーから来ました。
   Lwin is a student at Nagoya University, and is from Myanmar.
3. ルインさんが手紙を書いて、アリスさんがそれをポストに入れました。
   Lwin wrote a letter, and Alice put it into the mailbox.

B Usages of the -て form of verbs

The first clause ending with the -て form has the following usages.
(1) It describes a series of actions and events.
(2) It describes the two actions occurring at the same time and shows the means or methods of the action described in the following clause.

Examples

1. 教室に行って、日本語を勉強しました。
   I went to the classroom and studied Japanese. (Lit.)
2. 栄で降りて、デパートへ行きました。
   I got off at Sakae and went to a department store.
3. 漢字を書いて覚えました。
   I memorized the kanji while writing them.
4. 栄までバスに乗って行きます。
   I will go to Sakae by taking a bus.

III V-てきます

The -て form of a verb＋きます (V-てきます) means "(go somewhere to) do something and come back." This expression always implies that the actor who goes is intending to return again to where he/she is now.

Examples
1. 切手を買ってきます。
   I'll go and buy some postage stamps.
2. コーヒーを飲んできます。
   I'll go and drink some coffee.
3. 図書館へ行ってきます。
   I'm going to the library.
4. お金を出してきます。
   I'll go and withdraw some money.

IV Conjunction：それから

In Lesson 6, Notes on Grammar VI それから is used for indicating the chronological order of actions or states, and means "and then," "after that," or "secondly." Here それから is used for adding more information and means "in addition to that."

Examples
1. 教室にアリスさんがいます。それから、ルインさんもいます。
   Alice is in the classroom. And Lwin is, too.
2. はがきを5枚ください。それから、切手を10枚ください。
   I'll take five postcards. And I'll take ten stamps.
3. きのう、魚とサラダ、それから、ケーキを食べました。
   I ate fish, salad, and a piece of cake yesterday.

V Group 4 particles：から and が

A Reason：から

から means "because," "since," "as" and "so."

It belongs to Group 4 particles which connect two sentences. It follows the polite form or the non-polite form of a verb, -い adjective, -な adjective, and noun＋です or だ, the non-polite from of です. (For detailed information of the non-polite form, see Lesson 8, Notes on Grammar I.)

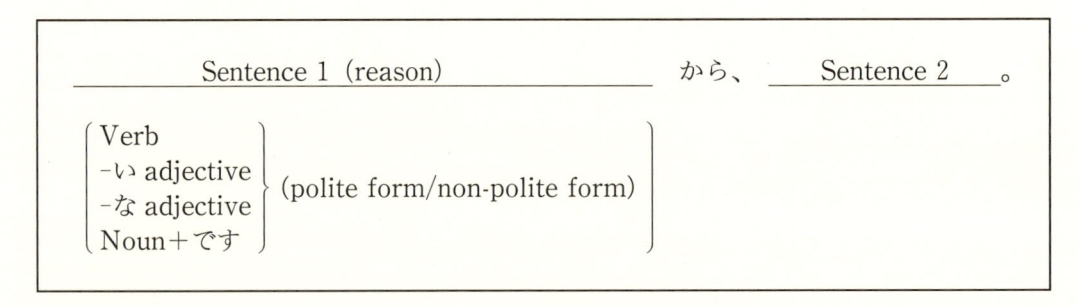

Sentence 1 (reason)	から、	Sentence 2 。
{ Verb / -い adjective / -な adjective / Noun＋です } (polite form/non-polite form)		

This から is different from から "from," Group 1 particle.

Examples

1. 宿題がありましたから、行きませんでした。
   しゅくだい
   As I had homework, I didn't go. / I had homework, so I didn't go.
2. 高かったですから、買いませんでした。
   たか   か
   Because it was expensive, I didn't buy it.
3. 学生ですから、よく勉強してください。
   がくせい   べんきょう
   Since you are a student, please study hard.

Note the following contrast.

1. 今12時ですから、ごはんを食べましょう。
   いま じ   た
   Let's have a meal because it is twelve o'clock. (Lit.)
2. 12時からごはんを食べましょう。
     じ   た
   Let's have a meal from twelve o'clock. (Lit.)

When you want to ask a reason, the question word どうして which means "why" is used.

Example

A：きょうパーティーへ行きますか。
                    い
Are you going to the party today?
B：いいえ。
No.
A：どうしてですか。
Why?
B：あしたテストがありますから。
Because I will have a test tomorrow.

B Opposition：が

が has been introduced in Lesson 5 as a conjunctive Group 4 particle to connect an introductory remark and the main part of a conversation. Another usage of が introduced in this lesson means "but," or "however."

Examples
1. わたしは元気ですが、ルインさんは元気じゃありません。
   I'm fine, but Lwin isn't.
2. EMS はちょっと高いですが、速くて、便利ですよ。
   EMS is a little expensive, but it is fast and convenient.

VI Group 1 particles：に and で

A Purpose：に

The particle に shows a purpose in the following sentence pattern.

$$\text{Place} \; へ \; \underbrace{(\text{Object} \; を) \; \text{Verb (base)}}_{\text{(purpose)}} \; に \; \begin{cases} 行きます。 \\ 来ます。 \\ 帰ります。 \end{cases}$$

In this pattern, verbs of motion like going or coming are used as main verbs.

Examples
1. あした栄へ映画を見に行きます。
   I will go to Sakae to see a movie tomorrow.
2. 大学へ先生に会いに来ました。
   I came to the university to see my teacher.
3. うちへ教科書を取りに帰りました。
   I went home to pick up my textbook.
4. A：図書館へ何をしに行きましたか。
   What did you go to the library for?
   B：新聞を読みに行きました。
   I went there to read a newspaper.

B で

1. Unit

で indicates a unit of things or a group of people and means "altogether."

Examples
1. 切手は5枚で600円です。
   きって　まい　　　えん
   Altogether the five stamps cost 600 yen.
2. 全部で3990円です。
   ぜんぶ　　　　えん
   It costs 3900 yen in total.

2. Period of time

で indicates a period of time within which an activity takes place.

Examples
1. 1時間でこの本を読んでください。
   じかん　　　　ほん　よ
   Please read this book in one hour.
2. A：航空便は何日ぐらいで着きますか。
   　　こうくうびん　なんにち　　　　つ
   How long does it take to reach there by airmail?
   B：1週間で着きます。
   　　いっしゅうかん　つ
   It will reach there in one week.
3. 1か月で専門の本を読みました。
   いっ　げつ　せんもん　ほん　よ
   I read a book on my major subject in one month.

VII Numbers as adverbs

Numbers which consist of "a numeral + a counter" often act like adverbs.

Examples
1. 学生が3人来ました。
   がくせい　にん き
   Three students came.
2. 紙が3枚あります。
   かみ　まい
   There are three sheets of paper.
3. りんごを3つ食べました。
   　　　　　みっ　た
   I ate three apples.
4. 肉を300グラム買いました。
   にく　　　　　　か
   I bought 300 grams of meat.
5. はがきを5枚ください。
   　　　　　まい
   I'll take five postcards.

Notes on Discourse

1 いいですね

Read the following conversation.

> A：コーヒー飲みに行きませんか。
> Would you like to come and have coffee with me ?
> B：いいですね。
> That's a great idea !

The speaker A invites B for a drink of coffee. The speaker B is willing to accept the invitation and says **いいですね** which means "That's good." **ね** should be pronounced with a prolonged falling intonation to show agreement.

In Dialogue 7-1 Alice accepts Lwin's invitation. But if you do not accept an invitation, **いいえ** is not a usual response word. **うーん**, **ああ** or even **ええ、でも〜** is used in a low, flat tone instead. And after **ああ** you give the reason why you can't accept the invitation with **んです**.

1. A：コーヒー飲みに行きませんか。
   Would you like to come and have coffee with me ?
   B：うーん、ちょっと……。
   Um I'm sorry but....
2. A：コーヒー飲みに行きませんか。
   Would you like to come and have coffee with me ?
   B：ああ、今から授業なんです。
   I have a class now.
   A：そうですか。
   Really.
   B：ええ。
   Yes.
   A：じゃ、また。
   Then, see you.

II　お願いします

お願いします is used to mean "Please do something for me" or "Please take care of this for me."

A

It is used when the speaker asks someone to do something without stating the particular verb, if the action to be taken is clear from the context or situation.
In Dialogue 7-2 Alice submits a letter at the post office and asks the clerk to send the letter.

   これ、航空便でお願いします。   Please send this by airmail.

These are some other examples where the context is obvious.

   魚フライ定食、お願いします。(at the cafeteria) A fried fish set, please.
   国際ホテル、お願いします。(to a taxi driver) Kokusai Hotel, please.
   駅までお願いします。(to a taxi driver) To the station, please.
   もう一度お願いします。(to ask to do it again) Once more, please.

B

When finishing a conversation in which one asks another to do or to take care of something, one often says お願いします or よろしくお願いします instead of ありがとうございます as you see in Dialogue 7-Supplement, Dialogue 8-3, etc.

III　これでいいですか

In Dialogue 7-2 Alice has to fill out the form to send a parcel by Express Mail Service at the post office.

  郵便局員：はい。じゃ、この用紙に記入してください。
      O.K. Then please fill out this form.
  アリス ：はい。(Filling out the form) これでいいですか。
      O.K.   Is it O.K. like this?

After filling it out she wants to confirm the form was filled out properly. これでいいですか is used for confirmation as in this case. The response to this question can be はい、けっこうです or はい、(これで)いいです, if it is O.K.

Drill

練習 1　Vて、Vて　(series of actions)

〈STRUCTURE〉

例) 日本語を勉強します。　研究室へ行きます。　うちへ帰ります。
　→ 日本語を勉強して、研究室へ行って、うちへ帰ります。

1. 8時にうちを出ます。　　大学に来ます。　　　　日本語を勉強します。
2. 生協へ行きます。　　　　ノートを買います。　　会館へ帰ります。
3. 朝起きます。　　　　　　シャワーを浴びます。　朝ごはんを食べます。
4. テレビを見ます。　　　　勉強します。　　　　　11時にねます。
5. 栄へ行きました。　　　　友達に会いました。　　いっしょにごはんを食べました。
6. 郵便局へ行きました。　　切手を買いました。　　手紙を出しました。

〈USAGE〉

例) A：Bさん、きょうは何をしますか。
　　B：図書館へ行って、勉強して、それから、研究室へ行きます。
　　A：そうですか。(いそがしいですね。)

1. きのう　　会館へ帰る　　　　ビデオを見る　　　　本を読む
2. あした　　栄で友達と会う　　いっしょに映画を見る　　お酒を飲む
3. きょう　　銀行へ行く　　　　円をドルにかえる　　　　会館へ帰る

練習 2　Vて　(two actions at the same time, method)

〈STRUCTURE〉

(大学へはどうやって来ますか。)
例) 自転車に乗る　来る　→　自転車に乗って来ます。

1. バスに乗る　　　　　来る
2. 歩く　　　　　　　　来る

(日本語はどうやって勉強しますか。)
3. テープを聞く　　　　勉強する

4. コンピューターを使う　　　勉強する
5. 日本人と話す　　　　　　　勉強する
6. テレビを見る　　　　　　　勉強する

（漢字はどうやって覚えますか。）
7. 書く　　　　　　　　　　　覚える
8. カードを作る　　　　　　　覚える
9. 辞書を使う　　　　　　　　覚える
10. コンピューターで練習する　覚える

〈USAGE〉

例）A：Bさんはどうやって漢字を覚えますか。
　　B：書いて覚えます。
　　A：ああ、それもいいですね。
　　B：Aさんは。
　　A：わたしはカードを作って覚えます。
　　B：ああ、そうですか。

練習3　　Nて／Aて／Vて

〈STRUCTURE〉

例1）図書館は広いです。　　図書館はきれいです。→　図書館は広くてきれいです。

1. 生協の食堂は安いです。　　　　　　生協の食堂はおいしいです。
2. このかばんは黒いです。　　　　　　このかばんは大きいです。
3. アリスさんは頭がいいです。　　　　アリスさんは親切です。
4. 図書館はきれいです。　　　　　　　図書館は静かです。
5. ルインさんはハンサムです。　　　　ルインさんは元気な人です。
6. カーリンさんはドイツ人です。　　　カーリンさんは経済学部の学生です。

例2）これは日本語の教科書です。　　あれは漢字の教科書です。
　→　これは日本語の教科書で、あれは漢字の教科書です。

1. こちらはナロンさんです。　　　　　あちらは佐藤さんです。
2. 新聞はテレビの上です。　　　　　　時計はベッドのそばです。
3. ルインさんのかばんは大きいです。　アリスさんのかばんは小さいです。
4. アリスさんはテレビを買いました。　ナロンさんは自転車を買いました。

〈USAGE〉

例）A：Bさん、インドネシアはどんな国ですか。

B：静かで、きれいな国です。
A：そうですか。

1. Bさんの部屋

練習4　Vてきます

〈STRUCTURE〉

例）ノートを買う　→　ノートを買ってきます。

1. 銀行へ行く　　4. テープレコーダーを取る
2. 先生に聞く　　5. 昼ごはんを食べる
3. 水を飲む　　　6. 手紙を出す

〈USAGE〉

（教室で、休み時間に）
例）A：ちょっと生協へ行ってきます。
　　B：あ、いってらっしゃい。

1. コーヒー　　買う
2. 友達　　　　電話する

練習5　Vに　　（purpose）

〈STRUCTURE〉

a.
例）栄へ行きます。（映画を見る）　→　栄へ映画を見に行きます。

1. デパートへ行きます。（くつを買う）
2. 生協へ行きます。（コピーをする）
3. 図書館へ行きます。（本を借りる）
4. 研究室へ行きます。（先生に会う）
5. 銀行へ行きました。（お金を出す）
6. 日本へ来ました。（専門の勉強をする）

b.
例）あした　　　栄　　　映画を見る　→　A：あした、どこかへ行きますか。
　　　　　　　　　　　　　　　　　　　　B：はい、栄へ行きます。
　　　　　　　　　　　　　　　　　　　　A：何をしに行きますか。
　　　　　　　　　　　　　　　　　　　　B：映画を見に行きます。

1. きょう　　　　　　生協　　　　　コーヒーを飲む
2. きのう　　　　　　研究室　　　　専門の先生に会う
3. 先週の日曜日　　　東京　　　　　コンサートを聞く

〈USAGE〉

例）A：Bさん、きっさてんへコーヒーを飲みに行きませんか。
　　B：いいですね。行きましょう。

1. プール　　　　　　　　泳ぐ
2. アリスさんのところ　　遊ぶ

練習6　　S1から、S2　　（reason）

〈STRUCTURE〉

例）友達が来ます。　うちへ帰ります。　→　友達が来ますから、うちへ帰ります。

1. あしたテストがあります。　　勉強します。
2. 復習が大変です。　　　　　　テレビは見ません。
3. 天気がいいです。　　　　　　公園へ行きましょう。
4. 時間がありません。　　　　　急いでください。
5. 予習しました。　　　　　　　分かります。
6. ひまでした。　　　　　　　　映画を見ました。

〈USAGE〉

例）A：きょうパーティーへ行きますか。
　　B：いいえ、行きません。
　　A：どうしてですか。
　　B：あしたテストがありますから。
　　A：そうですか。

1. ちょっといそがしいです。　　2. 時間がありません。

練習7　　S1が、S2　　（but）

〈STRUCTURE〉

例）漢字は難しいです。でも、ひらがなは簡単です。
　　→　漢字は難しいですが、ひらがなは簡単です。

1. てんぷらは好きです。でも、おすしは好きじゃありません。
2. 教科書は読みました。でも、テープは聞きませんでした。

3. パーティーへは行きました。でも、ピクニックへは行きませんでした。
4. ルインさんはひまでした。でも、どこへも行きませんでした。

練習 8　　Nで　　(altogether)

〈STRUCTURE〉

例）　（はがき　　　1枚 50円）　　　2枚　　　　100円
　　　　　　　　　　　　　　　　　　　→　2枚で 100円です。

1. （切手　　　　1枚 80円）　　　4枚　　　　320円
2. （りんご　　　1つ 80円）　　　3つ　　　　240円
3. （ノート　　　1冊 100円）　　　5冊　　　　500円
4. （とり肉　　　100グラム 150円）　200グラム　300円
5. （ビデオテープ 1本 400円）　　　3本　　　　1200円
6. ┌テレビ　　　6000円　┐
   │冷蔵庫　　　10000円　│　　　全部　　　20000円
   └自転車　　　4000円　┘

〈USAGE〉

例）A：すみません、はがきを 2枚 ください。
　　B：はい。2枚で 100円です。
　　A：はい。
　　B：はい。どうもありがとうございました。

1. 200円のりんご　　4つ
2. 100円のとり肉　　500グラム
3. 90円の切手　5枚　と　100円の切手　3枚

練習 9　　Nで　　(period of time)

〈STRUCTURE〉

例）レポートを書きました。（3日）　→　3日でレポートを書きました。

1. 専門の本を読みました。（1か月）
2. ドクターを取りました。（3年）
3. ひらがなを覚えました。（2日）
4. 手紙が着きます。（1週間）
5. 写真ができます。（1時間）

Aural Comprehension

I Listen to the conversations and answer the following questions.

(A) In the post office

1. タイまで航空便でいくらですか。
   こうくうびん

2. 何日ぐらいかかりますか。
   なんにち

(B) In the post office

1. はがきは1枚いくらですか。
   いちまい

2. 全部でいくらですか。
   ぜんぶ

(C) In the post office : sending a parcel

1. 何日ぐらいかかりますか。
   なんにち

2. 紙に何を書きましたか。
   かみ なに か

(D) In the bank : at the exchange counter   (かえる：to change   ドル：dollar)

1. 女の人は何を何にかえましたか。
   おんな ひと なに なに

2. きょうは1ドルいくらですか。

3. How much was the man charged as commission?

II (数字) Listen to the conversations and write down the numbers with the counters.
   すうじ

   1. _____   2. _____   3. _____   4. _____

III One of the people in each conversation is you.

Listen to what the other person says and write down the answer to your question.

Your question : いつできますか。 (1. laundry   2. photograph   3. photograph)
             (できる：to be ready)

   1. _____   2. _____   3. _____

Reading Comprehension

There are two types of writing in Japanese : horizontal lines and vertical lines.

手紙

古田さん、お元気ですか。わたしは毎日いそがしくて、大変です。
古田さんはいかがですか。
先月、日本語の授業が始まりました。授業は八時四十五分に始まって二時半に終わります。それから研究室へ行って、専門の本を読みます。毎日、五時に帰ります。日曜日には国の友達に会って、いっしょにごはんを食べます。
夏休みは七月十五日に始まります。夏休みには、古田さんに会いに京都へ行きますね。
きのう、国から小包が来ました。その中にきれいな切手がありましたから、送ります。

では、お元気で。　さようなら

五月三十日

バンバン

- 先月 last month
- 夏休み summer vacation
- 小包 parcel
- 送る to send

質問

1. だれがこの手紙を読みますか。
2. だれがいそがしいですか。
3. 日本語の授業はいつ始まりましたか。
4. 2時半からどこで、何をしますか。
5. いつ古田さんに会いますか。
6. 小包はどこから来ましたか。

Kanji Practice

New Kanji

No.	Kanji	Readings	Meaning
91. (11)	堂	どう	temple, hall
92. (7)	図	ず、と	drawing, plan
93. (16)	館	かん	(large) building, hall
94. (8)	国	こく、くに	country
95. (5)	外	がい、そと	outside
96. (10)	紙	し、かみ	paper
97. (4)	切	せつ、きる	to cut
98. (8)	枚	まい	counter for thin flat objects
99. (9)	送	おくる	to send
100. (11)	週	しゅう	week
101. (12)	間	かん、あいだ、ま	interval
102. (12)	着	つく、きる	arrival, to arrive, to put on
103. (5)	市	し	city, town
104. (14)	様	さま	Mr. Mrs. Miss.
105. (4)	方	ほう、かた	side, method, person

( ): Kanji stroke count
Bold letters: "on" readings
Underlined letters: "kun" readings

Essential Words

1. 食堂 (しょくどう) cafeteria
2. 図書館 (としょかん) library
3. 会館 (かいかん) hall, International Students' House
4. 国 (くに) country
5. 外国 (がいこく) foreign country
6. 外 (そと) outside
7. 紙 (かみ) paper
8. 手紙 (てがみ) letter
9. 切手 (きって) stamp
10. 一枚 (いちまい) a sheet of paper
11. 送る (おく) to send
12. 一週間 (いっしゅうかん) a week
13. 先週 (せんしゅう) last week
14. 今週 (こんしゅう) this week
15. 来週 (らいしゅう) next week
16. 着く (つ) to arrive
17. 着る (き) to put on
18. 市 (し) city
19. 使い方 (つかいかた) how to use

Words

1. 切る (き) to cut
2. 下着 (したぎ) underwear
3. この方 (かた) this person
4. 安田様 (やすだ さま) Mr. (Mrs. Miss) Yasuda
5. 何名様 (なんめいさま) how many people (polite expression)
6. 外国人 (がいこくじん) foreigner

Reading Practice

1. 図書館の前(まえ)に食堂があります。
2. 外国の友達(だち)に手紙を書きました。
3. 郵便局(ゆうびんきょく)で切手を五枚買いました。
4. 国へ手紙を送りました。
5. 手紙は一週間で着きます。

Lesson 8

Dialogue 体(からだ)の調子(ちょうし)

8-1 At the hospital

医者(いしゃ)： どうしました。

ルイン： あのう、2、3日前(にさんにちまえ)からのどがすごく痛(いた)いんです。

医者： そうですか。熱(ねつ)ははかりましたか。

ルイン： はい。8度(ど)5分(ぶ)ありました。

医者： はい。ちょっと口(くち)を開(あ)けて、のどを見(み)せてください。ああ、赤(あか)いですね。せきは出(で)ますか。

ルイン： はい、ときどき。

医者： はい。

ルイン： あのう、おなかもちょっと痛(いた)いんですけど。

医者： はい。じゃ、ちょっとそこに横(よこ)になってください。

◇　　　　◇　　　　◇

医者　：　かぜですね。薬を出しますから、食後に飲んでください。

ルイン：　はい。どうもありがとうございました。

医者　：　お大事に。

8-2 On campus

Nakayama meets Lwin by chance on campus in the morning.
Lwin is holding his elbow.

中山　：　ルインさん、どうしたんですか。

ルイン：　あのう、自転車で、転んだんです。

中山　：　ええっ。

ルイン：　坂でスピードを出しすぎて……。

中山　：　危ないですね。

ルイン：　ええ。

中山　：　痛いですか。

ルイン：　ええ。ひじがちょっと。

中山　：　病院に行きましたか。

ルイン：　いいえ。

中山　：　行ったほうがいいですよ。

ルイン：　そうですね。たぶん骨はだいじょうぶだと思うんですけど、今から行ってきます。

中山　：　お大事に。

ルイン：　どうも。

8-3 Making an appointment with the dentist

受付　　： 大川歯科です。
ルイン： あ、もしもし。
受付　　： はい。
ルイン： あのう、診察、お願いしたいんですが。
受付　　： はい。
ルイン： 初めてなんですが。
受付　　： はい。どうなさいましたか。
ルイン： あのう、虫歯だと思うんですけど、ちょっと痛いんです。
受付　　： そうですか。じゃ、きょう、4時40分、いかがですか。
ルイン： はい。4時40分ですね。
受付　　： はい。お名前は。
ルイン： あ、ルインと申します。
受付　　： はっ。
ルイン： ルインです。
受付　　： ルンさんですね。
ルイン： いえ、ちがいます。ルインです。
受付　　： あ、ルインさんですね。
ルイン： はい。
受付　　： 保険証を持ってきてくださいね。
ルイン： はい、分かりました。じゃ、お願いします。

Discourse Practice and Activity

Discourse Practice : Telling your symptom

Let's think about what you would say in response to the following task and carry out a conversation. Refer to **Dialogue 8-1**.

〈Task〉

You do not feel very well. Referring to the picture, describe your symptoms to your doctor.

医者　：どうしましたか。
あなた：　⋮

1　おなかが痛い
2　のどが痛い
3　頭が痛い

4　食欲がない
　　to have no appetite
5　熱がある
6　せきが出る

7　はき気がする
　　to feel sick
8　げりをしている
　　to have diarrhea
9　寒気がする
　　to have a chill

Vocabulary List

⟨ ⟩ : dictionary form
┐ : accent fall (for words only)

Dialogue

8-1

からだ	体	body
ちょうし	調子	condition
どうしました。		How is it?, What is the problem?
に┐さんにち	2、3日	two or three days
の┐ど		throat
すご┐く		very much
いた┐い	痛い	painful
ねつ┐	熱	fever, temperature
は┐かる　(〜が〜を)		to measure
はちどごぶ	8度5分	38.5 degrees centigrade
〜ど	〜度	degrees [counter]
くち	口	mouth
あける　(〜が〜を)	開ける	to open
みせ┐る　(〜が〜に〜を)	見せる	to show
あかい	赤い	red
せき┐		cough
ときどき		sometimes
おなか		stomach
け┐ど		[Group 4 particle, See Notes on Grammar]
よこになる　(〜が)	横になる	to lie down
くすり	薬	medicine
かぜ		common cold
だ┐す　(〜が〜を)	出す	to prescribe
しょくご	食後	after meals
の┐む（くすりを）　(〜が〜を)	飲む	to take (medicine)
おだいじに。	お大事に。	Get well soon.

8-2

どうしたんですか。		How is it?, What is the problem?

ころぶ	(〜が)	転ぶ	to take a fall
さか		坂	slope
スピード			speed
だす(スピードを)	(〜が〜を)	出す	to drive fast
〜すぎる			... too much [See Notes on G.]
あぶない		危ない	dangerous
ひじ			elbow
びょういん		病院	hospital
〜たほうがいい			You had better ...
たぶん			maybe, probably
ほね		骨	bone
だいじょうぶ			all right
と			[Group 5 particle for quotation]
おもう	(〜が〜と)	思う	to think

8-3

うけつけ		受付	reception
おおかわ		大川	[personal name]
しか		歯科	dental clinic
もしもし。			Hello. (on the phone)
しんさつ		診察	medical consultation
おねがいする	(〜が〜に〜を)	お願いする	to make a request
はじめて		初めて	first time
どうなさいましたか。			What seems to be the problem?
むしば		虫歯	bad tooth
はっ。			Pardon?
ほけんしょう		保険証	health insurance card
もってくる	(〜が〜を)	持ってくる	to bring

Drill

サッカー			soccer
じぶんで		自分で	by oneself
ビール			beer
おくる	(〜が〜に〜を)	送る	to send
たべもの		食べ物	food
ぶっか		物価	(commodity) prices
おおい		多い	many, much, a lot
きたない			dirty
やさしい			easy

もんだい		問題	question
じかん		時間	time
みじか｜い		短い	short
にぎ｜やか(な)			lively
やすみ｜		休み	being closed, holiday, break
〜さい			... years old [counter]
キャ｜ンパス			campus
しけ｜ん		試験	examination
は｜やく		早く	early, soon
たばこ			cigarette
すう(たばこを)	(〜が〜を)	吸う	to smoke
なが｜い		長い	long
つめたい		冷たい	cold
もの｜		物	thing, stuff
あたま｜		頭	head
い｜つも			always
げんきがない		元気がない	to be in low spirits
ピ｜ザ			pizza
め｜		目	eye
あし｜		足	leg, foot
うんどうする	(〜が)	運動する	to exercise
ひく(かぜを)	(〜が〜を)	引く	to catch (cold)
やす｜む	(〜が〜を)	休む	to be absent, to take a rest

Lesson 8

Related Vocabulary

Names of Parts of the Body

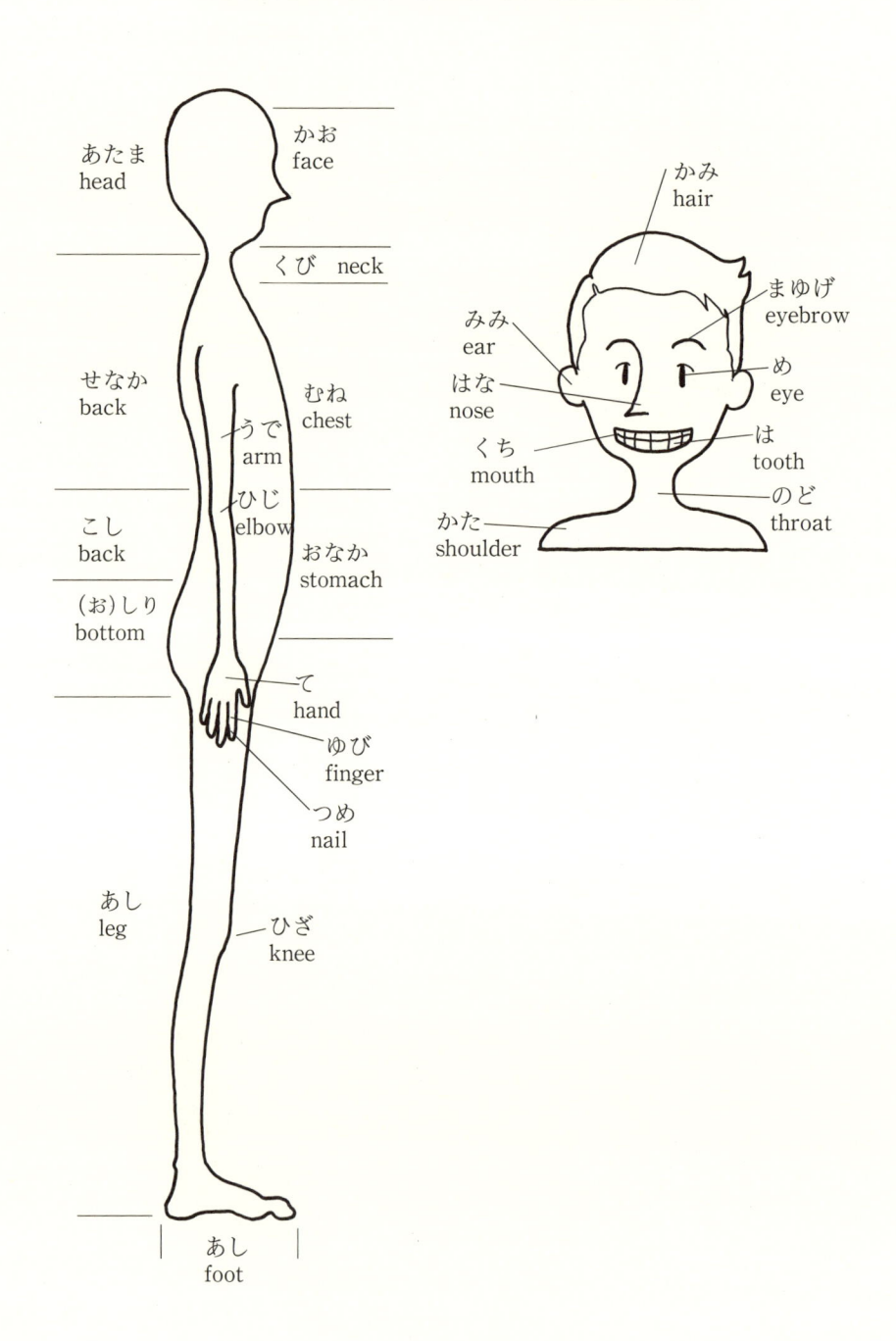

あたま	head
かお	face
くび	neck
せなか	back
むね	chest
うで	arm
ひじ	elbow
こし	back
おなか	stomach
(お)しり	bottom
て	hand
ゆび	finger
つめ	nail
あし	leg
ひざ	knee
あし	foot
かみ	hair
まゆげ	eyebrow
みみ	ear
め	eye
はな	nose
は	tooth
くち	mouth
のど	throat
かた	shoulder

Additional Vocabulary

Adjectives (1)

あおい	青い	blue
あかい	赤い	red
きいろい	黄色い	yellow
くろい	黒い	black
しろい	白い	white
みどりいろの	緑色の	green
ちゃいろの	茶色の	brown
あつい	暑い	hot
さむい	寒い	cold
あたたかい	暖かい	warm
すずしい		cool
むしあつい	むし暑い	humid
いい		good, nice
わるい	悪い	bad
おおきい	大きい	big, large
ちいさい	小さい	small, little
たかい	高い	high
ひくい	低い	low
たかい	高い	expensive
やすい	安い	cheap
ながい	長い	long
みじかい	短い	short
あたらしい	新しい	new
ふるい	古い	old
ひろい	広い	spacious
せまい		narrow, cramped
ちかい	近い	near
とおい	遠い	far
はやい	速い	fast
おそい		slow
はやい	早い	early
おそい		late

おおい	多い	many
すくない	少ない	few, little
いそがしい		busy
ひま(な)		not busy
むずかしい	難しい	difficult
やさしい		easy
かんたん(な)	簡単(な)	easy
おもしろい		interesting
つまらない		boring
きれい(な)		clean
きたない		dirty
しずか(な)	静か(な)	quiet
うるさい		noisy
にぎやか(な)		lively
おいしい		good, delicious
まずい		not good
いたい	痛い	to hurt(v)
ねむい		sleepy
すき(な)	好き(な)	to like(v)
きらい(な)		to dislike(v)
べんり(な)	便利(な)	convenient
ふべん(な)	不便(な)	inconvenient
きれい(な)		pretty
ハンサム(な)		handsome
まじめ(な)		serious-minded
しんせつ(な)	親切(な)	kind
げんき(な)	元気(な)	healthy
たいへん(な)	大変(な)	hard, tough
だめ(な)		unacceptable
いろいろ(な)		various
だいじ(な)	大事(な)	important

Notes on Grammar

I The non-polite form

There are two types of ending style in Japanese sentences. One is the polite style using the polite form of predicates, which you have been studying. The other one is the non-polite style using the non-polite form of predicates. The polite style is used between persons who are not close friends, as mentioned in Lesson 1, Notes on Grammar II. On the other hand, the non-polite style at the end of a sentence is used in informal speech among close friends or family members, and is also often used in written language, except in letters etc. For detailed information about informal speech, see Lessons 15 & 17 of Volume II.

In addition, the non-polite form has other usages according to certain grammatical rules. Some of them are introduced in this lesson, Notes on Grammar II.

A Formation rule: verbs

The non-polite form of verbs are formed from the dictionary form.

1. Group 1 verbs, or verbs ending in -eru or -iru

- Imperfective, affirmative form : the same as the dictionary form
- Imperfective, negative form   : Change the final -る to -ない.
- Perfective, affirmative form   : Change the final -る to -た.
- Perfective, negative form   : Drop the final -い of the imperfective, negative form -ない and add -かった.

† Table of the non-polite form of Group 1 verbs †

Dictionary form	Imperfective form		Perfective form	
	Affirmative	Negative	Affirmative	Negative
たべる to eat	たべる	たべない	たべた	たべなかった
ねる to sleep	ねる	ねない	ねた	ねなかった
おりる to get off	おりる	おりない	おりた	おりなかった
みる to see	みる	みない	みた	みなかった

2. Group 2 verbs, or verbs ending in -u

- Imperfective, affirmative form : the same as the dictionary form
- Imperfective, negative form : Change the final **-u** to **-anai**.
  - ⎡ verbs ending in a vowel -う : Change the final vowel -う to -わない.⎤
  - ⎣ verbs ending in -つ   : Change -つ to -たない.   ⎦
- Perfective, affirmative form : Change the final -て of the -て form to -た.
- Perfective, negative form   : Drop the final -い of the imperfective, negative form -ない and add -かった.

The imperfective, negative form of **ある** is **ない**.

† Table of the non-polite form of Group 2 verbs †

Dictionary form		Imperfective form		Perfective form	
		Affirmative	Negative	Affirmative	Negative
よむ	to read	よむ	よまない	よんだ	よまなかった
きく	to listen	きく	きかない	きいた	きかなかった
はなす	to speak	はなす	はなさない	はなした	はなさなかった
つかう	to use	つかう	つかわない	つかった	つかわなかった
まつ	to wait	まつ	またない	まった	またなかった
とる	to take	とる	とらない	とった	とらなかった
ある	there is...	ある	ない	あった	なかった

Note that the imperfective negative forms of verbs like 読_よまない, 聞_きかない, etc. are used as -い adjectives.

3. Irregular verbs

† Table of the non-polite form of Irregular verbs †

Dictionary form		Imperfective form		Perfective form	
		Affirmative	Negative	Affirmative	Negative
くる	to come	くる	こない	きた	こなかった
する	to do	する	しない	した	しなかった

B Formation rule : -い adjectives

	(polite form)	(non-polite form)
• Imperfective, affirmative form	: Change -いです	to -い.
• Imperfective, negative form	: Change -くありません	to -くない.
• Perfective, affirmative form	: Change -かったです	to -かった.
• Perfective, negative form	: Change -くありませんでした	to -くなかった.

ほしいです and V-たいです change to their non-polite forms in the same way as -い adjectives.

† Table of the non-polite form of -い adjectives †

Polite form	Imperfective form		Perfective form	
	Affirmative	Negative	Affirmative	Negative
やすいです cheap いいです good よみたいです to want to read	やすい いい よみたい	やすくない よくない よみたくない	やすかった よかった よみたかった	やすくなかった よくなかった よみたくなかった

C Formation rule : -な adjectives and noun+です

	(polite form)	(non-polite form)
• Imperfective, affirmative form	: Change です	to だ.
• Imperfective, negative form	: Change じゃありません	to じゃない.
• Perfective, affirmative form	: Change でした	to だった.
• Perfective, negative form	: Change じゃありませんでした	to じゃなかった.

The formal forms of じゃない and じゃなかった are ではない and ではなかった.

† Table of the non-polite form of -な adjectives and noun+です †

Polite form	Imperfective form		Perfective form	
	Affirmative	Negative	Affirmative	Negative
げんきです fine がくせいです to be a student	げんきだ がくせいだ	げんきじゃない ではない がくせいじゃない ではない	げんきだった がくせいだった	げんきじゃなかった ではなかった がくせいじゃなかった ではなかった

II Usages of the non-polite form according to grammatical rules

The non-polite form is required when used as a predicate in a subordinate clause, not at the end of a main clause. Here you will learn three usages.

A The non-polite form in a quoted sentence

ルインさんは病気だと思います。
I think Lwin is sick.

In the above sentence, the part ルインさんは病気だ "Lwin is sick" is called a quoted sentence.

The rules of a quoted sentence are:
(1) All sentences end in と, a quotative, Group 5 particle, and 思います "I think."
(2) All quoted sentences end in the non-polite form.

```
   quoted sentence        +    と思います。
  (non-polite form)
```

Examples

1. ルインさんは魚を食べると思います。
   I think Lwin eats fish.
2. カーリンさんは行かなかったと思います。
   I think Karin didn't go.
3. 日本語はおもしろいと思います。
   I think Japanese is interesting.
4. 漢字はあまり難しくないと思います。
   I think kanji aren't so difficult.
5. ルインさんはきのう元気だったと思います。
   I think Lwin was fine yesterday.
6. あの人は日本人だと思います。
   I think that man is Japanese.

B The non-polite form preceding んです : んです(2)

You have already learned んです(1) in Lesson 3, Notes on Grammar III. Predicates which precede んです are in the non-polite form, but as for the non-polite, imperfective, affirmative form of -な adjectives and noun＋です, change だ(＝the non-polite form of です) to な before んです.

```
 (non-polite form)   ＋   んです。
  -な adjective -な
  Noun         -な
```

† Table of the predicates＋んです †

Verb	-い adjective
読むんです 読まないんです 読んだんです 読まなかったんです	高いんです 高くないんです 高かったんです 高くなかったんです
-な adjective	Noun＋です
元気なんです 元気じゃないんです 元気だったんです 元気じゃなかったんです	学生なんです 学生じゃないんです 学生だったんです 学生じゃなかったんです

Examples

1. A：どうしたんですか。
      What happened to you?
   B：頭が痛いんです。
      I have a headache.

2. A：きのうコンピューターを買いました。
      Yesterday I bought a computer.
   B：へええ。高かったですか。
      Really? Was it expensive?
   A：いいえ、安かったです。3万円だったんです。
      No, it was cheap. It was 30000 yen.

C The non-polite form preceding からです

The non-polite form preceding からです is used to describe a reason in a formal answer to a question どうして〜か.

Examples

1. A：どうしてEMSは便利なんですか。
   Why is EMS convenient?
   B：速いからです。
   Because it's fast.

2. (About the Dialogue L. 7-2)
   Question：ルインさんは、どうしてアリスさんといっしょに郵便局へ行きますか。　　　　　　　　　　（〜と：with）
   Why is Lwin going to the post office with Alice?
   Answer　：ひまだからです。
   Because he is free.

III 〜ほうがいい／〜ほうがいいです

〜ほうがいいです can follow a sentence ending in the non-polite perfective or the non-polite imperfective negative form, and means "should/had better" or "should not/had better not," respectively when giving advice.

ほう is a noun and can not be used without a noun modifier.

```
Verb-た
〜-ない     } ほうがいいです。
```

Examples

1. 日本語を話したほうがいいですよ。
   You should speak Japanese.
2. 英語は話さないほうがいいですよ。
   You shouldn't speak English.
3. A：病院へ行きましたか。
   Did you go to the hospital?
   B：いいえ、まだです。
   No, not yet.
   A：早く行ったほうがいいですよ。
   You should go there soon.

IV Suffix：-すぎる／-すぎます

Added to the end of a sentence, -すぎる／-すぎます adds the meaning of an excessive degree "too much." It conjugates as a verb.

Examples

1. ルインさんは勉強(べんきょう)しすぎます。
   Lwin studies too much.
2. きのうビールを飲(の)みすぎました。
   I drank too much beer yesterday.
3. このかばんは大(おお)きすぎます。
   This bag is too big.
4. この部屋(へや)は静(しず)かすぎます。
   This room is too quiet.

-すぎる／-すぎます is added to the base form of a verb, an -い adjective, and a -な adjective.

```
      (base form)
Verb           -ます  ⎫
-いadjective   -い    ⎬ ＋ -すぎる／-すぎます。
-なadjective   -な    ⎭
```

† Table of verbs with -すぎる／-すぎます †

Dictionary form	Verb base	Non-polite form	Polite form
食(た)べる to eat	食(た)べ	食(た)べすぎる	食(た)べすぎます
使(つか)う to use	使(つか)い	使(つか)いすぎる	使(つか)いすぎます
する to do	し	しすぎる	しすぎます

Adjective	Adjective base		
大(おお)きい large	大(おお)き	大(おお)きすぎる	大(おお)きすぎます
静(しず)か quiet	静(しず)か	静(しず)かすぎる	静(しず)かすぎます

食(た)べすぎる, 使(つか)いすぎる, しすぎる, 大(おお)きすぎる, 静(しず)かすぎる, etc. are all Group 1 verbs.

V Group 4 particles：けど, けれど, けれども

けど, けれど and けれども mean "but" or "although." They are almost the same as が in meaning and can be also used to indicate an introductory remark. They sound less formal than が and are often used in conversation.

けれども sounds more polite than けれど, and けれど sounds more polite than けど.

Examples
1. 朝、頭が痛かったんですけど、熱はありませんでした。
   I had a headache this morning, but I didn't have a fever.
2. もしもし、ルインですけれども、……。
   Hello, this is Lwin speaking, but....

Notes on Discourse

I はっ ↗

Read the following conversation in Dialogue 8-3.

A：お名前は。
　　May I have your name ?
B：ルインと申します。
　　My name is Lwin.
A：はっ。
　　Pardon ?
B：ルインです。
　　Lwin.

The speaker A asked the name of B but failed to catch the exact sound of his name. So A conveys the signal はっ which shows that A didn't understand and asks B to repeat what he/she has said previously. はっ means "Excuse me ?" or "I beg your pardon?" It should be pronounced softly with a slightly rising intonation. はい or えっ with the same rising intonation are sometimes used in the same situation, though えっ sounds informal.

II ルインです

It will help the hearer if you break up the sounds of your name or word that is proving difficult to understand. For example :

A：ルンさんですね。
　　"Run ?"
B：いえ、ちがいます。ルインです。
　　No, it's "Ru-i-n."

Drill

【練習1】　V　と思います／V　ない　と思います

〈STRUCTURE〉

例）ルインさんは図書館にいますか。　→　はい、いると思います。
　　　　　　　　　　　　　　　　　　→　いいえ、いないと思います。

1. ルインさんはおさしみを食べますか。
2. ルインさんはお酒を飲みますか。
3. ルインさんはサッカーをしますか。
4. ルインさんはあした大学に来ますか。
5. ルインさんは毎日ニュースを見ますか。
6. ルインさんの部屋にテレビがありますか。
7. ルインさんはコンピューターを買いますか。
8. ルインさんは（自分で）料理を作りますか。

〈USAGE〉

例）A：Dさんはビールを飲みますか。
　　B：ええ、飲むと思います。
　　C：わたしは飲まないと思います。
　　A：そうですか。じゃ、聞きましょうか。
　　B：ええ。

【練習2】　Vた　と思います／V なかった　と思います

〈STRUCTURE〉

例）ルインさんはきのうテープを聞きましたか。　→　はい、聞いたと思います。
　　　　　　　　　　　　　　　　　　　　　　　→　いいえ、聞かなかったと思います。

1. ルインさんはきのうテレビを見ましたか。
2. ルインさんはきのう友達に会いましたか。
3. ルインさんはきのうビールを飲みましたか。
4. ルインさんはきのうスーパーへ行きましたか。

5. ルインさんはきのう国に電話しましたか。
6. ルインさんはきのうEメールを送りましたか。
7. ルインさんはきのう8時半に大学に来ましたか。
8. ルインさんはきのう先生と日本語で話しましたか。

〈USAGE〉

Guessing game: What do you think I did yesterday?
Students split into two groups, A & B, and must guess what students in the opposite team did yesterday.
If you are correct, your team receives 1 point. The teacher will be the judge.

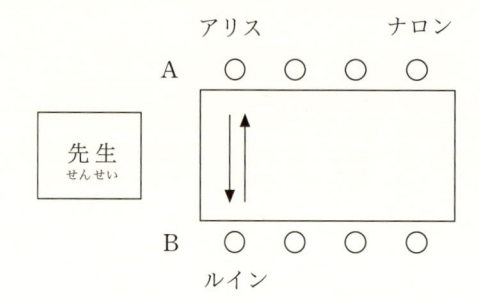

```
              アリス      ナロン
         A  ○   ○   ○   ○
┌────┐   ┌─────────────────┐
│ 先生 │   │   ↓     ↑       │
└────┘   └─────────────────┘
         B  ○   ○   ○   ○
              ルイン
```

例) アリス：ルインさん。

　　ルイン：はい。

　　アリス：ナロンさんはきのう国に電話しましたか。

　　ルイン：はい、電話したと思います。／いいえ、電話しなかったと思います。

　　先生　：ナロンさん、どうですか。

　　ナロン：(Showing either 　はい　 or 　いいえ　 card) 電話しました。

　　先生　：(The judge gives 1 point to team B.)

練習3　　いA　と思います／いAくない　と思います

〈STRUCTURE〉

（日本はどうですか。）

例) 食べ物は高いですか。　→　はい、高いと思います。
　　　　　　　　　　　　　→　いいえ、高くないと思います。

1. カメラは安いですか。
2. 物価は高いですか。
3. 人は多いですか。

（大学はどうですか。）

4. キャンパスは広いですか。

5. 食堂はいいですか。
6. 教室はきたないですか。
(日本語の勉強はどうですか。)
7. 漢字は難しいですか。
8. テストはやさしいですか。

〈USAGE〉

例) A：日本の食べ物はどうですか。安いですか。
   B：そうですね。安いと思います。／うーん、(あまり)安くないと思います。
   A：そうですか。

1. 日本のバス　　　高いです
2. 日本語の文法　　やさしいです

練習4　　いAかった　と思います／いAくなかった　と思います

〈STRUCTURE〉

(パーティーはどうでしたか。)

例) パーティーはいいです。　→　A：パーティーはよかったですか。
                            B：はい、よかったと思います。
                        →　A：パーティーはよかったですか。
                            B：いいえ、よくなかったと思います。

1. 食べ物はおいしいです。
2. 人は多いです。
(テストはどうでしたか。)
3. 漢字はやさしいです。
4. 問題は難しいです。
5. 時間は短いです。

(After looking at the picture of bags.)
(ルインさん／アリスさん／ナロンさんのかばんはどうでしたか。)
6. ルインさんのかばんは白いです。
7. ナロンさんのかばんは安いです。
8. アリスさんのかばんは大きいです。

〈USAGE〉

例) A：テストはどうでしたか。
   B：うーん、難しかったと思います。

ナロン　アリス　ルイン
1000円　15000円　5000円

A：Cさんは。

C：わたしも難しかったと思います。／
　　うーん、わたしは（あまり）難しくなかったと思います。

練習5　　なAだ　と思います／なAじゃない　と思います
　　　　　Nだ　と思います／　Nじゃない　と思います

〈STRUCTURE〉

例1）図書館は静かですか。　→　はい、静かだと思います。
　　　　　　　　　　　　　　→　いいえ、静かじゃないと思います。

例2）山田さんは学生ですか。　→　はい、学生だと思います。
　　　　　　　　　　　　　　→　いいえ、学生じゃないと思います。

1. 図書館はきれいですか。
2. 図書館は便利ですか。
3. 日本語は簡単ですか。
4. 栄はにぎやかですか。
5. 食堂はあした休みですか。
6. 食堂は10時からですか。
7. この人は日本人ですか。　→
8. この人は25さいぐらいですか。　→

〈USAGE〉

例）A：コンビニはどうですか。
　　B：そうですね。とても便利だと思います。

1. 大学のキャンパス　　きれいです
2. 図書館　　　　　　　あまり静かじゃありません
3. 日本　　　　　　　　車が多いです

練習6　　なAだった　と思います／なAじゃなかった　と思います
　　　　　Nだった　と思います／　Nじゃなかった　と思います

〈STRUCTURE〉

例）ルインさんはきのうひまでしたか。　→　はい、ひまだったと思います。
　　　　　　　　　　　　　　　　　　→　いいえ、ひまじゃなかったと思います。

1. （ルインさんはきのう来ませんでした。）ルインさんはきのう元気でしたか。
2. （ルインさんはきのう試験がありました。）ルインさんはきのう大変でしたか。
3. ルインさんは国では先生でしたか。

| 練習7 |　　　～ほうがいいです　　　(giving advice)

〈STRUCTURE〉

a. Vたほうがいいです

(not feeling well)

例) 病院に行く　→　病院に行ったほうがいいです。

1. 薬を飲む
2. うちへ帰る
3. 早くねる

(daily life in Japan)

4. 朝ごはんを食べる
5. 日本語を使う
6. 友達を作る

b. ～ないほうがいいです

(not feeling well)

例) たばこを吸う　→　たばこを吸わないほうがいいです。

1. お酒を飲む
2. 外に出る
3. シャワーを浴びる
4. 長い時間テレビを見る
5. 冷たい物を食べる
6. 遊びに行く

〈USAGE〉

例) A：ああ、頭が痛い……。
　　B：だいじょうぶですか。早く帰ったほうがいいですよ。
　　A：ええ、そうします。

1. 薬を飲む　　　3. 医者へ行く
2. お酒は飲まない

| 練習8 |　　V／Aすぎます

〈STRUCTURE〉

例) 毎日いそがしいです。　→　毎日いそがしすぎます。

1. このシャツは大きいです。
2. テストは難しいです。
3. 日本語の本は高いです。
4. この部屋は静かです。
5. いつもコーヒーを飲みます。
6. きのうテレビを見ました。
7. きのう勉強しました。
8. きのう食べました。

〈USAGE〉

例）A：Bさん、元気がありませんね。どうしましたか。
　　B：頭が痛いんです。
　　A：そうですか。
　　B：ええ。きのう、ちょっとテープを聞きすぎました。
　　A：ああ、そうですか。

1. おなか　　ピザを食べる
2. 目　　　　テレビを見る
3. 足　　　　運動する

練習9　　〜んです

〈STRUCTURE〉

例）（A：ナロンさん、今からコーヒーを飲みに行きませんか。）
　　　今、ちょっといそがしいです。
　　　　　（A：ナロンさん、今からコーヒーを飲みに行きませんか。）
　　→　B：ああ、今、ちょっといそがしいんです。

1. コーヒーはだめです。
2. 授業が5時までです。
3. あしたテストです。
4. これから授業があります。
5. あまり好きじゃありません。
（A：アリスさん、きのう、授業を休みましたね。どうしたんですか。）
6. 頭が痛かったです。
7. かぜでした。
8. 熱がありました。
9. 国から友達が来ました。

〈USAGE〉

例）A：Bさん、どうして授業を休んだんですか。
　　B：熱があったんです。

A：ああ、そうですか。

1. 病院へ行きました。　2. かぜを引きました。

練習 10　　どうして／〜からです

〈STRUCTURE〉

(Listen to what Alice says.)

> アリス：きのう、生協へ行きました。カメラがほしかったんです。でも、いいのがありませんでした。あした、デパートへ行って、いいカメラを買いたいです。

〈質問に答えてください。〉 (Now answer the questions.)

例) Q：アリスさんは、どうしてきのう生協へ行ったんですか。
　　A：カメラがほしかったからです。

1. アリスさんは、どうしてきのうカメラを買わなかったんですか。
2. アリスさんは、どうしてあしたデパートへ行くんですか。

Aural Comprehension

I Listen to the conversations and answer the following questions.

(A)　In the classroom　　（目:eye）

1. どちらの目が赤いですか。
2. どうして赤いですか。

(B)　On the campus　　（ひざ:knee）

1. 男の人はどうしてひざが痛いんですか。
2. 骨はどうですか。

(C)　Asking about a dentist

　　　　　　　　　　　　（歯:tooth　歯医者:dentist　本山:(name of a place)）

1. 歯医者さんはどこにありますか。
2. 電話番号は何番ですか。

(D)　Going to the Health Control Center　　（保健管理室:Health Control Center）

1. 男の人はどうして目が痛いですか。
2. お医者さんは何時までですか。

II （数字）Listen to the conversations and write down the numbers with the counters.

1.＿＿＿＿＿＿　2.＿＿＿＿＿＿　3.＿＿＿＿＿＿　4.＿＿＿＿＿＿

III One of the people in each conversation is you.

Listen to what the other person says and write down what you have to do or must not do.

Your action:何をしますか。

1.＿＿＿＿＿＿＿＿＿＿　2.＿＿＿＿＿＿＿＿＿＿　3.＿＿＿＿＿＿＿＿＿＿

Reading Comprehension

In written language, sentences often end in the non-polite form of a predicate.

数字のイメージ

　数字のイメージは、国によっていろいろだ。

　日本では、数字の読み方でイメージを作る。「4」は「よん」か「し」と読む。「し」は「死」と同じ読み方だ。それで、病院では部屋の番号は「4」を使わない。「9」は「きゅう」か「く」と読む。「く」は「苦」と同じ読み方だ。それで、人によっては少し気にする。

　漢字の形からも数字のイメージを作る。「8」はいい数字だ。漢字では「八」と書く。「八」は下が広いから、日本人は未来が広がると考える。

- 数字　　numeral
- か　　　or
- それで　therefore
- 気にする　to be worried
- 未来が広がる　to become richer and richer as time goes on
- イメージ　image
- 死　　　death
- 番号　　number
- 形　　　shape
- によって　depending on
- 同じ　　same
- 苦　　　pain
- 考える　to regard

質問

1. 日本ではどの数字がいい数字ですか。どの数字が悪い (bad) 数字ですか。
2. どうして病院では「4」の数字を使いませんか。
3. 「八」は未来が広がると考えますが、どうしてですか。
* 4. あなたの国ではどの数字がいい数字ですか。どの数字が悪い (bad) 数字ですか。

Kanji Practice

New Kanji

106.	休	やすむ　やすみ	to rest holiday	114.	医	い	medicine
(6)	イ 仁 什 休 休			(7)	一 テ ᄃ 三 ヂ 矢 医		
107.	少	しょう すこし すくない	a little little few	115.	者	しゃ	person
(4)	亅 小 小 少			(8)	一 十 土 耂 耂 者 者 者		
108.	体	からだ	body	116.	薬	くすり	medicine
(7)	イ 亻 什 什 休 体			(16)	艹 サ ヤ 芊 苩 渧 渧 薙 華 薬 薬		
109.	痛	いたい	painful	117.	電	でん	electricity
(12)	丶 亠 广 疒 疒 疒 疗 疠 痞 痞 痛			(13)	一 戸 币 币 雨 雪 雪 雷 電		
110.	熱	ねつ あつい	fever hot	118.	自	じ	self
(15)	一 十 土 夫 幸 幸 剌 剌 刲 勢 熱			(6)	亅 亻 冂 凢 自 自		
111.	度	ど	degree times	119.	転	てん ころぶ	to roll over to fall down
(9)	丶 亠 广 户 产 产 庐 度			(11)	一 亘 亘 車 転 転		
112.	病	びょう	illness	120.	思	おもう	to think to believe
(10)	丶 亠 广 疒 疒 疒 疠 病 病			(9)	亅 冂 四 用 田 田 思 思 思		
113.	院	いん	institution				
(10)	丶 丨 阝 阝' 阝宀 阝宀 院 院 院						

( ): Kanji stroke count
Bold letters: "on" readings
Underlined letters: "kun" readings

Essential Words

1. 休む (やす) — to be absent / to take a rest
2. 休み (やす) — holiday
3. 少し (すこ) — a little
4. 体 (からだ) — body
5. 痛い (いた) — painful
6. 熱 (ねつ) — fever
7. 38度 (ど) — 38 degrees
8. 病院 (びょういん) — hospital
9. 大学院 (だいがくいん) — graduate school
10. 医者 (いしゃ) — doctor
11. 薬 (くすり) — medicine
12. 電話 (でんわ) — telephone
13. 自転車 (じてんしゃ) — bicycle
14. 転ぶ (ころ) — to fall down
15. 思う (おも) — to think

Words

1. 少ない (すく) — few, little, small
2. 熱い (あつ) — hot(object)
3. 今度 (こんど) — next time
4. 病気 (びょうき) — sickness
5. 自分 (じぶん) — oneself

Reading Practice

1. あしたは休みです。
2. 体が少し痛いです。
3. 熱があります。
4. 熱は8度です。
5. 病院へ行きます。
6. 薬を飲みましたか。
7. 電話をしてください。
8. 自転車で行きました。
9. あの人は医者だと思います。
10. パーティーに何人来ると思いますか。

Lesson 9

Dialogue 研究室で

9-1 About Lwin's presentation

Prof. Honda has asked Lwin to come to the professor's office.

ルイン： （ノックする）

本田　： はい。

ルイン： ルインです。

本田　： あ、ルインさん、どうぞ。

ルイン： 失礼します。

本田　： 日本語の勉強はどうですか。

ルイン： 漢字を覚えるのが大変です。

本田　： そうですか。でも、がんばってくださいね。日本語は大事ですから。

ルイン： はい。

本田　： それで、ええと、来月の発表なんですけど。

ルイン： はい。

本田　： ルインさんにお願いしたいんですけど。

ルイン： はあ。あのう、日本語じゃなくてもいいですか。

本田： うーん。はい、いいですよ。英語で。

ルイン： はい、分かりました。

9-2 Asking permission to miss a Japanese language class

ルイン： 和田先生、ちょっとよろしいでしょうか。

和田： はい、何ですか。

ルイン： あのう、来週の月曜日の午後、研究室のゼミで発表するんですが、

和田： はい。

ルイン： 授業を休んでもいいでしょうか。

和田： あ、発表ですか。

ルイン： はい。

和田： はい。分かりました。いいですよ。

ルイン： すみません。午前中は来ますから。

和田： じゃ、休むのは午後だけですね。

ルイン： はい。

和田： 分かりました。

ルイン： あっ、それから、作文の宿題ですが、発表の準備をしなくてはいけないので、来週でもいいですか。

和田： うーん。しかたがありませんね。

ルイン： すみません。

Discourse Practice and Activity

Discourse Practice : Asking Permission

Let's think about what you would say in response to the following task and carry out a conversation. Refer to **Dialogue 9-2**.

⟨Task⟩

You have to be absent from your Japanese class for some reason.
Ask your teacher for permission to be absent and give the reason why.

あなた：あのう、ちょっとよろしいでしょうか。
先生(せんせい)：はい。何(なん)ですか。
あなた： ⋮

Vocabulary List

⟨ ⟩: dictionary form
⌐ : accent fall (for words only)

Dialogue

9-1

ノ⌐ックする	(〜が〜を)	to knock
しつれいします。	失礼します。	Excuse me.
の		[particle for nominalizing]
がんば⌐る	(〜が)	to try hard, to do one's best
だいじ(な)	大事(な)	important
それで		[conjunction for changing topic]
ら⌐いげつ	来月	next month
はっぴょう	発表	presentation
〜なんですけど		about [phrase used to present a topic]
〜なくてもいい		need not [See Notes on Grammar.]
えいご	英語	English language

9-2

ちょっとよろしいでしょうか。		May I disturb you for a moment?
らいしゅう	来週	next week
ご⌐ご	午後	afternoon
ゼ⌐ミ		seminar
はっぴょうする	(〜が〜を)	発表する	to present
ごぜんちゅう	午前中	in the morning
だけ⌐		just, only
さくぶん	作文	essay
じゅ⌐んび	準備	preparation
〜なくてはいけない		must [See Notes on Grammar.]
の⌐で		because [Group 4 particle for a reason clause]
〜でもいい		may, ... is O.K. [See Notes on Grammar.]
しかたがありませんね。		It can't be helped.

Drill

フランスご		フランス語	French
ジャ﹁ズ			jazz
テ﹁ニス			tennis
スパゲ﹁ティ			spaghetti
～てもいい			may [See Notes on Grammar.]
～てはいけない			must not [See Notes on Grammar.]
と﹁る(しゃしんを)	(～が～を)		to take (photo)
ふる﹁い		古い	old
ふ﹁べん(な)		不便(な)	inconvenient
こ﹁え		声	voice
じゅぎょうちゅう		授業中	during class
スト﹁ーブ			stove
とめる	(～が～を)	泊める	to put someone up for the night
ま﹁ど		窓	window
つけ﹁る	(～が～を)		to turn on
こま﹁る	(～が)	困る	to be troubled
すわる	(～が)	座る	to sit down
ちか﹁い		近い	near
で﹁る	(～が～に)	出る	to attend
あつ﹁い		暑い	hot
しめ﹁る	(～が～を)	閉める	to close
さむ﹁い		寒い	cold
がっこう		学校	school
ラ﹁ーメン			Chinese noodles
ねむい			sleepy
でかける	(～が)	出かける	to go out
そうじする	(～が～を)		to clean
やくそく		約束	appointment, promise
バ﹁ナナ			banana

Additional Vocabulary

Time Expressions

きのう		yesterday
きょう		today
あした		tomorrow
おととい		the day before yesterday
あさって		the day after tomorrow
せんしゅう	先週	last week
こんしゅう	今週	this week
らいしゅう	来週	next week
せんげつ	先月	last month
こんげつ	今月	this month
らいげつ	来月	next month
きょねん	去年	last year
ことし	今年	this year
らいねん	来年	next year

ごぜん(ちゅう)	午前(中)	in the morning, a.m.
ごご	午後	in the afternoon, p.m.
あさ	朝	morning
ひる	昼	noon, daytime
ゆうがた	夕方	evening
よる	夜	night
よなか	夜中	midnight
ゆうべ		last night
けさ		this morning
こんばん	今晩	tonight
まいあさ	毎朝	every morning
まいばん	毎晩	every night
まいにち	毎日	everyday
まいしゅう	毎週	every week
まいつき	毎月	every month
まいとし	毎年	every year

Notes on Grammar

I Nominalizing particle: の

A Function of の

This の is the nominalizing particle, or the particle which changes a sentence into a noun. Predicates preceding の are in the non-polite form which are the same forms as those before んです, explained in Lesson 8, Notes on Grammar II. The nominalizing particle の is different from の in "Noun 1 の Noun 2," introduced in Lesson 2, Notes on Grammar IV and also different from の in 赤いの or ルインさんの, introduced in Lesson 4, Notes on Grammar II. The nominal clauses preceding this particle の may sometimes be very long, but because it behaves as a noun, it can be followed by any particles which are added to a noun.

```
(non-polite form)
-な adjective -な     +  の
Noun         -な
```

Examples
1. 歌うのが好きです。
   I like singing.
2. テレビを見るのが好きです。
   I like watching the television.
3. テニスをするのはおもしろいです。
   Playing tennis is interesting.
4. 漢字を覚えるのは時間がかかります。
   It takes time to memorize kanji.
5. 友達に電話するのを忘れました。
   I forgot to call my friend.

B Some verbs with a の clause

The following verbs take a nominal clause ending with の as the object of a verb.

見る, 聞く, 感じる (to feel), 待つ, 手伝う (to help), etc.

Examples

1. 食べるのを見ました。
   I saw (someone) eat.
2. 歌うのを聞きました。
   I heard (someone) sing.
3. 授業が終わるのを待ちました。
   I waited for the class to finish.
4. 宿題をするのを手伝いました。
   I helped (someone) do homework.

C の in an emphatic sentence

When the speaker wants to give emphasis to the noun きのう in the sentence きのう友達に会いました, he/she can split it away from the rest of the sentence in the following way.

友達に会ったのはきのうです。
It was yesterday that I saw my friend.

Here, the rest of the sentence is indicated by the nominalizing particle の and is in the non-polite form. The emphasized noun is shifted to the end and is followed by です. In the following sentences, the subject is indicated by が in the clause preceding の.

Examples

1. （漢字が難しいです。）
   → 難しいのは漢字です。
   It is kanji that are difficult.
2. （アリスさんはテニスが好きです。）
   → a. テニスが好きなのはアリスさんです。
       It is Alice that likes tennis.
   → b. アリスさんが好きなのはテニスです。
       It is tennis that Alice likes.
3. （アリスさんはきのう友達に会いました。）
   → アリスさんが友達に会ったのはきのうです。
   It was yesterday that Alice saw her friend.

II Negative -て form

The negative -て form of verbs, -い adjectives, -な adjectives, and noun + だ are obtained by changing the final -ない to -なくて (negative -て form (1)).

Examples
1. アリスさんはエジプト人じゃなくてカナダ人です。
   Alice is not an Egyptian but a Canadian.
2. 佐藤さんは魚を食べなくて、ルインさんは肉を食べません。
   Mr. Sato doesn't eat fish and Lwin doesn't eat meat.

† Table of the negative -て form of verbs, -い adjectives, -な adjectives, and noun+だ †

Dictionary form		Non-polite negative form	Negative -て form (1)
みる	to see	みない	みなくて
たべる	to eat	たべない	たべなくて
よむ	to read	よまない	よまなくて
かう	to buy	かわない	かわなくて
くる	to come	こない	こなくて
する	to do	しない	しなくて
ひろい	spacious	ひろくない	ひろくなくて
いい	good	よくない	よくなくて
べんりだ	convenient	べんりじゃない	べんりじゃなくて
がくせいだ	to be a student	がくせいじゃない	がくせいじゃなくて

III Permission, prohibition, obligation

(1) 〜-てもいいです is used to give permission and means "may" or "be O.K."
(2) 〜-てはいけません is used to indicate prohibition and means "must not" or "should not."
(3) 〜-なくてもいいです is used to mean "do not have to."
(4) 〜-なくてはいけません is used to indicate an obligation and means "must," "have to" or "should."

Note that -て and -なくて above are -て forms.

Examples

1. 図書館で勉強してもいいです。
   You/We may study in the library.
2. 図書館で食べてはいけません。
   You/We must not eat in the library.
3. 日曜日は研究室に行かなくてもいいです。
   Someone* does not have to go to the professor's room on Sunday.
4. 朝、8時45分に教室に行かなくてはいけません。
   Someone* must go to the classroom at 8:45 in the morning.

(*"Someone" may be the speaker.)

いいです can be replaced by かまいません "do not mind." いけません can be replaced by なりません "must not," "should not," etc. -なくてはなりません has the same meaning as -なくてはいけません.

Examples

1. A：今、行ってもいいですか。
   May I go now?
   B：ええ、(行っても) いいですよ。
   Yes, you may (go).
2. A：ここでたばこを吸ってもいいですか。
   May I smoke here?
   B：いいえ、(ここで吸っては) いけません。
   No, you should not.
3. A：この本を借りてはいけませんか。
   Is it a problem if I borrow this book?
   B：はい、これは (借りては) いけません。
   Yes, that's right. You can't borrow this book.
4. A：このコンピューターを使ってはいけませんか。
   Is it a problem if I use this computer?
   B：いいえ、使ってもいいですよ。
   No, you can use it.
5. A：広くなくてもいいですか。
   Is it O.K. if it is not spacious?
   B：ええ、広くなくてもかまいませんよ。
   Yes, it is (also) all right even if it is not spacious.
6. A：日本語で話さなくてもいいですか。
   Is it O.K. even if I don't speak in Japanese?
   B：いいえ、日本語じゃなくてはいけません。

No, you have to speak in Japanese.

7. A：この宿題、出さなくてはいけませんか。
Do I have to hand in this homework?
B：ええ、出してください。
Yes, you have to.

8. A：きょう行かなくてはいけませんか。
Should I go today?
B：いいえ、きょうじゃなくてもいいです。あしたでもかまいません。
It's all right if you don't go today. Tomorrow is (also) O.K.

9. A：この雑誌を借りてもいいですか。
May I borrow this magazine?
B：ええ、どうぞ。
Yes, go ahead.

10. A：英語でもいいですか。
Is it all right even in English?
B：英語はちょっと……。
English is no good.

IV Particles：ので and だけ

A Group 4 particle：ので

ので means "as," "since" or "because." It is almost the same as から (See Lesson 7, Notes on Grammar V). ので follows verbs and -い adjectives in the non-polite/(polite) form. です of a -な adjective and a noun+です change to な before ので.

```
 (non-polite form)
-な adjective  -な      +    ので
 Noun          -な
```

Examples

1. かぜを引いたので授業を休みます。
As I caught a cold, I won't go to the class.
2. 暑かったので窓を開けました。
I opened the window since it was hot.

3. この漢字は簡単なので分かります。
   I can read this kanji, because it's easy.

B Group 2 particle：だけ

The particle だけ means "only." The location of だけ in the sentence is restricted. だけ is located just after a word or phrase which the speaker wants to emphasize.

Examples

1. けさ、サラダだけ食べました。
   Someone* ate only salad this morning.
2. きのうルインさんにだけ会いました。
   Someone* met only Lwin yesterday.
3. 1週間だけ待ってください。
   Please wait for only one week.
4. 少しだけ勉強しました。
   Someone* studied only a little.

(*"Someone" may be the speaker.)

V でしょうか

When asking superiors or unfamiliar people in a modest manner, でしょうか is used instead of ですか, whether the question sentence is a nominal one or an adjectival one. どこですか changes to どこでしょうか, and いいですか changes to いいでしょうか.

Examples

1. A：先生、これは先生のかばんでしょうか。
   Is this your bag, sir?
2. B：いえ、わたしのじゃありません。
   No, it isn't.
3. A：先生、あした休んでもいいでしょうか。
   May I be absent from classes tomorrow?
   B：ええ、いいですよ。
   Yes, you may.

VI Conjunction: それで

A "therefore"

それで is a conjunction used to show that what has been mentioned in the preceding sentence is thought to be the reason for what will be said in the sentence following it. It is equivalent to the English "because of that," "therefore," "so."

Examples
1. 歯がちょっと痛いんです。それで、授業を休みたいんですが。
   I have a toothache. So, I'd like to be absent from class.
2. EMSはとても便利です。それで、EMSで送ったんです。
   EMS is very useful. So, I sent it by EMS.

B Changing the topic

それで is also used to change the topic of a conversation, as shown in Dialogue 9-1, line 11 of Lesson 9.

本田：日本語の勉強はどうですか。
How is your Japanese going?

ルイン：漢字を覚えるのが大変です。
Memorizing kanji is difficult.

本田：そうですか。でも、がんばってくださいね。日本語は大事ですから。
I see. But do your best. Because Japanese is important for you, isn't it?

ルイン：はい。
Yes.

本田：それで、ええと、来月の発表なんですけど。
Well, I am going to talk about the next month's presentation.

Notes on Discourse

I ちょっとよろしいでしょうか ↘

Read the following conversation in Dialogue 9-2.

　　学生：和田先生、ちょっとよろしいでしょうか。
　　　　　Ms. Wada, may I disturb you for a moment ?
　　先生：はい、何ですか。
　　　　　Yes, what is it ?

When we have something to talk about with a senior, we can open a conversation with the expression ちょっとよろしいでしょうか, the polite expression of ちょっといいですか, meaning "May I talk with you now ?" or "May I disturb you for a moment ?" 〜でしょうか is pronounced with a falling intonation though it is a question sentence.

II 〜んですが、〜てもいいでしょうか ↘

Lwin asks permission from Ms. Wada to miss a Japanese class in Dialogue 9-2. Lwin has to explain his/her situation (or reason) why he misses the class, using 〜んですが, starting with あのう in a low, flat tone before he says 休んでもいいでしょうか. He has to finish the conversation with すみません, expressing his apology for being absent and gratitude for her permission.

　　〈function〉
calling (the teacher)	和田先生、	Ms. Wada,
start conversation	今ちょっとよろしいでしょうか。	May I disturb you for a moment ?
response	はい。何でしょうか。	Yes, what is it ?
explain the situation	あのう、ゼミで発表するんですが、	I have a presentation for my seminar.
ask permission	授業を休んでもいいでしょうか。	May I miss class ?

give permission　　　　　はい。分かりました。（いいですよ）　Yes, O.K.
express apology and gratitude　すみません。　　　　　　Thank you.

Here is another example.

    A：すみません。
       Excuse me.
    B：はい、何でしょうか。
       Yes, what is it?
    A：あのう、ちょっと頭が痛いんですが、帰ってもいいでしょうか。
       I have a headache. May I go home?
    B：あ、はい。分かりました。
       Yes, sure.
    A：すみません。
       I'm sorry.
    B：お大事に。
       Take care.
    A：ありがとうございます。
       Thank you.

The situation (or reason) can be explained using -たいんですが, -なくてはいけないんですが.

    専門のゼミに出たいんですが、休んでもいいでしょうか。
    I'd like to attend the seminar on my speciality. May I miss class?
    病院に行かなくてはいけないんですが、休んでもいいでしょうか。
    I have to go to the hospital. May I miss class?

Drill

練習1　　〜の　　（nominalizing particle）

〈STRUCTURE〉

例1） ひらがなを読みます。やさしいです。　→　ひらがなを読むのはやさしいです。
例2） サッカーをします。好きです。　　　　→　サッカーをするのが好きです。
例3） ルインさんが食堂にいます。見ました。→　ルインさんが食堂にいるのを見ました。

1. 日本語を話します。おもしろいです。
2. はしを使います。簡単です。
3. 映画を見ます。好きです。
4. 朝ごはんを食べません。よくありません。
5. 歩いて行きます。時間がかかります。
6. タクシーで行きます。お金がかかります。
7. アリスさんがタクシーに乗ります。見ました。
8. ルインさんがフランス語を話します。聞きました。

〈USAGE〉

例） A：Bさんは何をするのが好きですか。
　　 B：音楽を聞くのが好きです。
　　 A：どんな音楽ですか。
　　 B：ジャズです。
　　 A：ジャズですか。

練習2　　〜のは　Nです　　（emphatic sentence）

〈STRUCTURE〉

例） 漢字が難しいです。（何）　→　A：難しいのは何ですか。
　　　　　　　　　　　　　　　　　B：難しいのは漢字です。

1. 目が痛いです。（どこ）
2. のどが痛かったです。（どこ）
3. ひらがなは簡単です。（何）

4. テニスが好きです。(何)
5. きのうスパゲティを食べました。(いつ、何)
6. アリスさんはパーティーに行きません。(だれ、何)

〈USAGE〉
例) 先生：Aさん、きのう何をしましたか。
　　A　：デパートへ行きました。
　　先生：Bさんは何をしましたか。
　　B　：友達に会いました。
　　先生：Cさんは。
　　C　：映画を見ました。

(Can you remember who did what? Let's ask each other.)
　　A　：きのう映画を見たのはだれですか。
　　B　：ええと、きのう映画を見たのはCさんです。
　　　　　デパートへ行ったのはだれですか。
　　C　：デパートへ行ったのはAさんです。
　　　　　友達に会ったのはだれですか。
　　A　：友達に会ったのはBさんです。

| 練習3 | 〜てもいいです／〜てはいけません |

〈STRUCTURE〉
a. 〜てもいいです

(昼休みに教室で)
例) 昼ごはんを食べる　→　昼ごはんを食べてもいいです。

1. ジュースを飲む
2. 勉強する
3. テレビを見る
4. 写真をとる

(アパートを借ります。)
5. 古い
6. 不便
7. １階

b. 〜てはいけません

(図書館では)
例) ごはんを食べる　→　ごはんを食べてはいけません。

1. ジュースを飲む
2. 大きい声で話す
3. たばこを吸う
4. 写真をとる

c.

（教室のルール）

例) A：授業中、教科書を見てもいいですか。
　　B：はい、（見ても）いいです。／
　　　　いいえ、（見ては）いけません。

1. ジュースを飲む
2. 英語を使う
3. 電話をしに行く
4. となりの人と話す

d.

（会館のルール）

例) A：会館では、お酒を飲んではいけませんか。
　　B：はい、（飲んでは）いけません。／
　　　　いいえ、（飲んでも）いいです。

1. 部屋でたばこを吸う
2. 部屋でストーブを使う
3. パーティーをする
4. 友達を泊める

〈USAGE〉

① （教室で）

例) A　：先生、今、写真をとってもいいですか。
　　先生：ええ、（いいですよ。）どうぞ。

1. 教科書を見る　　4. 英語で話す
2. 窓を開ける　　　5. トイレへ行く
3. エアコンをつける

② (to a stranger)

例) A：たばこを吸ってもいいですか。
　　B：ええ、どうぞ。／あ、すみませんが、たばこはちょっと（困るんですが）。

1. ここに座る　2. ここに自転車を置く

練習 4　～なくてもいいです／～なくてはいけません

〈STRUCTURE〉

a. ～なくてもいいです

（あしたは授業がありません。）

例）テープを聞く　→　テープを聞かなくてもいいです。

1. 予習をする
2. 宿題をする
3. 漢字を覚える
4. あした8時45分に来る

（アパートを借ります。）

5. 大学に近い
6. 静か
7. 2階

b. ～なくてはいけません

（日本語コースでは）

例）テープを聞く　→　テープを聞かなくてはいけません。

1. 予習をする
2. 宿題をする
3. 漢字を覚える
4. 毎日8時45分に来る

c.

（専門の勉強）

例）A：レポートを書かなくてもいいですか。
　　B：はい、（書かなくても）いいです。／
　　　　いいえ、（書かなくては）いけません。

1. 日本語の本を読む
2. 毎日研究室に行く
3. ゼミに出る
4. ゼミで発表する

〈USAGE〉

①

例）A：ルインさんに手紙を書きましょうか。
　　B：いいえ、書かなくてもいいですよ。電話しますから。

1. エアコンをつける　　暑くない
2. 窓を閉める　　　　　寒くない
3. タクシーに乗る　　　近い

②
例) A：Bさん。
　　B：はい。
　　A：ごはんを食べに行きませんか。
　　B：うーん。勉強しなくてはいけないんです。
　　A：そうですか。
　　B：ええ。
　　A：じゃ、また。

1. 宿題をする
2. 銀行へ行く
3. 国へ電話をする

練習5　　S1ので、S2

〈STRUCTURE〉

例) 熱があります。　　学校を休みます。
　　→　熱があるので、学校を休みます。

1. 友達が来ます。　　　　　　　　　料理を作ります。
2. きょうはいそがしいです。　　　　パーティーには行きません。
3. 自転車が便利です。　　　　　　　バスにはあまり乗りません。
4. きょうは金曜日です。　　　　　　早く帰ります。
5. お金がありません。　　　　　　　ラーメンを食べます。
6. きょうは天気がよくありません。　出かけません。
7. 2時まで勉強しました。　　　　　今とてもねむいです。
8. テレビが安かったです。　　　　　買いました。
9. きのうは休みでした。　　　　　　友達のところへ行きました。
10. きのうあまりねませんでした。　　頭が痛いです。

〈USAGE〉

例) A：きょう、ひまですか。
　　B：いいえ、友達が来るので、そうじしなくてはいけないんです。
　　A：ああ、そうですか。じゃ、また。

1. 友達と約束がある　　今から行く
2. あしたテストだ　　勉強する

練習6　　〜だけ

〈STRUCTURE〉

例1) 何か食べましたか。
　　　→　はい、サラダだけ食べました。

例2) どこかへ行きましたか。
　　　→　はい、東京へだけ行きました。

1. 何か飲みましたか。
2. 研究室にだれか来ましたか。
3. きのう、勉強しましたか。
4. 国で日本語を勉強しましたか。
5. ルインさんは研究室へ行きますか。
6. だれかと話しましたか。

1 ビール ㊉水 ジュース	2 ナロンさん アリスさん ルインさん ㊉さとうさん	3 30分
4 1か月	5 ㊉月 火 水 木 金	6 ㊉ナロンさん アリスさん ルインさん さとうさん

〈USAGE〉

例) A：Bさん、けさ何か食べましたか。
　　B：はい、バナナを食べました。
　　A：バナナだけですか。
　　B：ええ、バナナだけです。(時間がありませんでしたから。)／
　　　　いいえ、パンも食べました。

Aural Comprehension

I   Listen to the conversations and answer the following questions.

   (A)   Asking the teacher about a tape recorder

   1. 女の人はどこでテープレコーダーを使いたいですか。

   2. どこで使いますか。

   (B)   The woman is going to make a speech at the party.   (スピーチ：speech)

   1. あしたのパーティーは日本人が多いですか。

   2. 女の人はスピーチを何語でしますか。

   (C)   Asking permission from the teacher   (空港：airport)

   1. 男の人は午後の授業を休みますか。

   2. 男の人は今からどこへ行きますか。それはどうしてですか。

   (D)   Going to the department store   (バーゲン：sale　ジーンズ：jeans)

   1. アリスさんはデパートに行きますか。

   2. どうしてですか。

II   (数字) Listen to the conversations and write down the numbers with the counters.

   1.＿＿＿＿＿＿   2.＿＿＿＿＿＿   3.＿＿＿＿＿＿   4.＿＿＿＿＿＿

III   One of the people in each conversation is you.

   Listen to what the other person says and write down what you will do.

   Your action：どうしますか。

   1.＿＿＿＿＿＿＿＿＿＿＿＿＿＿   2.＿＿＿＿＿＿＿＿＿＿＿＿＿＿

Reading Comprehension

ゼミの発表

　わたしの研究室には、日本人の学生が5人と留学生が3人いる。ゼミでは、毎週、学生が発表しなくてはいけない。

　日本人の学生の発表を聞くのは大変だ。日本語だからだ。辞書でハンドアウトの言葉を調べるが、時間がかかる。

　留学生の発表は日本語じゃなくてもいいので、わたしは英語で発表する。でも、日本人の学生は日本語で質問する。その日本語が分からない。だから、もっと日本語を勉強して、日本人の学生と日本語で話したいと思う。

- 毎週　　every week
- 調べる　to look up
- だから　so, therefore
- ハンドアウト　hand-out
- 時間がかかる　it takes time
- もっと　more
- 言葉　word
- 質問する　to ask

質問

1. 研究室の学生は全部で何人ですか。
2. ハンドアウトの言葉はどうやって調べますか。
3. どうして日本人の発表を聞くのが大変ですか。
4. 留学生は日本語で発表しなくてはいけませんか。
5. どうしてもっと日本語を勉強したいですか。
* 6. あなたの研究室には留学生が何人いますか。
* 7. あなたの研究室では留学生の発表は日本語ですか。

Kanji Practice

New Kanji

No.	Kanji	Reading	Meaning	No.	Kanji	Reading	Meaning
121.	研	けん	to sharpen	129.	業	ぎょう	business
(9)	一 ナ 丆 石 石 矴 矴 研 研			(13)	丨 丷 丷 业 业 业 業 業		
122.	究	きゅう	to investigate	130.	英	えい	short for England
(7)	丶 宀 宀 宀 究 究 究			(8)	一 十 艹 艹 艹 苹 英 英		
123.	室	しつ	room	131.	語	ご	language
(9)	丶 宀 宀 宀 宀 宀 宀 室 室			(14)	丶 亠 言 言 語 語 語 語		
124.	発	はつ	to depart	132.	科	か	academic course division
(9)	フ ヌ ブ 癶 癶 癶 癶 発 発			(9)	一 二 千 禾 禾 禾 科 科 科		
125.	表	ひょう / おもて	chart, to express surface	133.	専	せん	entirely exclusively
(8)	一 十 キ 主 丰 表 表 表			(9)	一 冂 冂 百 甫 甫 甫 専 専		
126.	勉	べん	effort	134.	事	じ / こと	thing affair
(10)	ノ ク ク 夕 免 免 免 勉			(8)	一 一 亓 亓 写 写 写 事		
127.	強	きょう / つよい	strong	135.	法	ほう	law
(11)	フ コ 弓 引 弘 弘 弘 強 強			(8)	丶 丶 氵 氵 汁 注 法 法		
128.	授	じゅ	to grant to teach				
(11)	扌 扌 扌 扌 扩 抒 抒 授 授						

( ): Kanji stroke count
Bold letters: "on" readings
Underlined letters: "kun" readings

Essential Words

1. 研究(する)　けんきゅう　research
2. 研究室　けんきゅうしつ　professor's office, laboratory
3. 研究生　けんきゅうせい　research student
4. 教室　きょうしつ　classroom
5. 発表(する)　はっぴょう　presentation
6. 勉強(する)　べんきょう　study
7. 強い　つよい　strong
8. 授業　じゅぎょう　class
9. 授業中　じゅぎょうちゅう　during class
10. 日本語　にほんご　Japanese
11. 英語　えいご　English
12. 教科書　きょうかしょ　textbook
13. 専門　せんもん　major
14. 大事(な)　だいじ　important
15. 食事(する)　しょくじ　meal
16. 法学　ほうがく　study of law

Words

1. 表　おもて　surface
2. 教授　きょうじゅ　professor
3. 研究科　けんきゅうか　post graduate course
4. 火事　かじ　fire

Reading Practice

1. 日本で専門の研究をします。
2. ナロンさんは法学部の学生ですか。
3. 研究室で専門について発表します。
4. 研究室では英語で話します。
5. 山田先生は法学研究科の教授です。
6. 毎日、日本語を勉強します。
7. 日本語の授業は何時からですか。
8. 専門の勉強は大事です。

Lesson 10

Dialogue　お茶を飲みながら話す

10-1　About Alice's family

鈴木　：　アリスさん、もうすぐ休みですね。
アリス：　ええ。
鈴木　：　休みはどうするんですか。
アリス：　国へ帰ります。家族が待っていますから。
鈴木　：　あ、そうですか。いいですね。
アリス：　兄弟もみんな集まるんです。
鈴木　：　ご兄弟は何人ですか。
アリス：　妹が2人います。
鈴木　：　そうですか。
アリス：　あ、今、写真を持っています。
鈴木　：　あ、見せてください。
アリス：　どうぞ。
鈴木　：　こちらはご両親ですか。
アリス：　ええ。
　　　　　めがねをかけているのが上の妹です。

鈴木　：　そうですか。アリスさんに似ていますね。
アリス：　そうですか。
鈴木　：　ええ。学生さんですか。
アリス：　いいえ。銀行で働いています。下の妹は大学生です。
鈴木　：　あ、そうですか。

10-2　About daily life

After working together in the laboratory

佐藤　：　ああ、つかれた！
ルイン：　つかれましたね。お茶でも飲みましょうか。
佐藤　：　ああ、いいですね。
ルイン：　あれ、コーヒーしかありませんね。コーヒーでいいですか。
佐藤　：　ええ、いいです。

佐藤　：　日本の生活にはもう慣れましたか。
ルイン：　ええ、だいぶ慣れました。
佐藤　：　そうですか。言葉も文化もちがうから大変でしょうね。
ルイン：　ええ、まあ。
佐藤　：　日曜日は何をしているんですか。
ルイン：　日曜日は友達のところへ行ったり、映画を見たりしています。
佐藤　：　あ、そうですか。

佐藤　：　ルインさんの自転車、いい自転車ですね。
ルイン：　ああ。

佐藤　：　あれ、どこで買ったんですか。
ルイン：　あれは会館のせんぱいにもらったんです。
佐藤　：　へええ、そうですか。
ルイン：　ええ。せんぱいが自転車とか、テレビとか、いろいろくれましたから、助かりました。
佐藤　：　それはよかったですね。日本は物価が高いから……。
ルイン：　ええ。

Discourse Practice and Activity

Activity : Interview

Ask a Japanese person about his/her daily life. Also tell him/her about your daily life in Japan or in your country. Refer to **Dialogue 10-1, 10-2**. Think about possible questions, and write them below.

質問1
しつもん

質問2
⋮

(Example)

質問1　大学では何を勉強していますか。
しつもん　だいがく　なに　べんきょう

質問2　日曜日には何をしていますか。
　　　　にちようび　　なに

質問3　スポーツは何が好きですか。
　　　　　　　　なに　す

Vocabulary List

⟨ ⟩ : dictionary form
˥ : accent fall (for words only)

Dialogue

10-1

おちゃ		お茶	tea
のみな˥がら		飲みながら	while drinking
もうす˥ぐ			soon
か˥ぞく		家族	family
きょ˥うだい		兄弟	brothers and sisters
みんな˥			all
あつま˥る	(〜が)	集まる	to gather
〜にん		〜人	person(s) [counter]
いもうと˥		妹	(my) younger sister
も˥つ	(〜が〜を)	持つ	to have
りょ˥うしん		両親	parents
め˥がね			glasses
かけ˥る(めがねを)	(〜が〜を)		to wear (glasses)
うえ		上	older
にる	(〜が〜に)	似る	to look like, to resemble
はたらく	(〜が)	働く	to work
した		下	younger
だいが˥くせい		大学生	college student

10-2

つかれた。			I'm tired.
つかれ˥る	(〜が)		to get tired
で˥も			or something [Group 2 particle]
しか			only [Group 2 particle]
〜でいい			to be O.K. [See Notes on Grammar.]
せいかつ		生活	life
も˥う			already
なれ˥る	(〜が〜に)	慣れる	to get accustomed to
だいぶ			quite a lot
ことば˥		言葉	language

ぶ￢んか		文化	culture
ちがう	(～が～と)		to be different
～でしょうね。			must be ....
まあ。			well ....
～たり～たりする			[See Notes on Grammar.]
せんぱい			senior students
もらう	(～が～に～を)		to receive
と￢か			and so on [Group 1 particle]
くれる	(～が～に～を)		to give (me)
へええ。			Oh, really?
たすか￢る	(～が)	助かる	to be helped
よかったですね。			That's nice.

Drill

ロ￢ビー			lobby
ジョ￢ン			[personal name]
まいあさ		毎朝	every morning
ま￢いばん		毎晩	every night
まいしゅう		毎週	every week
かいしゃ		会社	company
つとめ￢る	(～が～に)	勤める	to work for
スポ￢ーツ			sport
しゅうまつ		週末	weekend
ネ￢クタイ			necktie
はく	(～が～を)		to wear
シャ￢ツ			shirt
きる	(～が～を)	着る	to wear
ズボ￢ン			trousers, pants
ぼうし			hat, cap
かぶ￢る	(～が～を)		to wear (hat, cap)
あおき		青木	[personal name]
にし￢かわ		西川	[personal name]
ふと￢る	(～が)	太る	to get fat
やせる	(～が)		to lose weight
た￢つ	(～が)	立つ	to stand
ハ￢ン			[personal name]
ア￢リ			[personal name]
けっこんする	(～が～と)	結婚する	to get married
す￢む	(～が～に)	住む	to live

しる	(〜が〜を)	知る	to know
みどりく		緑区	[name of a ward]
がくせいしょう		学生証	student ID card
あげる	(〜が〜に〜を)		to give
プレゼント			present
チケット			ticket
はは		母	(my) mother
セーター			sweater
ちち		父	(my) father
あに		兄	(my) elder brother
つま		妻	(my) wife
かない		家内	(my) wife
ネックレス			necklace
おとうと		弟	(my) younger brother
こども		子供	child
おっと		夫	(my) husband
しゅじん		主人	(my) husband
あね		姉	(my) elder sister
ハンカチ			handkerchief
チョコレート			chocolate
ペン			pen
かいもの		買い物	shopping
せんたくする	(〜が〜を)		to wash
ばんごはん		晩ごはん	dinner, supper
なつやすみ		夏休み	summer vacation
うみ		海	sea
やま		山	mountain
のぼる	(〜が〜に)	登る	to climb
ハンバーガー			hamburger
ドライブ			drive
みせ		店	shop, store
はいる	(〜が〜に)	入る	to go in
おなかがすく			to be hungry
たくさん			a lot, many
〜かい		〜回	[counter for times (frequency)]
ほっかいどう		北海道	[name of a place]
すこし		少し	a little
ガールフレンド			girl friend

Additional Vocabulary

家族：family members
かぞく

上：わたしの家族：my family members
うえ　　　　　　かぞく
(下：ほかの人の家族：other's family members)
した　　　　　ひと　かぞく

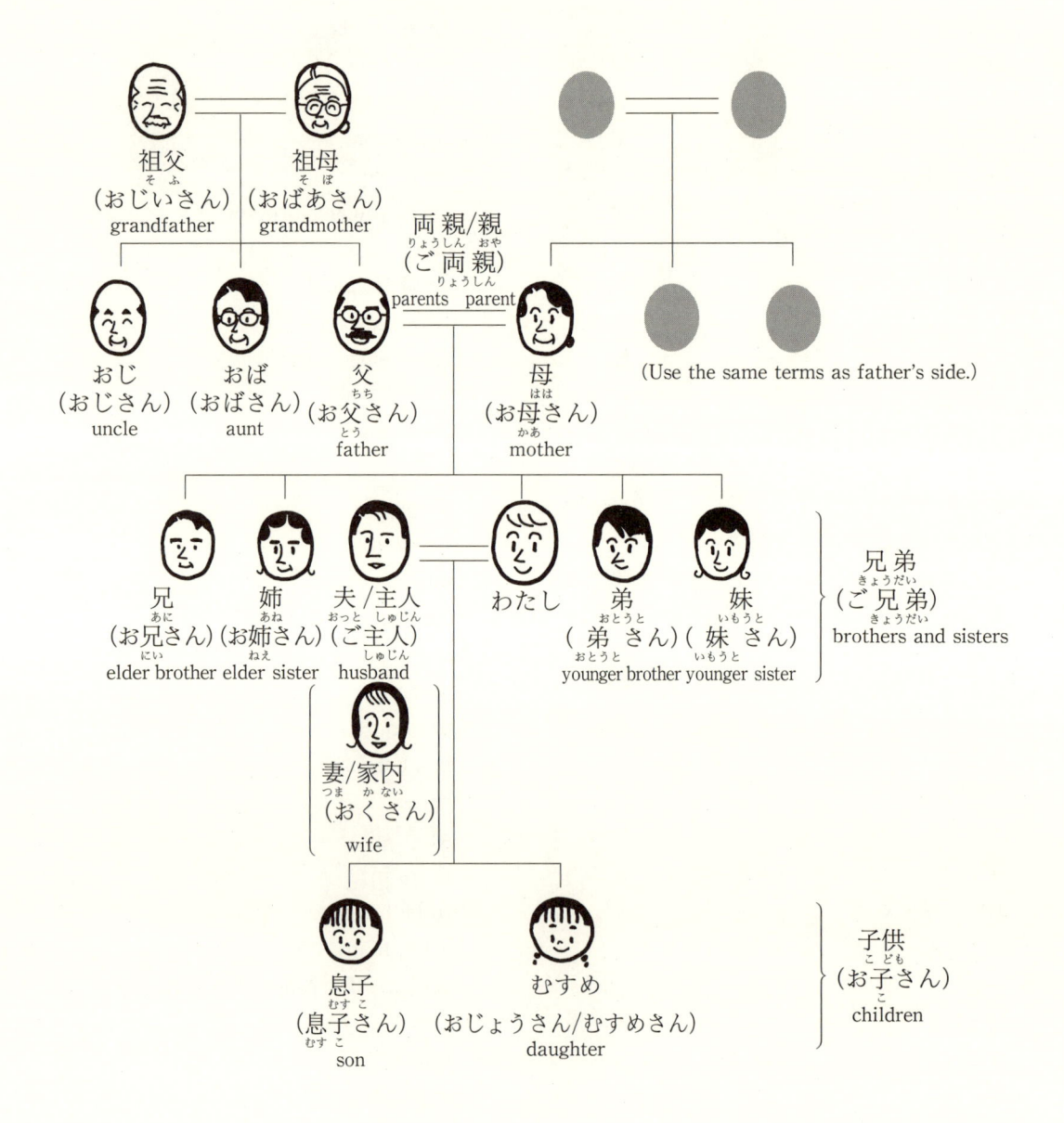

- 祖父（おじいさん） grandfather
そふ
- 祖母（おばあさん） grandmother
そぼ
- 両親/親（ご両親） parents / parent
りょうしん おや　　りょうしん
- おじ（おじさん） uncle
- おば（おばさん） aunt
- 父（お父さん） father
ちち　　とう
- 母（お母さん） mother
はは　　かあ

(Use the same terms as father's side.)

- 兄（お兄さん） elder brother
あに　　にい
- 姉（お姉さん） elder sister
あね　　ねえ
- 夫/主人（ご主人） husband
おっと しゅじん　しゅじん
- わたし
- 弟（弟さん） younger brother
おとうと おとうと
- 妹（妹さん） younger sister
いもうと いもうと
- 兄弟（ご兄弟） brothers and sisters
きょうだい きょうだい
- 妻/家内（おくさん） wife
つま かない
- 息子（息子さん） son
むすこ　むすこ
- むすめ（おじょうさん/むすめさん） daughter
- 子供（お子さん） children
こども　　こ

Notes on Grammar

I V-ている

As shown below, the -て form of a verb＋いる(V-ている) is used in the following ways.

A Progressive action

The -て form of a verb＋いる(V-ている) shows a progressive action.

Examples
1. ルインさんは本を読んでいます。
   Lwin is reading a book.
2. アリスさんは魚を食べていました。
   Alice was eating fish.
3. カーリンさんはテープを聞いていると思います。
   I think Karin is listening to the tape.
4. A：ナロンさん、何をしているんですか。
   What are you doing now, Naron?
   B：友達を待っているんです。
   I am waiting for my friend.
5. 雨が降っています。
   It is raining.

B Habitual action

This construction shows one's habitual action. Also it is often used with adverbs like 毎日, よく "often," ときどき "sometimes." Some verbs used for this purpose are 教える, 働く "to work," 勤める "to work," etc.

Examples
1. 毎週ビデオを借りて見ています。
   Every week I rent video tapes and watch them.
2. ルインさんは国では電子工学を教えていました。
   Lwin was teaching electronic engineering in his country.

3. A：仕事は何をしていますか。
    What are you doing for your work? (Lit.)
    B：銀行に勤めています。
    I work for a bank.
4. 山田さんは郵便局で働いています。
    Mr. Yamada works at a post office.

C Resultant state

The following are verbs used to express a state or condition of a person or thing as a result of an action.

The V-ている in the right column of the following table indicates the present state as a result of the action, whereas the dictionary form of the verbs in the left column indicates the action itself.

† Table of the V-ている †

Dictionary form		V-ている	
結婚する	to get married	結婚している	to be married
立つ	to stand up	立っている	to be standing
座る	to sit down	座っている	to be seated
行く	to go	行っている	to be in that place
来る	to come	来ている	to be in this place
乗る	to get on a vehicle	乗っている	to be in/on a vehicle
出る	to appear in (a book)	出ている	to be in (a book)
太る	to get fat	太っている	to be fat
やせる	to get thin	やせている	to be thin
着る	to put on (clothes for the upper half of the body)	着ている	to be wearing (clothes for the upper half of the body)
（くつ、ズボンを）はく	to put on (shoes, pants)	（くつ、ズボンを）はいている	to be wearing (shoes, pants)
（めがねを）かける	to put on (glasses)	（めがねを）かけている	to be wearing (glasses)
（ぼうしを）かぶる	to put on (a hat)	（ぼうしを）かぶっている	to be wearing (a hat)
（ネクタイを）する	to put on (a tie)	（ネクタイを）している	to be wearing (a tie)
（ドアが）開く	(the door) to open	（ドアが）開いている	(the door) to be open

(電気が)つく (the light) to turn on	(電気が)ついている (the light) to be on

Examples

1. 和田先生は結婚しています。
   Prof. Wada is married.
2. ルインさんは今、東京へ行っています。
   Lwin is now in Tokyo.
3. アリスさんはやせています。
   Alice is thin.
4. ルインさんは青いシャツを着ています。
   Lwin is wearing a blue shirt.

Note that there are some verbs which are normally used in the V-ている form.

住む − 住んでいる　to live
持つ − 持っている　to have
知る − 知っている　to know, etc.

Examples

1. ルインさんは名古屋に住んでいます。
   Lwin lives in Nagoya.
2. 和田先生はいい辞書を持っています。
   Prof. Wada has a good dictionary.
3. カーリンさんは漢字をよく知っています。
   Karin knows kanji very well.
4. A：ミャンマー語を知っていますか。
   Do you know Myanmarese?
   B：いいえ、知りません。
   No, I don't.

Note that the negative form of 知っています is 知りません, not 知っていません.

II Giving and receiving verbs (1)：あげる，くれる，もらう

There are three verbs which are used to express the idea "someone gives something to someone" or "someone receives something from someone." These verbs are used with three nouns, i.e. the giver, the receiver, and the thing given or received. The differences in usage among these three verbs are decided from the speaker's viewpoint (👁).

(Hereafter, the giver, the receiver and the thing will be abbreviated as G, R and T, respectively.)

A あげる

あげる means "to give." This verb is used when G is the speaker or a member of his/her group. R is never the speaker. It is used in the following pattern.

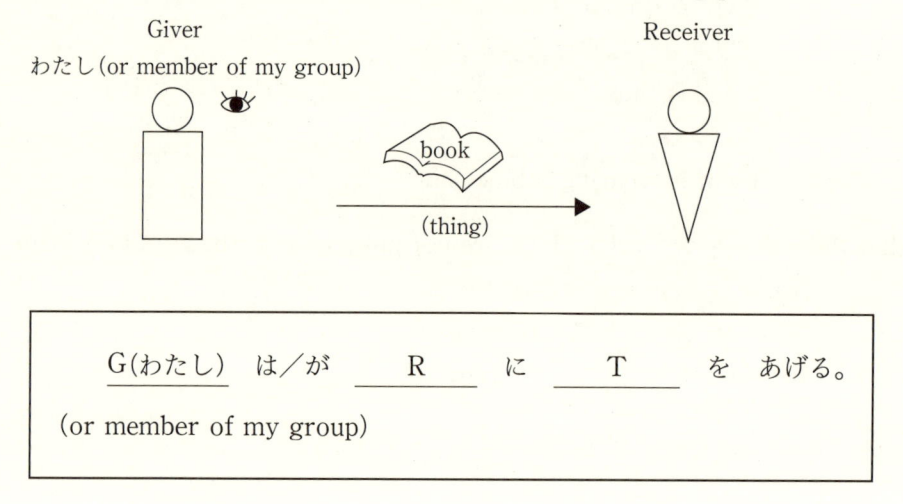

$$\underline{G(わたし)}\ は/が\ \underline{\ \ R\ \ }\ に\ \underline{\ \ T\ \ }\ を\ あげる。$$
(or member of my group)

In this pattern, に means "to."

Examples
1. わたしはカーリンさんにテープをあげました。
   I gave a tape to Karin.
2. ルインさんはアリスさんに本をあげます。
   Lwin gives a book to Alice.
3. （あなたは）ルインさんに何をあげましたか。
   What did you give to Lwin?

B くれる

くれる means "to give." G is never the speaker, and R is always the speaker or a member of his/her group. It is used in the following pattern.

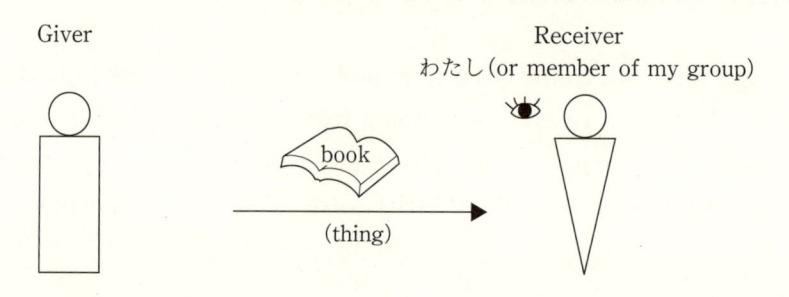

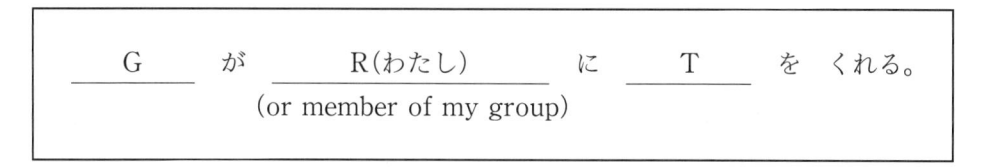

```
    G      が    R(わたし)        に    T    を    くれる。
                (or member of my group)
```

In this pattern, に means "to."

Examples

1. ルインさんがわたしに辞書をくれました。
   Lwin gave me a book.
2. 弟がわたしに本をくれました。
   My younger brother gave a book to me.
3. アリスさんが弟にカメラをくれました。
   Alice gave a camera to my younger brother.
4. ルインさんは（あなたに）何をくれましたか。
   What did Lwin give to you?

C もらう

もらう means "to receive." This verb is used when R is the speaker or a member of his/her group. It is used in the following pattern.

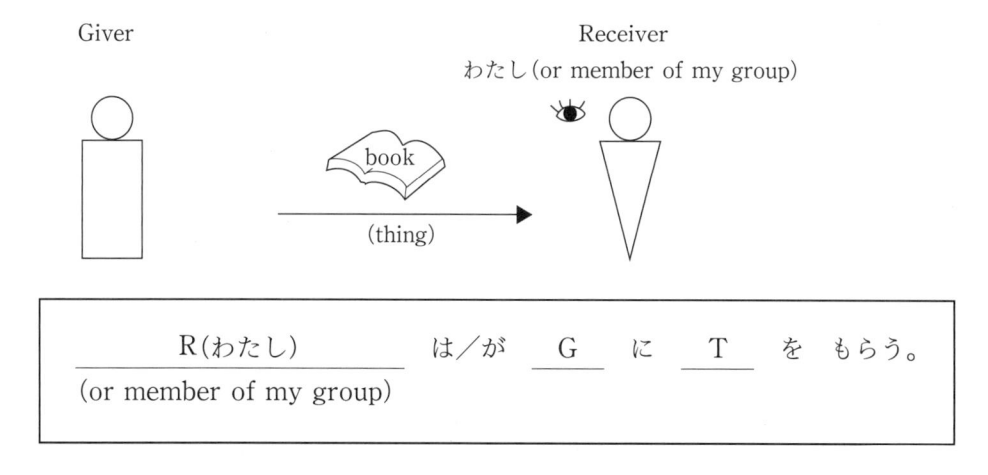

```
        R(わたし)           は／が    G    に    T    を    もらう。
    (or member of my group)
```

In this pattern, に means "from."

Examples

1. わたしはルインさんに本をもらいました。
   I received a book from Lwin.
2. 弟がアリスさんにテープをもらいました。
   My younger brother received a tape from Alice.
3. （あなたは）カーリンさんに何をもらいましたか。

What did you receive from Karin?
4. アリスさんはルインさんに辞書をもらいました。
Alice received a dictionary from Lwin.

III Construction：〜-たり〜-たりする

A Formation rule of the -たり form

Add り to the non-polite, perfective form.

† Table of the -たり form †

Dictionary form		Affirmative -たり form	Negative -たり form
みる	to see	みたり	みなかったり
たべる	to eat	たべたり	たべなかったり
よむ	to read	よんだり	よまなかったり
いく	to go	いったり	いかなかったり
する	to do	したり	しなかったり
やすい	cheap	やすかったり	やすくなかったり
いい	good	よかったり	よくなかったり
げんきだ	fine	げんきだったり	げんきじゃなかったり
がくせいだ	to be a student	がくせいだったり	がくせいじゃなかったり

B Usages of the -たり form

1. Representative actions or states

One usage of the -たり form is to indicate one or some representative actions or states.

Examples
1. 日曜日にはテレビを見たり本を読んだりします。
   Someone* watches TV, reads a book, and so on on Sundays.
2. 毎日、わたしは図書館でテープを聞いたり、漢字を書いたりしています。
   I do things like listening to tapes, writing kanji, and so on at the library everyday.

(*"Someone" may be the speaker.)

Sometimes only one -たり form can be used with する following it.

> **Example**　日曜日に、公園へ行ったりします。
> I often do things such as going to the park on Sunday.

2. Repetition

The other usage of -たり indicates the repetition of two opposite actions, condition or states.

> **Examples**
> 1. アリスさんは専門の先生の研究室を探して、行ったり来たりしました。
>   (探す：to look for)
>   Alice kept coming and going looking for her academic adviser's room. (Lit.)
> 2. このごろは寒かったり暑かったりします。
>   It keeps getting cold and getting warm these days. (Lit.)

When -たり is used in this sense, there must be two -たり. The latter one is directly followed by する.

IV　Particles：でも，とか，しか

A　Group 2 particle：でも

でも is a Group 2 particle meaning "... or something like that." It is usually used when offering suggestions.

が and を are replaced by でも, but other particles in Group 1 precede でも.

> **Examples**
> 1. 映画でも見ましょうか。
>   Shall we go to a movie or do something like that?
> 2. ルインさんのところへでも行きましょうか。
>   How about going to Lwin's or someplace else?

B　Group 1 particle：とか

とか is a particle used to combine two or more nouns. The difference between と and とか is that the former is used when the speaker mentions all the nouns he/she wants to refer to, but the latter is used when he/she mentions only some examples among all the nouns.

Examples 1. いろいろな物をもらいました。自転車とかテレビとか……。
I received various things, a bicycle, a television, etc.
2. パーティーにはルインさんとかアリスさんとかが来ました。
Lwin, Alice and some others came to the party.

C Group 2 particle：しか

しか is a Group 2 particle used in a negative sentence. It means "only" or "nothing but." It follows a noun or noun＋a Group 1 particle except が and を.

Examples 1. a．ルインさんが来ました。
Lwin came.
b．ルインさんしか来ませんでした。
No one came but Lwin.
2. a．魚を食べました。
I ate fish.
b．魚しか食べませんでした。
I didn't eat anything but fish.
3. a．日本にあります。
It's in Japan.
b．日本にしかありません。
It's only in Japan.

V でしょう（1）

でしょう indicates the speaker's supposition. The non-polite form of four types of predicates precede でしょう, except that the imperfective form of -な adjectives and noun＋だ drop だ before them.
The non-polite form of でしょう is だろう.

Examples 1. あしたは雨でしょう。
It will rain tomorrow.
2. A：ルインさんは来るでしょうか。
Will Lwin come?
B：たぶん来るだろうと思います。
Maybe he will come.

VI Expressions：～でいいです and ～がいいです

Examples

1. A：コーヒー、ありますか。
   Do you have coffee?
   B：いいえ、ありません。
   No, I don't.
   A：紅茶は。
   How about tea?
   B：紅茶はあります。
   I have tea.
   A：じゃ、紅茶でいいです。
   Then, tea is all right.

2. A：何を飲みますか。
   What do you drink?
   B：何がありますか。
   What do you have?
   A：コーヒーと紅茶とミルクがあります。
   I have coffee, tea and milk.
   B：じゃ、紅茶がいいです。
   Tea is fine.
   A：そうですか。
   O.K.

Example 1 shows that A can be satisfied with tea, although his first choice is coffee. On the other hand, Example 2 shows that B likes tea best among the three.

Examples

1. A：日本語が分からないんですが。
   I don't understand Japanese.
   B：じゃ、英語でいいですよ。
   Well, English will be fine.

2. A：ボールペン、ありますか。
   Do you have a ballpoint pen?
   B：いいえ。
   No, I don't.
   A：ペンは。

How about a pen?

B：あります。

I have some.

A：じゃ、ペンでいいです。

Then, a pen will do.

VII Demonstrative pronouns (3)：あれ，あの，あそこ

あれ is used to refer to something far from the speaker and the hearer. あれ is also used to refer to something which the speaker thinks the hearer can understand without mentioning the name of the thing. The latter usage of あれ is common to all words such as あの, あそこ, etc.

Examples
1. A：アリスさんにテレビをもらいました。
   I received a television from Alice.
   B：あのテレビもらったんですか。あれ、新しいですよね。
   Did you receive that television? That television is new, isn't it?
2. A：きのう東山公園へ行きましたよ。
   I went to Higashiyama Park yesterday.
   B：そうですか。あそこはいつもきれいですね。
   Oh, that place is always beautiful, isn't it?

VIII Family terms

The following is a list of family terms. When talking about your own family members, use the non-polite terms. When talking about other people's family members, use the polite terms.

† Table of family terms †

	My family members	Other's family members
parents	両親（りょうしん）	ご両親（りょうしん）
father	父（ちち）	お父さん（とう）
mother	母（はは）	お母さん（かあ）
husband	夫／主人（おっと／しゅじん）	ご主人（しゅじん）

wife	妻／家内 (つま／かない)	おくさん
elder brother	兄 (あに)	お兄さん (にい)
elder sister	姉 (あね)	お姉さん (ねえ)
younger brother	弟 (おとうと)	弟さん (おとうと)
younger sister	妹 (いもうと)	妹さん (いもうと)
child	子供 (こども)	お子さん (こ)
son	息子 (むすこ)	息子さん (むすこ)
daughter	むすめ	むすめさん
baby	赤んぼう (あか)	赤ちゃん (あか)
grandfather	祖父 (そふ)	おじいさん
grandmother	祖母 (そぼ)	おばあさん
uncle	おじ	おじさん
aunt	おば	おばさん

Notes on Discourse

I そうですか ↗

Read the following conversation from Dialogue 10-1.

アリス：めがねをかけているのが上の妹です。
　　　　The one wearing glasses is the older of my two younger sisters.
鈴木　：そうですか。アリスさんに似ていますね。
　　　　I see. She resembles you.
アリス：そうですか。
　　　　Really?

In Notes on Discourse in Lesson 1, そうですか↘, meaning "I see" was introduced. On the other hand そうですか↗ with rising intonation is used to express the speaker's doubt. In the above conversation from Dialogue 10-1 Suzuki says about one of Alice's sisters "She resembles Alice." Alice responds そうですか↗ because Alice doesn't think so.

II 大変でしょうね

Read the following conversation from Dialogue 10-2.

A：日本の生活にはもう慣れましたか。
　　Have you become used to life in Japan?
B：ええ、だいぶ慣れました。
　　Yes, I am quite used to it now.
A：そうですか。言葉も文化もちがうから大変でしょうね。
　　Really. It must be quite difficult as the language and culture are quite different.

〜でしょうね in 大変でしょうね is used to sympathize with the referred person. It is pronounced with a prolonged intonation.

A：自転車で転んだんですか。
　　Did you fall over on your bicycle?
B：ええ、スピードを出しすぎて……。
　　Yes, I was going too fast.
A：それは痛かったでしょうね。
　　I bet it hurt, didn't it?

大変ですね is also an expression used to show sympathy.

A：毎日12時まで働いています。
　　I work until 12 o'clock everyday.
B：そうですか。大変ですね。
　　Really. That sounds like hard work.

Drill

練習1　Vている　(progressive action)

〈STRUCTURE〉

a.

（公園で）

例）音楽を聞く　→　音楽を聞いています。

1. ジュースを飲む
2. 手紙を書く
3. 本を読む
4. ごはんを食べる
5. 写真をとる
6. 電話をする

b.

例）A：この人は何をしていますか。
　　B：音楽を聞いています。

(Use the words in a. above.)

〈USAGE〉

(会館(かいかん)のロビーで)

例) A：すみません、ルインさん、いますか。
　　B：あ、あそこで新聞(しんぶん)を読(よ)んでいます。
　　A：(ルインさんを見(み)て) あ、どうも。

1. アリスさん
2. バンバンさん
3. ジョンさん

練習2　　Vている　　(habitual action)

〈STRUCTURE〉

例) 毎朝(まいあさ)、サラダを食(た)べる　→　毎朝(まいあさ)、サラダを食(た)べています。

1. 毎晩(まいばん)、日本語(にほんご)を勉強(べんきょう)する
2. 毎日(まいにち)、日本人(にほんじん)と話(はな)す
3. 毎週(まいしゅう)、土曜日(どようび)はプールで泳(およ)ぐ
4. 日本(にほん)では大学(だいがく)で日本語(にほんご)を勉強(べんきょう)する
5. 国(くに)では英語(えいご)を教(おし)えた
6. 国(くに)では会社(かいしゃ)で働(はたら)いた
7. 国(くに)では会社(かいしゃ)に勤(つと)めた

〈USAGE〉

例) A：Bさんは何(なに)かスポーツをしていますか。
　　B：はい、テニスをしています。
　　A：そうですか。

1. 週末(しゅうまつ)は何(なに)をする

練習3　　Vている　　(state or condition)

〈STRUCTURE〉

例) 佐藤(さとう)さん　めがねをかける
　　→　佐藤(さとう)さんはめがねをかけています。

1. 佐藤(さとう)さん　　　　　ネクタイをする
2. 佐藤(さとう)さん　　　　　黒(くろ)いくつをはく
3. 佐藤(さとう)さん　　　　　シャツを着(き)る

4. 佐藤さん　　　　　　　　　ズボンをはく
5. 佐藤さん　　　　　　　　　時計をする
6. 佐藤さん　　　　　　　　　ぼうしをかぶる

7. 青木さん　　　　　　　　　太る
8. 西川さん　　　　　　　　　やせる
9. ジョンさん　　　　　　　　立つ
10. ハンさん　　　　　　　　　座る
11. ナロンさんとカーリンさん　　車に乗る
12. アリさん　　　　　　　　　結婚する

7 8	9 10	11	12
青木　西川	ジョン　ハン	ナロン　カーリン	アリ

練習4　　住んでいる／持っている／知っている

〈STRUCTURE〉

a. 住む

例）A：Bさんはどこに住んでいますか。
　　B：緑区に住んでいます。

1. 本山　　2. 留学生会館　　3. アパート

b. 持つ

例）A：カメラを持っていますか。
　　B：はい、持っています。／いいえ、持っていません。

1. 自転車　　2. テレビ　　3. 学生証

c. 知る

例）A：タンさんを知っていますか。
　　B：はい、知っています。／いいえ、知りません。

1. 安田先生　　2. この漢字　　3. 留学生センターの電話番号

練習5　　　あげる／くれる／もらう

〈STRUCTURE〉

a.

例）A：Bさん、これ、どうぞ。
　　B：ありがとう。

　→　A：（わたしは）Bさんにプレゼントをあげました。
　→　B：Aさんが（わたしに）プレゼントをくれました。
　　　　：（わたしは）Aさんにプレゼントをもらいました。

1．写真（しゃしん）　2．CD　3．テレビ　4．映画（えいが）のチケット

b.

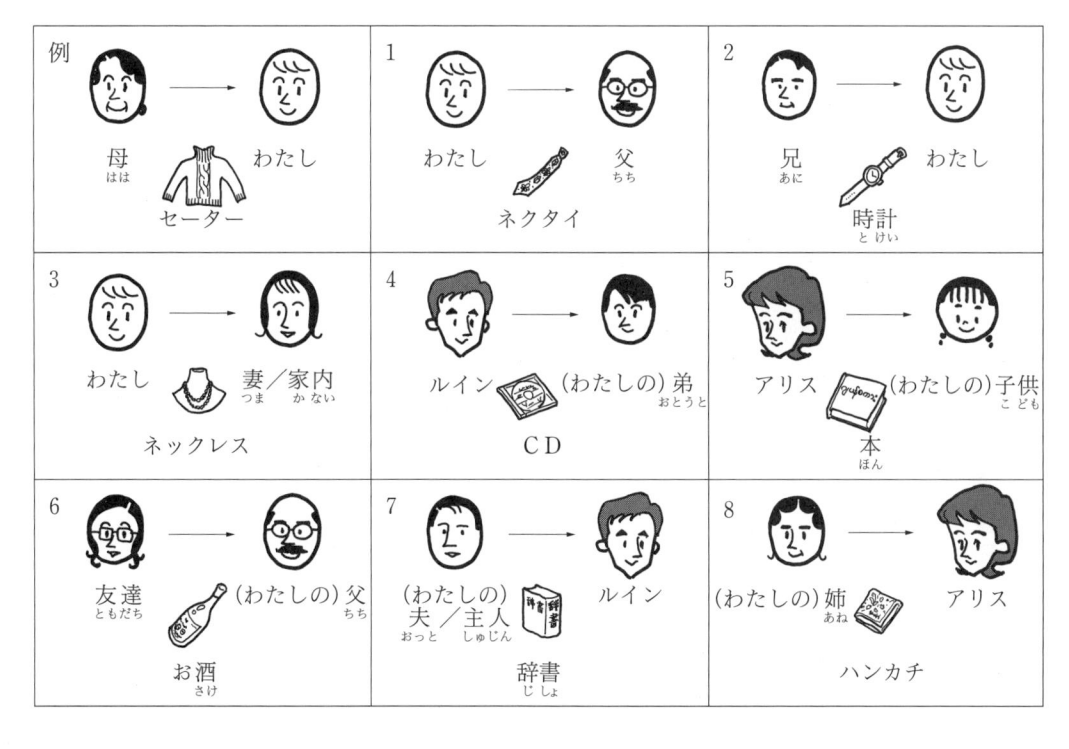

例）わたし：母（はは）が（わたしに）セーターをくれました。
　　　　　　（わたしは）母（はは）にセーターをもらいました。

例 母→わたし セーター	1 わたし→父 ネクタイ	2 兄→わたし 時計
3 わたし→妻／家内 ネックレス	4 ルイン→（わたしの）弟 CD	5 アリス→（わたしの）子供 本
6 友達→（わたしの）父 お酒	7 （わたしの）夫／主人→ルイン 辞書	8 （わたしの）姉→アリス ハンカチ

〈USAGE〉

①

例）A：Bさんは誕生日に何かもらいましたか。
　　B：はい、もらいました。
　　A：何をもらいましたか。

B：チョコレートをもらいました。
　　　A：だれにもらいましたか。／　A：だれがくれましたか。
　　　B：友達にもらいました。　　　　B：友達がくれました。

② (Present exchange)
例）A：Bさん、何をあげましたか。
　　B：コピーカードをあげました。
　　A：だれにあげましたか。
　　B：Cさんにあげました。
　　A：ああ、そうですか。じゃ、何をもらいましたか。
　　B：ペンをもらいました。
　　A：いいですね。だれがくれましたか。
　　B：Dさんがくれました。
　　A：ああ、そうですか。

| 練習6 |　　〜たり　〜たりする |

〈STRUCTURE〉

例）（休みの日には）友達に会う　　買い物をする
　　　→　友達に会ったり、買い物をしたりします。

　1．（休みの日には）そうじする　　せんたくする
　2．（晩ごはんは）自分で作る　　　外で食べる
　3．（研究室では）日本語で話す　　英語で話す
　4．（夏休みには）海へ行く　　　　山に登る

〈USAGE〉
例）A：Bさん、休みの日には何をしますか。
　　B：音楽を聞いたり、テニスをしたりします。
　　A：ああ、テニスですか。どこでするんですか。

　1．週末　　2．夏休み

| 練習7 |　　Nでも　　（...or something like that） |

〈STRUCTURE〉
例1）お茶を飲む　→　お茶でも飲みませんか。
例2）きっさてんへ行く　→　きっさてんへでも行きませんか。

1. ハンバーガーを食べる
2. 映画を見る
3. ドライブに行く
4. あの店に入る
5. アリスさんのところへ行く

〈USAGE〉
例) A：ひまですね。
　　B：そうですね。
　　A：ビデオでも見ましょうか。
　　B：ええ、そうしましょう。

1. いい天気　　　　　ドライブに行く
2. つかれた　　　　　コーヒーを飲む
3. おなかがすいた　　ハンバーガーを食べる

練習8　　しか〜ない

〈STRUCTURE〉
例1) いろいろ食べましたか。
　　→　いいえ、サラダしか食べませんでした。
例2) いろいろな人に会いましたか。
　　→　いいえ、ルインさんにしか会いませんでした。

1. いろいろ飲みましたか。
2. みんな来ましたか。
3. ゼミは毎日ありますか。
4. 日本でいろいろなところへ行きましたか。
5. 研究室に留学生はたくさんいますか。
6. テープは10回ぐらい聞きましたか。
7. 今、5000円ありますか。
8. ビールはたくさん飲みましたか。

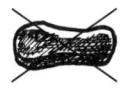

⟨USAGE⟩

例) A：ここからアパートまで時間がかかりますか。
　　B：いいえ、5分しかかかりません。
　　A：近いですね。

1. いろいろな国の新聞を読みますか。
2. 復習も予習もしましたか。
3. 留学生会館には先生もいますか。
4. きょうはお金をたくさん持っていますか。
5. ガールフレンドはたくさんいますか。

Aural Comprehension

I Listen to the conversations and answer the following questions.

(A)　At the party

　　1．いとうさんは何(なに)をしていますか。

　　2．リーさんの勉強(べんきょう)はどうですか。

(B)　About the bag the woman has　　　(悪(わる)い：bad　〜と言(い)っている：to say〜)

　　1．女(おんな)の人(ひと)はかばんをだれにもらいましたか。

　　2．女(おんな)の人(ひと)はどうして大変(たいへん)ですか。

(C)　Aikidoo　　(合気道(あいきどう)：[a kind of Japanese traditional sports]　練習(れんしゅう)する：to practice)

　　1．何曜日(なんようび)と何曜日(なんようび)に練習(れんしゅう)しますか。

　　2．日本語(にほんご)は分(わ)かりますか。

　　3．それはどうしてですか。

(D)　About the earrings the woman wears 〈Informal speech style〉

　　　(イヤリング：earring　買(か)ったの↗＝買(か)ったんですか　もらったの↘＝もらったんです
　　　　　　　　　　　　　　　　　　　　　　　　ぼく：I　ピンク：pink)

　　1．このイヤリングは女(おんな)の人(ひと)が買(か)いましたか。

　　2．男(おとこ)の人(ひと)があげたのは何色(なにいろ)のイヤリングですか。

II　(数字(すうじ))Listen to the conversations and write down the numbers with the counters.

　　　1._____　2._____　3._____　4._____

III One of the people in each conversation is you.

　　Listen to what the other person says and write down the answer to your question.

　　Your question：リーさんはいっしょに行(い)きますか。

　　　1._____　2._____　3._____

Reading Comprehension

年賀状
ねんがじょう

　年賀状は日本の習慣のひとつだ。会社の人とか友達とか、いろいろな人に出す。年賀状は「年賀はがき」に書く。ふつうのはがきでもいい。12月20日までに書いてポストに入れる。その年賀状は1月1日に着く。

　年賀状には「あけましておめでとうございます。今年もよろしくお願いします」と書く。「元気です」とか、「毎日いそがしいです」とか短い文も書く。人によって、絵をかいたり家族の写真をプリントしたりする。

　年賀状はいろいろな人からもらうが、特に遠くの友達や昔の友達からもらうのはうれしい。その人の近況が分かるからだ。

• 年賀状	New Year's card	• 習慣のひとつ	one of the custom
• 年賀はがき	government postcard for the New Year	• ふつうの	ordinary
• までに	by, not later than	• 短い文	short sentence
• 人によって	depending on the people	• 絵をかく	to draw a picture
• 特に	especially	• 遠く	long distance
• 昔	old days	• うれしい	glad
• 近況	the recent condition		

質問

1. 年賀状はだれに出しますか。
2. 年賀状は「年賀はがき」に書かなくてはいけませんか。
3. 「あけましておめでとうございます」は英語で何だと思いますか。
* 4. あなたの国にも年賀状がありますか。
* 5. カードにはどんなことを書きますか。

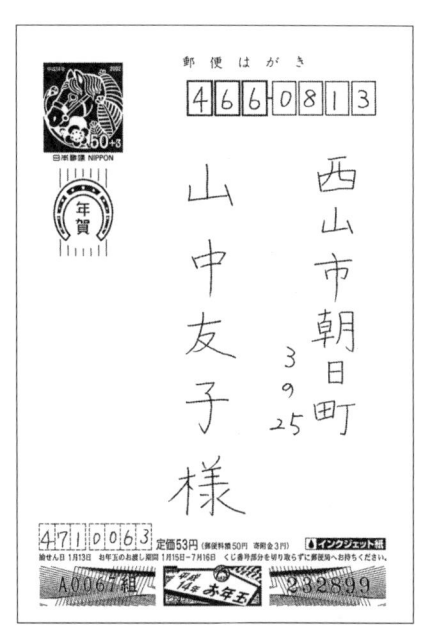

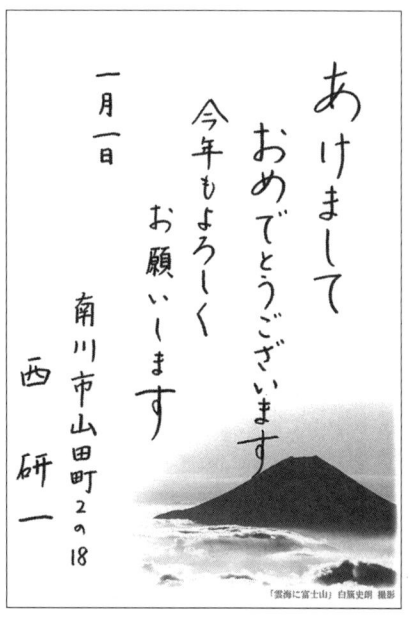

Kanji Practice

New Kanji

No.	Kanji	Reading	Meaning	No.	Kanji	Reading	Meaning
136.	家 (10)	**か** / いえ	house	144.	両 (6)	**りょう**	both
137.	族 (11)	**ぞく**	family, tribe	145.	親 (16)	**しん** / おや	intimacy, parent
138.	父 (4)	ちち	father	146.	働 (13)	はたらく	to work
139.	母 (5)	はは	mother	147.	主 (5)	**しゅ** / おも(な)	master, main
140.	兄 (5)	**きょう** / あに	elder brother	148.	内 (4)	ない	inside
141.	姉 (8)	あね	elder sister	149.	仕 (5)	**し**	to serve, to work
142.	弟 (7)	**だい** / おとうと	younger brother	150.	毎 (6)	**まい**	every, each
143.	妹 (8)	いもうと	younger sister				

( ): Kanji stroke count
Bold letters: "on" readings
Underlined letters: "kun" readings

Essential Words

1. 家 (いえ) house
2. 家族 (かぞく) family
3. 父 (ちち) father
4. 母 (はは) mother
5. 兄 (あに) elder brother
6. 姉 (あね) elder sister
7. 弟 (おとうと) younger brother
8. 妹 (いもうと) younger sister
9. 両親 (りょうしん) parents
10. 兄弟 (きょうだい) brothers, brothers and sisters
11. 親切(な) (しんせつ) kind
12. 働く (はたらく) to work
13. 主人 (しゅじん) husband
14. 家内 (かない) wife
15. 仕事 (しごと) work, job
16. 毎日 (まいにち) everyday
17. 毎月 (まいつき) every month
18. 毎年 (まいとし) every year

Words

1. お父さん (とう) father
2. お母さん (かあ) mother
3. お兄さん (にい) elder brother
4. お姉さん (ねえ) elder sister
5. 親 (おや) parent
6. 両方 (りょうほう) both
7. 主(な) (おも) main

Reading Practice

1. わたしの家族は父と母と兄の4人です。
2. 姉が1人、弟が2人います。
3. 兄弟は何人ですか。
4. 両親が日本へ来ます。
5. ご主人の仕事は何ですか。
6. わたしの家内は病院で働いています。
7. わたしの妹は大学生です。
8. 毎日、家族に手紙を書きます。

Appendix

- Japanese Conjugation Patterns (1)
- Numbers (Numerals+Counters) (Lesson 1~10)

Japanese Conjugation Patterns (1)

1. Verbs

Dictionary form		English	Polite form	Base form	-て form
(L 1)			(L 1)	(L 6)	(L 6)
Group 1					
食べる	たべる	to eat	たべます	たべ	たべて
ねる	ねる	to go to bed	ねます	ね	ねて
見る	みる	to see	みます	み	みて
着る	きる	to wear	きます	き	きて
Group 2					
	-u		-i	-i	
書く	かく	to write	かきます	かき	かいて
行く	いく	to go	いきます	いき	いって*
急ぐ	いそぐ	to hurry up	いそぎます	いそぎ	いそいで
話す	はなす	to speak	はなします	はなし	はなして
待つ	まつ	to wait	まちます	まち	まって
作る	つくる	to make	つくります	つくり	つくって
買う	かう	to buy	かいます	かい	かって
死ぬ	しぬ	to die	しにます	しに	しんで
遊ぶ	あそぶ	to play	あそびます	あそび	あそんで
読む	よむ	to read	よみます	よみ	よんで
ある	ある	to exist	あります	あり	あって
Irregular					
来る	くる	to come	きます	き	きて
する	する	to do	します	し	して

2. -い adjectives

(L 3)			(L 3)	(L 8)	(L 7)
高い	たかい	high, expensive	たかいです	たか	たかくて
おいしい	おいしい	delicious	おいしいです	おいし	おいしくて
いい	いい	good	いいです	よ	よくて
ほしい	ほしい	to want	ほしいです	ほし	ほしくて
V-たい	V-たい	to want to do	V-たいです	V-た	V-たくて

3. -な adjectives & Noun + です

(L 3/L 2)			(L 3/L 2)	(L 8)	(L 7)
便利	べんり	convenient	べんりです	べんり	べんりで
きれい	きれい	beautiful, clean	きれいです	きれい	きれいで
学生	がくせい	to be a student	がくせいです	がくせい	がくせいで

＊：exception

Japanese Conjugation Patterns (1)

Non-polite form			
Imperfective		Perfective	
Affirmative	Negative	Affirmative	Negative
(L 8)			
たべる	たべない	たべた	たべなかった
ねる	ねない	ねた	ねなかった
みる	みない	みた	みなかった
きる	きない	きた	きなかった
	-a		-a
かく	かかない	かいた	かかなかった
いく	いかない	いった*	いかなかった
いそぐ	いそがない	いそいだ	いそがなかった
はなす	はなさない	はなした	はなさなかった
まつ	またない	まった	またなかった
つくる	つくらない	つくった	つくらなかった
かう	かわない	かった	かわなかった
しぬ	しなない	しんだ	しななかった
あそぶ	あそばない	あそんだ	あそばなかった
よむ	よまない	よんだ	よまなかった
ある	ない*	あった	なかった*
くる	こない	きた	こなかった
する	しない	した	しなかった

(L 8)			
たかい	たかくない	たかかった	たかくなかった
おいしい	おいしくない	おいしかった	おいしくなかった
いい	よくない	よかった	よくなかった
ほしい	ほしくない	ほしかった	ほしくなかった
V-たい	V-たくない	V-たかった	V-たくなかった

(L 8)			
べんりだ	べんりじゃない	べんりだった	べんりじゃなかった
きれいだ	きれいじゃない	きれいだった	きれいじゃなかった
がくせいだ	がくせいじゃない	がくせいだった	がくせいじゃなかった

＊：exception

Numbers (Numerals + Counters) (Lesson 1〜10)

Counter	L 1 Numerals (typeA)	number L 4 〜番（ばん）	[building number] L 4 〜号館（ごうかん）	[flat things] L 7 〜枚（まい）
1	いち	いちばん	いちごうかん	いちまい
2	に	にばん	にごうかん	にまい
3	さん	さんばん	さんごうかん	さんまい
4	し、よん	よんばん	よんごうかん	よんまい
5	ご	ごばん	ごごうかん	ごまい
6	ろく	ろくばん	ろくごうかん	ろくまい
7	しち、なな	ななばん	ななごうかん	ななまい
8	はち	はちばん	はちごうかん	はちまい
9	きゅう、く	きゅうばん	きゅうごうかん	きゅうまい
10	じゅう	じゅうばん	じゅうごうかん	じゅうまい
Question word	いくつ	なんばん	なんごうかん	なんまい

Counter	gram(s) L 7 〜グラム	degree(s), time(s) L 8 〜度（ど）*1	yen L 1 〜円（えん）	year(s), 〜th grade L 2 〜年（ねん）
1	いちグラム	いちど	いちえん	いちねん
2	にグラム	にど	にえん	にねん
3	さんグラム	さんど	さんえん	さんねん
4	よんグラム	よんど	よえん	よねん
5	ごグラム	ごど	ごえん	ごねん
6	ろくグラム	ろくど	ろくえん	ろくねん
7	ななグラム	しちど、ななど	ななえん	ななねん、しちねん
8	はちグラム	はちど	はちえん	はちねん
9	きゅうグラム	きゅうど（くど*2）	きゅうえん	きゅうねん
10	じゅうグラム	じゅうど	じゅうえん	じゅうねん
Question word	なんグラム	なんど	なんえん、いくら	なんねん

＊1 〜分（ぷん）(1/10 degree, L 8) もこのタイプ。
＊2 body temperature

Counter	hour(s) L 5 〜時間（じかん）	o'clock L 1 〜時（じ）	[name of the month] L4 〜月（がつ）	〜th floor L 4 〜階（かい）[k-]
1	いちじかん	いちじ	いちがつ	**いっかい**
2	にじかん	にじ	にがつ	にかい
3	さんじかん	さんじ	さんがつ	さんがい
4	**よじかん**	**よじ**	**しがつ**	よんかい
5	ごじかん	ごじ	ごがつ	ごかい
6	ろくじかん	ろくじ	ろくがつ	**ろっかい**
7	しちじかん、ななじかん	**しちじ**	**しちがつ**	ななかい
8	はちじかん	はちじ	はちがつ	はちかい、**はっかい**
9	**くじかん**	**くじ**	**くがつ**	きゅうかい
10	じゅうじかん	じゅうじ	じゅうがつ	**じ（ゅ）っかい**
Question word	なんじかん	なんじ	なんがつ	なん**がい**

Counter	time(s) L 10 〜回（かい）[k-]	〜th lesson L 6 〜課（か）[k-]	month(s) L 7 〜か月（げつ）[k-]	week(s) L 2 〜週間（しゅうかん）[s-]
1	**いっかい**	**いっか**	**いっかげつ**	**いっしゅうかん**
2	にかい	にか	にかげつ	にしゅうかん
3	さんかい	さんか	さんかげつ	さんしゅうかん
4	よんかい	よんか	よんかげつ	よんしゅうかん
5	ごかい	ごか	ごかげつ	ごしゅうかん
6	**ろっかい**	**ろっか**	**ろっかげつ**	ろくしゅうかん
7	ななかい	ななか	ななかげつ	ななしゅうかん
8	はちかい、**はっかい**	はちか、**はっか**	はちかげつ、**はっかげつ**	**はっしゅうかん**
9	きゅうかい	きゅうか	きゅうかげつ	きゅうしゅうかん
10	**じ（ゅ）っかい**	**じ（ゅ）っか**	**じ（ゅ）っかげつ**	**じ（ゅ）っしゅうかん**
Question word	なんかい	なんか	なんかげつ	なんしゅうかん

Numbers (Numerals + Counters)

Counter	book(s), etc. L 7 ～冊 [s-] さつ	year(s) old L 8 ～さい [s-]	minute(s) L 1 ～分 [h-] ふん	[long things] L 7 ～本 [h-] ほん
1	いっさつ	いっさい	いっぷん	いっぽん
2	にさつ	にさい	にふん	にほん
3	さんさつ	さんさい	さんぷん	さんぼん
4	よんさつ	よんさい	よんぷん	よんほん
5	ごさつ	ごさい	ごふん	ごほん
6	ろくさつ	ろくさい	ろっぷん	ろっぽん
7	ななさつ	ななさい	ななふん	ななほん
8	はっさつ	はっさい	はっぷん、はちふん	はっぽん、はちほん
9	きゅうさつ	きゅうさい	きゅうふん	きゅうほん
10	じ(ゅ)っさつ	じ(ゅ)っさい	じ(ゅ)っぷん	じ(ゅ)っぽん
Question word	なんさつ	なんさい	なんぷん	なんぼん

Counter	L 4 Numerals (TypeB)*3	[day of the month] L 4 ～日 *4 にち／か	day(s) L 7 ～日 *4 にち／か	person(s) L 4 ～人 にん
1	ひとつ	ついたち	いちにち	ひとり
2	ふたつ	ふつか	ふつか	ふたり
3	みっつ	みっか	みっか	さんにん
4	よっつ	よっか	よっか	よにん
5	いつつ	いつか	いつか	ごにん
6	むっつ	むいか	むいか	ろくにん
7	ななつ	なのか	なのか	ななにん、しちにん
8	やっつ	ようか	ようか	はちにん
9	ここのつ	ここのか	ここのか	きゅうにん
10	とお	とおか	とおか	じゅうにん
Question word	いくつ	なんにち	なんにち	なんにん

*3　11からはTypeA。　*4　11からはTypeA。
　　　14、24：～よっか、17、27：～しちにち、
　　　19、29：～くにち、20：はつか。

Vocabulary Index (Lesson 1～10)

N: noun, V: verb, iA: -い adjective, naA: -な adjective, Adv: adverb, E: expression
P: particle, C: conjunction, G: [See Notes on Grammar], preN: pre-nominal, Q: question word, prefix, suffix, counter, Arabic Numeral: Lesson No.(φ: Dialogue, D: Drill, S: Dialogue Supplement, A: Additional Vocabulary), 〈 〉: -masu form

【あ】

あ　E　oh　1
ああ　E　oh　4
あいだ　間　N　between　4 D
あう〈あいます〉　会う　V　to meet　5 D
あお　青　N　blue　4 S
あおい　青い　iA　blue　4 D
あおき　青木　N　[personal name]　10 D
あか　赤　N　red　4 S
あかい　赤い　iA　red　4 D
あける　開ける　V　to open　8
あげる　V　to give　10 D
あさ　朝　N　morning　7 D
あさごはん　朝ごはん　N　breakfast　7 D
あさって　N　the day after tomorrow　9 A
あし　足　N　leg, foot　8 D
あした　N　tomorrow　1 D
あそこ　N　there　4 D
あそぶ　遊ぶ　V　to play　7 D
あたま　頭　N　head　8 D
あたまがいい　頭がいい　iA　smart　7 D
あちら　N　that way　6
あつい　暑い　iA　hot　9 D
あつまる　集まる　V　to gather　10
あに　兄　N　(my) elder brother　10 D
あね　姉　N　(my) elder sister　10 D
あの　preN　that... [used before a noun]　2
あのう　E　Um...　4
アパート（あぱあと）　N　apartment　4 D
あびる〈あびます〉（シャワーを）　浴びる　V　to take a shower　7 D
あぶない　危ない　iA　dangerous　8
あまり　Adv　not very　3
アリ　N　[personal name]　10 D
ありがとうございました。　E　Thank you.　1
ありがとうございます。　E　Thank you.　3
アリス（ありす）　N　Alice [personal name]　1
ある〈あります〉　V　There is... [used for non-living things]　4
あるいて　歩いて　on foot　5 D
あれ　N　that　2 D
あれっ。　E　Oh !?　6

いい　iA　good　3 D
いいえ、ちがいます。　E　No, it isn't.　2 D
いいえ。　E　No.　1
いいえ。　E　No problem.　4
イーエムエス　EMS　N　Express Mail Service　7
いいですか。　E　Is that O.K. ?　7
いいですね。　E　That's a good idea.　7
いいですよ。　E　Sure.　6
イーメール（いいめいる）　Eメール　N　e-mail　3 D
いかが　Q　how [polite form of どう]　6 D
いく〈いきます〉　行く　V　to go　1
いくら　Q　how much　4 S
いしゃ　医者　N　medical doctor　2 D
いす　N　chair　4 D
いそがしい　iA　busy　3
いそぐ　急ぐ　V　to hurry　6 D
いたい　痛い　iA　painful　8
いただきます。　E　Please. [Lit. I would like to receive...]　1
いちねん　1年　N　first grade　2
いちねんせい　1年生　N　first grade　2 D
いつ　Q　when　2
いつごろ　Q　around what time　6
いっしょに　Adv　together　7 D
いってらっしゃい。　E　[greeting to person leaving a place to come back]　7 D
いつも　Adv　always　8 D
いぬ　犬　N　dog　4 D
いま　今　N　now　2
いる〈います〉　V　There is... [used for living things]　4
いもうと　妹　N　(my) younger sister　10
いらっしゃいませ。　E　Can I help you ?　4 S
いる〈いります〉　要る　V　to need　7
いれる〈いれます〉　入れる　V　to put in　6
いろ　色　N　color　4 S
いろいろ（な）　naA　various　4
インドネシア　N　Indonesia　7 D
うえ　上　N　on, above　4 D
うえ　上　N　older　10
ウォークマン（うぉうくまん）　N　Walkman　5 D

うけつけ 受付 N reception 8
うしろ 後ろ N behind 4 D
うち N house, home 5 D
うみ 海 N sea 10 D
うりば 売り場 N section of a dept. store 4 S
うーん。 E Well ..., let me see. 4 S
うんどうする 運動する V to exercise 8 D
エアコン(えあこん) N air conditioner 4 D
えいが 映画 N movie 3 D
えいご 英語 N English language 9
ええ。 E Yes. 1
ええと E Let me see. 4
エスカレーター(えすかれいたあ) N escalator 4 D
えらぶ〈えらびます〉 選ぶ V to choose 6
エル L(える) N large size 4 S
エレベーター(えれべいたあ) N elevator 4 D
〜えん 〜円 counter yen 1
えんぴつ N pencil 2 D
おいしい iA delicious 3
おおい 多い iA many, much, a lot 8 D
おおかわ 大川 N [personal name] 8
おおきい 大きい iA large 3 D
おおさか 大阪 N [name of a place] 6 D
おかげさまで。 E I'm fine, thank you. [Lit. Thanks to you.] 3
(お)かね (お)金 N money 7
おきる〈おきます〉 起きる V to get up 7 D
おく N behind, beyond 4
おく〈おきます〉 置く V to put 6
おくに お国 N your country [shows respect to the listener] 2
おくる 送る V to send 8 D
おげんきですか。 お元気ですか。 E How are you? 3
(お)さけ お酒 N alcohol 7 D
(お)さしみ N raw fish 3
おしえる〈おしえます〉 教える V to teach 6
おす〈おします〉 押す V to push 6
(お)すし N [name of Japanese food] 7 D
おだいじに。 お大事に。 E Get well soon. 8
おちゃ お茶 N tea 10
おっと 夫 N (my) husband 10 D
おとうと 弟 N (my) younger brother 10 D
おとこ 男 N man 2 D
おととい N the day before yesterday 9 A
おともだち お友達 N your friend [shows respect to the listener] 2
おなか N stomach 8
おなかがすく V to be hungry 10 D
おねがいします。 お願いします。 E Please. 1
おねがいする お願いする V to make a request 8
おはようございます。 E Good morning. 1
おぼえる〈おぼえます〉 覚える V to memorize 7 D
おもう 思う V to think 8
おもしろい iA interesting 3
およぐ 泳ぐ V to swim 7 D
おりる〈おります〉 降りる V to get off 5
おりる〈おります〉 降りる V to go down (the stairs) 6
おんがく 音楽 N music 1 D
おんな 女 N woman 2

【か】
か P [Group 3 particle for question sentences] 1
か 課 N lesson 6 D
が P [Group 1 particle for indicating actor, subject] 1 D
が P [Group 4 particle for introductory remarks] 5
が P but [Group 4 particle] 7
カード N card 6
カーリン(かありん) N Karin [personal name] 1
〜かい 〜階 counter [counter for floor] 4
〜かい 〜回 counter [counter for times] 10 D
かいかん 会館 N (International Students') House 1 D
かいしゃ 会社 N company 10 D
かいしゃいん 会社員 N company employee 2 D
かいだん 階段 N stairs 4
かいもの 買い物 N shopping 10 D
かう〈かいます〉 買う V to buy 3 D
かえる〈かえります〉 帰る V to go back, to return 3 D
かえる V to change 7 D
かかる〈かかります〉 V it takes, it costs 5
かく〈かきます〉 書く V to write 5 D
がくせい 学生 N student 2 D
がくせいしょう 学生証 N student ID card 10 D
がくぶ 学部 N faculty 2 D
〜かげつ 〜か月 counter ... month(s) 7 D
かける(めがねを) V to wear (glasses) 10
かさ N umbrella 4 D
かぜ N common cold 8
かぞく 家族 N family 10
〜かた 〜方 G method, way 6
かたかな N "katakana" 1 D
〜がつ 〜月 counter month 4 D
がっこう 学校 N school 9 D

かない　家内　N　(my) wife　10 D
カナダ(かなだ)　N　Canada　2
かね　金　N　money　7
かばん　N　bag　2 D
かぶる　V　wear (hat, cap)　10 D
かみ　紙　N　paper　6
カメラ(かめら)　N　camera　3 D
かようび　火曜日　N　Tuesday　2 D
から　P　from [Group 4 particle for source]　2
から　P　because [Group 4 particle for reason clauses]　7
からだ　体　N　body　8
かりる〈かります〉　借りる　V　to borrow, to rent　6
カレーライス(かれいらいす)　N　curry　1 D
～がわ　～側　suffix　on the side of ...　6
かんじ　漢字　N　Chinese character　1 D
かんたん(な)　簡単(な)　naA　easy, simple　3 D
かんぱい。　E　Cheers！[word of toast]　3
がんばる　V　to try hard, to do one's best　9
き　木　N　tree　4 D
きいろ　黄色　N　yellow　9 A
きかい　機械　N　machine　6
きく〈ききます〉　聞く　V　to listen　1
きく〈ききます〉　聞く　V　to ask　5
きた　北　N　north　4 D
きたない　iA　dirty　8 D
きっさてん　N　coffee shop　7
きって　切手　N　postal stamp　7
きにゅうする〈きにゅうします〉　記入する　V　to fill in　7
きのう　N　yesterday　1
キャンパス　N　campus　8 D
きょう　N　today　1 D
きょうかしょ　教科書　N　textbook　1
きょうしつ　教室　N　classroom　4
きょうだい　兄弟　N　brothers and sisters　10
きょうと　京都　N　[name of a place]　6 D
きょねん　去年　N　last year　6
きらい(な)　naA　to dislike　3 D
きる　着る　V　to wear　10 D
きれい(な)　naA　beautiful, clean　3 D
ぎんこう　銀行　N　bank　5 D
きんようび　金曜日　N　Friday　2 D
くうこう　空港　N　airport　5 D
くがつ　九月　N　September　4 A
くすり　薬　N　medicine　8
ください。　E　I'll take ...　4 S
くち　口　N　mouth　8
くつ　N　shoes　4 D
くに　国　N　country　2
～ぐらい　suffix　about ...　5
グラム　counter　gram　7 D
くる〈きます〉　来る　V　to come　2
くるま　車　N　car　5 D
グレー(ぐれい)　N　gray　4 S
くれる　V　to give (me)　10
くろい　黒い　iA　black　4 D
けいざいがくぶ　経済学部　N　Faculty of Economics　2 D
けさ　N　this morning　4 D
けしゴム(ごむ)　N　eraser　2 D
けっこうです。　E　That's fine.　7 S
けっこんする　結婚する　V　to get married　10 D
げつようび　月曜日　N　Monday　2 A
けど　P　[Group 4 particle]　8
けんがく(する)　見学(する)　N　study visit, field trip　7 S
げんき(な)　元気(な)　naA　fine, healthy, energetic　3
げんきがない　元気がない　E　to be in low spirits　8 D
けんきゅうしつ　研究室　N　professor's office, laboratory　1 D
けんきゅうせい　研究生　N　research student　2 D
～ご　～語　suffix　[language]　6 D
こう　Adv　this way, like this　6
こうえん　公園　N　park　7 D
こうがくぶ　工学部　N　Faculty of Engineering　2 D
～ごうかん　～号館　counter　Building No. 4
こうくうびん　航空便　N　airmail　7
こうじょう　工場　N　factory, plant　7 S
こうちゃ　紅茶　N　(black) tea　4 D
こうむいん　公務員　N　government officer　2 D
こえ　声　N　voice　9 D
コーナー　N　corner　6
コーヒー(こうひい)　N　coffee　1 D
こくさいほう　国際法　N　international law　2
ここ　N　here　4 D
ごご　午後　N　afternoon　9
ございます　V　[polite form of あります]　4 S
ごぜん　午前　N　in the morning　9 A
ごぜんちゅう　午前中　N　in the morning　9
ごせんもん　ご専門　N　your major subject of study　2
こちら　N　this [polite form of これ]　2
こちらこそ　E　I should say that ...　2
ことし　今年　N　this year　9 A
ことば　言葉　N　language　10
こども　子供　N　child　10 D
この　preN　this [used before a noun]　2 D
このごろ　N　nowadays　3
ごはん　N　meal, cooked rice　1 D

コピーカード　N　photocopying card　6
コピーき　コピー機　N　copy machine　6
コピーする〈コピーします〉　V　to copy　6
こまる　困る　V　to be troubled　9 D
これ　N　this　2 D
これでいいですか。　E　Is this O.K.?　7
ころぶ　転ぶ　V　to take a fall　8
こんげつ　今月　N　this month　9 A
コンサート　N　concert　7 D
こんしゅう　今週　N　this week　9 A
こんにちは。　E　Hello., Good afternoon.　3
こんばん　今晩　N　tonight, this evening　9 A
コンピューター（こんぴゅうたあ）　N　computer　4 D
コンピュータールーム（こんぴゅうたあるうむ）　N　computer room　4 D

【さ】

さあ…。　E　I have no idea.　5
～さい　counter　... years old　8 D
さいごに　最後に　C　finally　6
サイズ　N　size　6
さいふ　財布　N　wallet, purse　7
サイン　N　signature　7
サインする　V　to sign　6 D
さか　坂　N　slope　8
さかえ　栄　[name of a place]　5
さかな　魚　N　fish　3
さかなフライ（ふらい）ていしょく　魚フライ定食　N　fried fish set meal　1
さきに　Adv　first, before the rest　7
さくぶん　作文　N　essay　9
さけ　酒　N　alcohol　7 D
さしみ　N　raw fish　3
サッカー　N　soccer　8 D
ざっし　雑誌　N　magazine　1 D
～さつ　～冊　counter　[counter of books]　7 D
さとう　佐藤　N　[personal name]　2
さとう　砂糖　N　sugar　6 D
さむい　寒い　iA　cold　9 D
サラダ（さらだ）　N　salad　1
～さん　suffix　Mr., Ms.　1
サンドイッチ（さんどいっち）　N　sandwich　1 D
さんびゃくきゅうじゅう　390　N　390　1
～じ　～時　counter　o'clock　2
シーディー（しいでぃい）　N　CD　1 D
しか　歯科　N　dental clinic　8
しか　P　only [Group 2 particle]　10
しかたがありませんね。　E　It can't be helped.　9
じかん　時間　counter　... hour(s)　5 D
じかん　時間　N　time　7 D
しけん　試験　N　examination　8 D

ししょ　司書　N　librarian　6
じしょ　辞書　N　dictionary　2 D
しずか（な）　静か（な）　naA　quiet　3 D
した　下　N　under, below　4 D
した　下　N　younger　10
しつれいします。　失礼します。　E　Good-bye.　2
しつれいします。　失礼します。　E　Excuse me.　9
じてんしゃ　自転車　N　bicycle　3 D
じぶんで　自分で　Adv　by oneself　8 D
じむしつ　事務室　N　office　7 S
しめる　閉める　V　to close　9 D
じゃ　C　well, then　2
シャープペンシル（しゃあぷぺんしる）　N　mechanical pencil　2 D
～じゃありません　G　was, were [negative form of です]　2 D
～じゃありませんでした　G　[negative form of でした]　2 D
じゃ、また。　E　See you again.　2
しやくしょ　市役所　N　City Hall　5
しゃしん　写真　N　picture　7 D
ジャズ　N　jazz　9 D
シャツ（しゃつ）　N　shirt　4 D
シャワー　N　shower　7 D
しゅうかん　週間　counter　weeks　2
しゅうし　修士　N　master course　2
じゅうしょ　住所　N　address　7 S
ジュース　N　juice　6 D
しゅうまつ　週末　N　weekend　10 D
じゅぎょう　授業　N　class　2
じゅぎょうちゅう　授業中　N　during class　9 D
しゅくだい　宿題　N　homework　3
しゅじん　主人　N　(my) husband　10 D
しゅみ　N　hobby　9 D
じゅんび（する）　準備（する）　N　preparation　9
しょうかい　N　introduction　2
しょうかいする〈しょうかいします〉　V　to introduce　2
しょうがくきん　奨学金　N　scholarship　7 S
しょくご　食後　N　after meals　8
しょくどう　食堂　N　cafeteria　1
しょくどうのひと　食堂の人　N　staff of cafeteria　1
ジョン　N　[personal name]　10 D
しる　知る　V　to know　10 D
しろい　白い　iA　white　4
～じん　～人　suffix　[nationality]　2 D
しんかんせん　新幹線　N　the Shinkansen　5 D
しんさつ（する）　診察（する）　N　medical consultation　8
しんせつ（な）　親切（な）　naA　kind　3 D
しんぶん　新聞　N　newspaper　1 D
すいようび　水曜日　N　Wednesday　2 A

Vocabulary Index 289

すう（たばこを）　吸う　V　to smoke　8 D
スーパー（すうぱあ）　N　supermarket　5 D
すき（な）　好き（な）　naA　to like　3
〜すぎる　suffix　... too much　8
スケジュール　N　schedule　6 D
すごく　Adv　very much　8
すこし　少し　a little　10 D
すし　N　[name of Japanese food]　7 D
ストーブ　N　stove　9 D
スパゲティ　N　spaghetti　9 D
スピード　N　speed　8
スプーン（すぷうん）　N　spoon　5 D
スポーツ　N　sport　10 D
ズボン　N　trousers, pants　10 D
すみません。　E　Thank you.　3
すみません。　E　Excuse me.　4
すみません。　E　I'm sorry.　7
すむ　住む　V　to live　10 D
する〈します〉　V　to do　1 D
すわる　座る　V　to sit down　9 D
せいかつ（する）　生活（する）　N　life　10
せいきょう　生協　N　co-op　4 D
せいぶつがく　生物学　N　biology　2
セーター　N　sweater　10 D
せき　N　cough　8
ゼミ　N　seminar　9
せんげつ　先月　N　last month　9 A
せんしゅう　先週　N　last week　2 D
せんせい　先生　N　teacher　2 D
せんたくする　V　to wash, to launder　10 D
せんぱい　N　senior students　10
ぜんぶ　全部　Adv　all　7
せんもん　専門　N　major subject of study　2
そうじする　V　clean (room/house)　9 D
そうですか。　E　I see.　1
そうですね。　E　That's right.　4
そうですねえ。　E　Well ... [thinking]　5
そこ　N　there　4 D
そして　C　and then　5
そと　外　N　outside　4 D
その　preN　that [used before a noun]　2 D
そば　N　near　4 D
それ　N　it　2 D
それから　C　and then　6
それで　C　so [for changing topic]　9

【た】
タイ（たい）　N　Thailand　2
〜たい　G　to want to ...　6
だいがく　大学　N　university　1
だいがくいん　大学院　N　graduate school　2 D
だいがくせい　大学生　N　college student　10

タイご　タイ語　N　Thai language　6 D
だいじ（な）　大事（な）　naA　important　9
だいじょうぶ（な）　naA　all right　8
たいてい　Adv　usually, mostly　10 A
だいぶ　Adv　quite a lot　10
たいへん（な）　大変（な）　naA　hard, difficult　3
たかい　高い　iA　expensive　3 D
たかい　高い　iA　high, tall　4
たくさん　Adv　a lot, many, much　10 D
タクシー（たくしい）　N　taxi　5 D
だけ　P　just, only　9
だす〈だします〉　出す　V　to mail, to hand in　7
だす〈だします〉　出す　V　to withdraw (money)　7
だす（くすりを）　出す　V　to prescribe　8
だす（スピードを）　出す　V　to drive fast　8
たすかりました。　E　Thanks for helping me.　6
たすかる　助かる　V　to be helped　10
たつ　立つ　V　to stand　10 D
たてもの　建物　N　building　4
たばこ　N　cigarette　8 D
たぶん　Adv　maybe, probably　8
たべもの　食べ物　N　food　8 D
たべる〈たべます〉　食べる　V　to eat　1
〜たほうがいい　G　You had better ...　8
だめ（な）　naA　no good, unacceptable　3
〜たり〜たりする　G　10
だれ　Q　who　1 D
だれか　N　somebody　5
たんじょうび　誕生日　N　birthday　4 D
ちいさい　小さい　iA　small　3 D
ちか　地下　N　underground　6
ちかい　近い　iA　near　9 D
ちがう　V　to be different　10
ちかてつ　地下鉄　N　subway　5
チケット　N　ticket　10 D
ちち　父　N　(my) father　10 D
ちゃいろ　茶色　N　brown　9 A
ちょうし　調子　N　condition　8
チョコレート　N　chocolate　10 D
ちょっと　Adv　a little　3
ちょっとうかがいますが。　E　Excuse me, may I ask a question?　5
ちょっとよろしいでしょうか。　E　May I disturb you for a moment?　9
つかう〈つかいます〉　使う　V　to use　6
つかれた。　E　I'm tired.　10
つかれる　V　to get tired　10
つぎに　次に　C　next　6
つく〈つきます〉　着く　V　to arrive　7
つくえ　机　N　desk　4 D
つくる　作る　V　to make　6 D
つける　V　to turn on　9 D

つとめる　勤める　V　to work for　10 D
つま　妻　N　(my) wife　10 D
つめたい　冷たい　iA　cold　8 D
て　手　N　hand　5 D
で　P　[Group 1 particle for action place]　1
で　P　by, with [Group 1 particle for means]　5 D
で　P　in [Group 1 particle for period of time]　7
で　P　[Group 1 particle for unit of things]　7
～でいい　G　to be O.K.　10
テープ（てぷ）　N　tape　1
テープレコーダー　N　tape recorder　7 D
でかける　出かける　V　to go out　9 D
てがみ　手紙　N　letter　5 D
できる＜できます＞　V　to be ready, to be made　7 D
～てください　G　Please …　6
～てくださいませんか　G　Will you … for me ?　6
～てくる＜～てきます＞　to do something and come back　7
～でした　G　was, were [perfect form of です]　2 D
～でしょうね。　E　must be …　10
～です　G　be　2
テスト　N　test　7 D
テニス　N　tennis　9 D
デパート（でぱあと）　N　department store　4 S
～てはいけない　G　must not　9 D
でも　C　but, however　3
でも　P　or something [Group 2 particle]　10
～てもいい　G　may　9 D
～でもいい　G　may, … is O.K.　9
でる＜でます＞　出る　V　to leave　5 D
でる＜でます＞　出る　V　to come out　6
でる　出る　V　to attend　9 D
テレビ（てれび）　N　television　1 D
てんいん　店員　N　sales clerk　4
てんき　天気　N　weather　7 D
でんしこうがく　電子工学　N　electronic engineering　2
でんしじしょ　電子辞書　N　electronic dictionary　6 D
でんしゃ　電車　N　train　5 D
てんぷら　N　[name of Japanese food]　7 D
でんわ　電話　N　telephone　4 D
でんわする　電話する　V　to make a phone call　6 D
でんわばんごう　電話番号　N　telephone number　6 D
と　P　with [Group 1 particle]　5 D
と　P　[Group 5 particle for quotation]　8
～ど　～度　counter　degrees　8
と　P　and [Group 1 particle]　1
ドイツ（どいつ）　N　Germany　2 D
トイレ（といれ）　N　toilet, restroom　4 D
どう　Q　how　3

どういたしまして。　E　You are welcome.　6
とうきょう　東京　N　[name of a place]　5 D
どうしたんですか。　E　How is it ?, What is the problem ?　8
どうして　Q　why　7 D
どうしました。　E　How is it ?, What is the problem ?　8
どうぞ　E　please　1
どうぞよろしく。　E　Nice to see you.　2
どうぞよろしくおねがいします。　E　Very nice to see you.　2
どうなさいましたか。　E　What seems to be the problem ?　8
どうも。　E　Thank you.　4
どうもありがとうございました。　E　Thank you very much.　4
どうもすみません。　E　I'm sorry.　4
どうやって　Q　how, by what means　5
とおる＜とおります＞　通る　V　to go through, to pass through　5 D
とか　P　and so on [Group 1 particle]　10
ときどき　Adv　sometimes　8
ドクター　N　doctor ('s degree)　7 D
とけい　時計　N　clock, watch　4 D
どこ　Q　where　1 D
どこか　N　somewhere　5
ところ　N　place　7 D
としょかん　図書館　N　library　1 D
どちら　Q　where [polite form of どこ, どれ]　2
とても　Adv　very　3
となり　N　next to　4 D
どの　Q　which [used before a noun]　2
どのぐらい　Q　how long, how much　5
どのへん　どの辺　Q　whereabout　4
とめる　泊める　V　to put someone up for the night　9 D
～ともうします。　E　My name is ….　2
ともだち　友達　N　friend　2
どようび　土曜日　N　Saturday　2 A
ドライブ（する）　N　drive　10 D
とりにく　とり肉　N　chicken　7 D
ドル　N　dollar　7 D
とる＜とります＞　取る　V　to take　3
とる（しゃしんを）　V　to take (photo)　9 D
どれ　Q　which　2 D
どんな　Q　what kind of　3 D

【な】
ナイフ（ないふ）　N　knife　5 D
なか　中　N　inside　4 D
ながい　長い　iA　long　8 D
～ながら　suffix　while doing …　11

Vocabulary Index 291

~なくてはいけない G must 9
~なくてもいい G need not 9
なごやえき 名古屋駅 N Nagoya Station 5 D
なごやこう 名古屋港 N Nagoya Port 5
なごやじょう 名古屋城 N Nagoya Castle 5
なごやだいがく 名古屋大学 N Nagoya University 2 D
なつやすみ 夏休み N summer vacation 10 D
なに 何 Q what 1
なにか 何か N something 5 D
なにも 何も N not anything 5 D
なま 生 N raw 3
なまえ 名前 N name 5 D
なれる 慣れる V to get accustomed to 10
ナロン(なろん) N [personal name] 1 D
なん 何 Q what 2
~なんですけど。 E about [phrase used to present a topic] 9
に P to [Group 1 particle for place of arrival] 2
に P on, at [Group 1 particle for time] 2
に P in, at [particle for existence place] 4
に P on, at [Group 1 particle for place] 6
に P [Group 1particle for purpose of motion] 7
にぎやか(な) naA lively 8 D
にく 肉 N meat 3 D
にさんにち 2,3日 N two or three days 8
にし 西 N west 4 D
にしかわ 西川 N [personal name] 10 D
~にち ~日 counter day 4 D
にちようび 日曜日 N Sunday 2 A
にほん 日本 N Japan 2
にほんご 日本語 N Japanese language 1 D
ニュース(にゅうす) N news 5 D
にる 似る V to look like, to resemble 10
~にん ~人 counter person 10
ね P [Group 3 particle for agreement, confirmation] 3
ネクタイ N necktie 10 D
ねこ N cat 4 D
ねつ 熱 N fever, temperature 8
ネックレス N necklace 10 D
ねむい iA sleepy 9 D
ねる〈ねます〉 V to go to bed, to sleep 7 D
~ねん ~年 counter year(s), ...th grade 2
の P of, 's [Group 1 particle for modification] 2
の P one [particle for noun substitution] 4
の P [particle for nominalizing] 9
ノート(のうと) N notebook 2 D
ノックする V to knock 9
ので P because [Group 4 particle for a reason clause] 9
のど N throat 8
のぼる 登る V to climb 10 D
のむ〈のみます〉 飲む V to drink 1 D
のむ(くすりを) 飲む V to take (medicine) 8
のりかえる 〈のりかえます〉 乗りかえる V to change (trains/buses) 5
のる〈のります〉 乗る V to get on, to take, to ride 5

【は】

は P as for [Group 2 particle for topic, contrast] 1
はっ。 E Pardon ?, Yes. 8
パーティー(ぱあてぃい) N party 3
はい、そうです。 E Yes, that's right. 2 D
はい、どうぞ。 E Here it is. 1
はい。 E Yes. 1
はいる 入る V to go in 10 D
はがき N postcard 7
はかる V to measure 8
はく V to wear 10 D
バザー(ばざあ) N bazaar 3 D
はし N chopsticks 5 D
はじまる〈はじまります〉 始まる V to begin 2
はじめて 初めて Adv first time 8
はじめまして。 E How do you do ? 2
バス(ばす) N bus 3 D
はたらく 働く V to work 10
はちどごぶ 8度5分 N 38.5 degrees centigrade 8
バックナンバー N back issue 6
はっぴょう(する) 発表(する) N presentation 9
はなす〈はなします〉 話す V to speak, to tell, to talk 5 D
バナナ N banana 9 D
はは 母 N (my) mother 10 D
はやい 速い iA fast 7
はやく 早く Adv fast, early 8 D
はん 半 N and half 5 D
ハン N [personal name] 10 D
~ばん ~番 counter Number ... 4
パン(ぱん) N bread 5 D
ハンカチ N handkerchief 10 D
ばんごはん 晩ごはん N dinner, supper 10 D
ハンサム(な) naA handsome 7 D
はんたい 反対 N the other way around 6
ハンバーガー N hamburger 10 D
バンバン(ばんばん) N [personal name] 1 D
ビール N beer 8 D
ひがし 東 N east 4 D
ひく(かぜを) 引く V to catch (cold) 8 D
ピクニック N picnic 7 D
ひこうき 飛行機 N airplane 5 D

ピザ　N　pizza　8 D
ひさしぶりですね。　E　I haven't seen you for a long time.　3
ひじ　N　elbow　8
ひだり　左　N　left　4
ビデオ　N　video　6 D
ビデオテープ　N　video tape　7 D
ひと　人　N　person　2
ひま(な)　naA　free, to have time　3 D
びょういん　病院　N　hospital　8
ひらがな　N　"hiragana"　1 D
ひる　昼　N　noon, daytime　9 A
ひるごはん　昼ごはん　N　lunch　7 D
ひろい　広い　iA　spacious, big　4
プール　N　swimming pool　7 D
フォーク(ふぉおく)　N　fork　5 D
ふくしゅう(する)　復習(する)　N　review　7 D
ふたつ　2つ　N　two　4 S
ふつか　2日　N　two days　7 D
ぶっか　物価　N　(commodity) prices　8 D
ふとる　太る　V　to get fat　10 D
ふべん(な)　不便(な)　naA　inconvenient　9 D
フライ(ふらい)　N　fried (food)　3
フランスご　フランス語　N　French　9 D
プリント　N　handout　6 D
ふるい　古い　iA　old　9 D
プレゼント　N　present　10 D
~ふん/ぷん　~分　counter　minute(s)　4 D
ぶんか　文化　N　culture　10
ぶんぽう　文法　N　grammar　1 D
へ　P　to [Group 1 particle for direction]　1
へええ。　E　Oh, really?　10
ベッド　N　bed　7 D
へや　部屋　N　room　4 D
~へん　~辺　suffix　around, nearby, in the vicinity　4
ペン　N　pen　10 D
べんきょう　勉強　N　study　3
べんきょうする〈べんきょうします〉　勉強する　V　to study　1 D
べんり(な)　便利(な)　naA　useful, convenient　3 D
ほうがくけんきゅうか　法学研究科　N　Graduate School of Law　2
ぼうし　N　hat, cap　10 D
ボールペン(ぼうるぺん)　N　ball-point pen　2 D
ほか　N　other　4 S
ほけんかんりしつ　保健管理室　N　health control center　4 D
ほけんしょう　保険証　N　health insurance card　8
ほしい　iA　to want　6 D
ボタン　N　button　6

ほっかいどう　北海道　N　[name of a place]　10 D
ほね　N　bone　8
ほん　本　N　book　1 D
~ほん　~本　counter　[for tapes, long cylindrical things]　7 D
ほんだ　本田　N　[personal name]　4

【ま】
まあ。　E　well...　10
~まい　~枚　counter　[for flat objects]　7
まいあさ　毎朝　N　every morning　10 D
まいしゅう　毎週　N　every week　9 A
まいつき　毎月　N　every month　9 A
まいとし　毎年　N　every year　9 A
まいにち　毎日　N　everyday　3
まいばん　毎晩　N　every night　10 D
まえ　前　N　ago, before　2
まえ　前　N　in front of　4 D
~ましょう　G　Let's ...　3 D
~ましょうか　G　Shall I/we ... ?　3
まず　C　first of all　6
~ませんか　G　Would you like to ... ?　3
また　Adv　again　2
まつ　待つ　V　to wait　6 D
まで　P　to, as far as [Group 1 particle for goal]　5
まど　窓　N　window　9 D
みぎ　右　N　right　4
みじかい　短い　iA　short　8 D
みず　水　N　water　7 D
みせ　店　N　shop, store　10 D
みせる　見せる　V　to show　8
みっか　3日　N　three days　7 D
みどりいろ　緑色　N　green　9 A
みどりく　緑区　N　[name of a ward]　10 D
みなみ　南　N　south　4 D
ミャンマー(みゃんまあ)　N　Myanmar　2 D
みる〈みます〉　見る　V　to see, to watch　1 D
みんな　N　all　10
むこう　N　over there, that away　4
むしば　虫歯　N　bad tooth　8
むずかしい　難しい　iA　difficult　3 D
め　目　N　eye　8 D
めいだいまえ　名大前　N　[name of a bus stop]　5 D
メールボックス　N　mailbox　6 D
めがね　N　glasses　10
メモ　N　memorandum　6 D
も　P　too [Group 2 particle]　1
もう　Adv　already　10
もういちど　もう一度　Adv　once more　6
もうしこみ(をする)　申しこみ(をする)　V　application (to apply)　7 S

もうすぐ　Adv　soon　10
もくようび　木曜日　N　Thursday　2 A
もしもし。　E　Hello. (on the phone)　8
もつ　持つ　V　to have　10
もってくる　持ってくる　V　to bring　8
もとやま　本山　N　[name of a place]　5
もの　物　N　thing, stuff
もらう　V　to receive　10
もんだい　問題　N　question　8 D

【や】
やくそく(する)　約束(する)　N　appointment, promise　9 D
やさしい　iA　easy　8 D
やすい　安い　iA　inexpensive　3 D
やすみ　休み　N　being closed, holiday, no class/work　8 D
やすみじかん　休み時間　N　break (time)　7 D
やすむ　休む　V　to be absent, to take a rest　8 D
やせる　V　to lose weight　10 D
やま　山　N　mountain　10 D
やまかわ　山川　N　[personal name]　2 D
やました　山下　N　[personal name]　5
ゆうびんきょく　郵便局　N　post office　4 D
ゆうびんきょくいん　郵便局員　N　post office clerk　7
ゆうがた　N　evening　9 A
ゆうべ　N　last evening　9 A
〜ゆき　〜行き　suffix　for ...　5
よ　P　[Group 3 particle for emphatical statement]　3
ようし　用紙　N　form (to fill in)　7
よかったですね。　E　That's nice.　10
よこになる　横になる　V　to lie down　8
よしゅう(する)　予習(する)　N　preparation for class　3
よぶ　呼ぶ　V　to call　6 D
よむ〈よみます〉　読む　V　to read　1

よる　夜　N　night　9 A

【ら】
ラーメン　N　Chinese noodles　9 D
らいげつ　来月　N　next month　9
らいしゅう　来週　N　next week　9
らいねん　来年　N　next year　9 A
ラジオ(らじお)　N　radio　1 D
りゃく　略　N　abbreviation, acronym　7
りゅうがくせい　留学生　N　international student　2 D
りゅうがくせいかいかん　留学生会館　N　International Students' House　1 D
りゅうがくせいセンター(せんたあ)　留学生センター　N　Education Center for International Students　4 D
りょうしん　両親　N　parents　10
りょうり(する)　料理(する)　N　cooking　6 D
りんご　N　apple　7 D
ルイン(るいん)　N　Lwin [personal name]　1
れいぞうこ　冷蔵庫　N　refrigerator　4 D
レジ(れじ)　N　cashier　1
レジ(れじ)のひと　レジの人　N　staff at cash register　1
レポート　N　report　7 D
れんしゅうする　練習する　N　to practice　7 D
ロビー　N　lobby　10 D

【わ】
ワープロ　N　word processor　6 D
わかる〈わかります〉　分かる　V　to understand　6
わすれる〈わすれます〉　忘れる　V　to forget　7
わだ　和田　N　[personal name]　2 D
わたし　N　I　1
を　P　[Group 1 particle for direct object]　1
を　P　through, from, along [Group 1 particle]　5 D
〜んです　G　3

Index for Notes on Grammar (Lesson 1~10)

Arabic numeral : Lesson number
Roman numeral & alphabet : Item number

【a】
ああ (verb modifier)	6 V
ああやって	5 IV
あちら	2 IIIC
adjective sentences	3 I
adverb	3 V
あげる	10 IIA
alternative questions	2 II
あまり (～ない)	3 VB
あの	2 IIIB
あの (mutually understood)	10 VII
approximate amounts	5 V
あれ	2 IIIA
あれ (mutually understood)	10 VII
あります (existence)	4 IA
あります (possession)	6 IIIA
あります (to take place)	6 IIIB
あそこ	4 IB
あそこ (mutually understood)	10 VII

【c】
ちがいます (answering)	2 IC
ちょっと	3 VA
classification of particles	1 VI
classification of verbs	1 IIA
conjugation	
-い adjectives	3 IA
-な adjectives	3 IB
noun＋です	2 IB
verbs	1 IIB
conjunction	3 VI
conjunctive particle	5 III
counter	1 IX

【d】
だけ	9 IVB
だれ	1 IVB
だれか	5 IA
だれも	5 IB
だろう	10 V
で (by means of)	5 IIA
で (period of time)	7 VIB
で (place of action)	1 IIIB
で (unit)	7 VIB
では (conjunction)	4 VI
では (じゃ)	2 IB
ではありません	2 IB
でいい	10 VI
でも (but)	3 VI
でも (or something like that)	10 IVA
demonstrative pronouns (1)	2 III
demonstrative pronouns (2) (what was just mentioned)	4 IV
demonstrative pronouns (3) (mutually understood)	10 VII
でしょう (1) (supposition)	10 V
でしょうか	9 V
desire	6 II
です	2 IA
です (substitute for a verb)	4 III
dictionary form	1 IIA
どちら	2 IIIC
どちらも	5 IB
どこ	1 IVB
どこか	5 IA
どこも	5 IB
どんな	3 VIIB
どの	2 IIIB
どのぐらい/どのくらい	5 V
どれ	2 IIIA
どれも	5 IB
どう	3 VIIA
どう (one's desire)	6 IIC
どう (verb modifier)	6 V
どうして	7 VA
どうやって	5 IV
ええ (yes)	1 IVA

【e】
emphatic sentence	9 IC
existential sentences	4 IA

【f】
family terms	10 VIII

Index for Notes on Grammar 295

formation rule	
non-polite form	
-い adjectives	8 IB
-な adjectives	8 IC
noun＋です	8 IC
verbs	8 IA
polite form of verbs	1 IIB
-たり form	10 IIIA
-て form	
-い adjectives	7 IA
-な adjectives	7 IB
noun＋です	7 IB
verbs	6 IB
分 (ふん)	1 IXB
function of の (nominalizing particle)	9 IA
function of the -て form	7 IIA

【g】

が (but)	7 VB
が (direct object)	3 IB, 6 IIA, 6 IIB
が (introductory remark)	5 III
が (subject)	1 I
がいい	10 VI
giving and receiving verbs (1) (あげる, くれる, もらう)	10 II
ご- (prefix)	2 VI
ございます (humble form)	4 ID
Group 1 particles	1 VI
Group 1 verbs	1 IIA
Group 2 particles	1 VI
Group 2 verbs	1 IIA
Group 3 particles	1 VI
Group 4 particles	5 III
Group 5 particle	8 IIA
ぐらい	5 V

【h】

は (topic)	1 VA
～は～にあります/います	4 IC
はい (yes)	1 IVA
へ (direction)	1 IIIA
ほしい	6 IIA
ほうがいい	8 III

【i】

-い adjective sentences	3 IA
いいえ (no)	1 IVA
いかが (one's desire)	6 IIC
いくら	1 IXB, 4 VA
いくつ	1 IXA, 4 VB, 4 VIIA
います	4 IA
imperfective form	
-い adjectives	3 IA
-な adjectives	3 IB
noun＋です	2 IB
verbs	1 IIB
Irregular verbs	1 IIA
いつ	2 V
いつか	5 IA
いつも	5 IB

【j】

じゃ (conjunction)	4 VI
時 (じ)	1 IXB
invitation	3 II

【k】

日 (か)	4 VIIB
か (question marker)	1 IVA
から (from, since)	2 IVB
から (reason)	7 VA
からです	8 IIC
-かた	6 IV
けど	8 V
けれど	8 V
けれども	8 V
きらい	3 IB
こちら	2 IIIC
ここ	4 IB
この	2 IIIB
これ	2 IIIA
こう (verb modifier)	6 V
こうやって	5 IV
くらい	5 V
くれる	10 IIB

【l】

location	4 I

【m】

まで (as far as, until)	5 IIC
-ませんか	3 IIA
-ましょう	3 IIA
-ましょうか	3 IIB
-ます	1 I
まず (temporal sequence)	6 VI
も (topic) (too, also)	1 VB
もらう	10 IIC

【n】

-な adjective sentences	3 IB
-なくて	9 II
-なくてはいけない	9 III
-なくてはならない	9 III
-なくてもいい	9 III
-なくてもかまわない	9 III
何（なん／なに）	2 IIIA
何＋で (in what way)	5 IV
何円（なんえん）	1 IXB
何（なに）	1 IVB
何か（なにか）	5 IA
何も（なにも）	5 IB
何時（なんじ）	1 IXB
何日（なんにち）	4 VIIB
何人（なんにん）	4 VIIB
何分（なんぷん）	1 IXB
んです (1)	3 III
んです (2) (with the non-polite form)	8 IIB
ね	3 IV
negative -て form (1)	9 II
に (from)	10 IIC
に (indirect object)	1 I
に (place of arrival)	2 IVC
に (place of location)	4 IA
に (place to be put or written)	6 VII
に (time)	2 IVC
～に～があります／います	4 IA
に＋verbs of motion (purpose)	7 VIA
日（にち）	4 VIIB
人（にん）	4 VIIB
の (nominalizing particle)	9 I
の (Noun 1 の Noun 2)	2 IVA
の (substitute for a noun)	4 II
ので	9 IVA
non-polite form	8 I
noun modifiers	
-い adjective	3 IA
-な adjective	3 IB
noun	2 IVA
noun phrase	1 I
noun sentences	2 I
nouns of place	4 IB
numbers as adverbs	7 VII
numbers (1) (Chinese origin)	1 IX
numbers (2) (Japanese origin)	4 VII
numerals (1) (Chinese origin)	1 IX
numerals (2) (Japanese origin)	4 VII

【o】

お- (prefix)	2 VI
obligation	9 III
omission of particles	3 VIII
omission of some noun phrases	1 VIII

【p】

particle	1 I
particles (classification)	1 VI
perfective form	1 IIB
perfective form	
-い adjectives	3 IA
-な adjectives	3 IB
noun＋です	2 IB
verbs	1 IIB
permission	9 III
polite command	6 I
polite form	1 IIB
polite form of verbs	1 IIB
prohibition	9 III

【q】

question sentences	
noun sentences	2 IC
-い adjective sentences	3 IA
-な adjective sentences	3 IB
verbal sentences	1 IV
question word	1 IVB
question words＋か	5 IA
question words＋も	5 IB
questions with question words	
noun sentences	2 IC
verbal sentences	1 IVB
quotative particle	8 IIA
quoted sentence	8 IIA

【r】

request	6 I

【s】

しか (～ない)	10 IVC
そちら	2 IIIC
そこ	4 IB
その	2 IIIB
その (what was just mentioned)	4 IV
それ	2 IIIA
それ (what was just mentioned)	4 IV
それで (changing the topic)	9 VIB
それで (therefore)	9 VIA
それから (adding more information)	7 IV
それから (temporal sequence)	6 VI
そして	5 VI
そう (verb modifier)	6 V
そうです (answering)	2 IC
そうやって	5 IV
suggestion	3 II
-すぎる (suffix)	8 IV

好き	3 IB	とか	10 IVB
少し	3 VA	と思います	8 IIA
		とても	3 VA
【t】			
-たい	6 IIB	**【u】**	
-たり (repetition)	10 IIIB	usages	
-たり (representative actions)	10 IIIB	non-polite form (grammatical rules)	8 II
-たり～-たりする	10 III	-たり form	10 IIIB
-て form		-て form of verbs	7 IIB
verb	6 IA		
-い adjectives	7 I	**【v】**	
-な adjectives	7 I	verb base	6 IIB
noun＋です	7 I	verbal sentences	1 I
-てはいけない	9 III	verbs	1 II
-てはならない	9 III	verbs with a の clause	9 IB
-ている	10 I		
-ている (habitual action)	10 IB	**【w】**	
-ている (progressive action)	10 IA	を (from)	5 IIB
-ている (resultant state)	10 IC	を (object)	1 I
-てください	6 IA	を (through)	5 IIB
-てくださいませんか	6 IC		
-てくる (do ～ and come back)	7 III	**【y】**	
-てもいい	9 III	Yes-No questions	
-てもかまわない	9 III	noun sentences	2 IC
time expressions	1 VII	verbal sentences	1 IVA
と (connecting two nouns) (and)	1 IIIC	よ	3 IV
と (quotative particle)	8 IIA		

Index for Kanji Strokes (Lesson 1〜10)

The number in brackets 【 】 indicates the stroke counts.
The number following the Kanji indicates the lesson number.

【1】 一 1

【2】 二 1　七 1　八 1　九 1　十 1　人 2

【3】 三 1　千 1　万 1　山 2　川 2　女 2　子 2　土 2　口 3　大 3　小 3
　　　上 4　下 4　工 4

【4】 五 1　六 1　円 1　日 2　月 2　火 2　水 2　木 2　手 3　友 3　中 4
　　　分 5　今 5　元 5　切 7　方 7　少 8　父 10　内 10

【5】 四 1　田 2　目 3　生 3　本 3　右 4　左 4　北 4　白 4　半 5　広 5
　　　古 5　外 7　市 7　母 10　兄 10　主 10　仕 10

【6】 百 1　年 1　耳 3　先 3　好 3　西 4　名 4　安 5　多 5　気 5　行 6
　　　会 6　休 8　自 8　両 10　毎 10

【7】 車 2　足 3　男 3　何 4　赤 5　利 5　言 6　見 6　来 6　図 7　体 8
　　　医 8　究 9　弟 10

【8】 門 2　金 2　学 3　明 3　東 4　青 4　使 6　国 7　枚 7　者 8　表 9
　　　英 9　事 9　法 9　姉 10　妹 10

【9】 南 4　便 5　食 6　送 7　度 8　思 8　研 9　室 9　発 9　科 9　専 9

【10】 時 5　高 5　書 6　通 6　紙 7　病 8　院 8　勉 9　家 10

【11】 部 4　教 6　堂 7　週 7　転 8　強 9　授 9　族 10

【12】 飲 6　買 6　間 7　着 7　痛 8

【13】 新 5　話 6　電 8　業 9　働 10

【14】 読 6　聞 6　様 7　語 9

【15】 熱 8

【16】 館 7　薬 8　親 10

General Editors

FUJIWARA, Masanori	藤原雅憲	
KANDA, Toshiko	神田紀子	

Authors

DAKE, Itsuko	嶽　逸子	(Dialogue, Reading Comprehension)
FUJIWARA, Masanori	藤原雅憲	(Notes on Grammar, Notes on Discourse)
HATTORI, Atsushi	服部　淳	(Dialogue, Aural Comprehension)
KANDA, Toshiko	神田紀子	(Dialogue, Aural Comprehension, Notes on Discourse)
KASHIMA, Tanomu	鹿島　央	(Pronunciation and Writing System)
SOORIN, Yuka	宗林由佳	(Kanji, Notes on Grammar, Reading Comprehension)
TAKAHASHI, Nobuko	高橋伸子	(Drill, Notes on Grammar)
TAKAYASU, Yooko	高安葉子	(Notes on Grammar)
TSUBAKI, Yukiko	椿由紀子	(Dialogue, Aural Comprehension)
TSUBOTA, Masako	坪田雅子	(Dialogue, Reading Comprehension)
UOZUMI, Tomoko	魚住友子	(Drill, Notes on Grammar)
YASUI, Sumie	安井澄江	(Kanji)
HARRISON, Richard	リチャード・ハリソン	(English Editor)
PRESTON, Judith	ジュディス・プレストン	(English check (Pronunciation and Writing System))
FUJISHIMA, Kaoru	藤嶋かおる	(Illustration)

A COURSE IN MODERN JAPANESE [REVISED EDITION] VOLUME ONE

2002年4月20日　初版第1刷発行
2014年7月15日　初版第3刷発行

定価はカバーに表示しています

編　者　名古屋大学日本語教育研究グループ

発行者　石井三記

発行所　一般財団法人　名古屋大学出版会
〒464-0814　名古屋市千種区不老町名古屋大学構内
電話(052)781-5027／FAX(052)781-0697

Ⓒ名古屋大学日本語教育研究グループ, 2002　　Printed in Japan
印刷・製本　㈱クイックス　　ISBN978-4-8158-0425-1
乱丁・落丁はお取替えいたします。

Ⓡ〈日本複製権センター委託出版物〉
本書の全部または一部を無断で複写複製（コピー）することは，著作権法上での例外を除き，禁じられています。本書からの複写を希望される場合は，日本複製権センター(03-3401-2382)にご連絡ください。

●コミュニケーション能力の養成に重点をおいた日本語教科書

〈初級編〉
A Course in Modern Japanese
[Revised Edition] Vol. 2

名古屋大学日本語教育研究グループ編

基礎文法力，ディスコース能力，社会言語学的能力の養成と，音声言語理解力が獲得できるように編集した好評テキストの改訂版．

Vol.1	CD 3枚組	A 5判・本体 4,800 円
Vol.2	テキスト	B 5判・336頁・本体 2,800 円
	CD 3枚組	A 5判・本体 4,800 円

〈中級編〉
現代日本語コース中級 I, II
－A Course in Modern Japanese Vol.3, 4－

名古屋大学日本語教育研究グループ編

ことばのもつ機能を重視し，円滑なコミュニケーションを支える口頭表現能力を養成することを目的とした日本語教科書．A Course in Modern Japanese Vol. 1, 2 の続刊．

Vol. 3	テキスト	B 5判・348頁・本体 2,800 円
	テープ	B 6判・C 60×2，C 45×1・本体 7,000 円
	聴解ワークシート	A 4判・238頁＋テープ（C 46×1）・本体5,000円
Vol. 4	テキスト	B 5判・330頁・本体 2,800 円
	テープ	B 6判・C 45×2，C 90×1・本体 7,000 円
	聴解ワークシート	A 4判・218頁＋テープ（C 46×1）・本体5,000円

日本地図 Map of Japan
にほんちず

地方 region
ちほう

都道府県 （県庁所在地・市） prefectures (location of the prefectural govt.)
とどうふけん　けんちょうしょざいち　し

中国地方
ちゅうごくちほう

31　鳥取県　（鳥取市）
　　とっとりけん　とっとりし
32　島根県　（松江市）
　　しまねけん　まつえし
33　岡山県　（岡山市）
　　おかやまけん　おかやまし
34　広島県　（広島市）
　　ひろしまけん　ひろしまし
35　山口県　（山口市）
　　やまぐちけん　やまぐちし

近畿地方
きんきちほう

25　滋賀県　（大津市）
　　しがけん　おおつし
26　京都府　（京都市）
　　きょうとふ　きょうとし
27　大阪府　（大阪市）
　　おおさかふ　おおさかし
28　兵庫県　（神戸市）
　　ひょうごけん　こうべし
29　奈良県　（奈良市）
　　ならけん　ならし
30　和歌山県　（和歌山市）
　　わかやまけん　わかやまし

中部地方
ちゅうぶちほう

15　新潟県　（新潟市）
　　にいがたけん　にいがたし
16　富山県　（富山市）
　　とやまけん　とやまし
17　石川県　（金沢市）
　　いしかわけん　かなざわし
18　福井県　（福井市）
　　ふくいけん　ふくいし
19　山梨県　（甲府市）
　　やまなしけん　こうふし
20　長野県　（長野市）
　　ながのけん　ながのし
21　岐阜県　（岐阜市）
　　ぎふけん　ぎふし
22　静岡県　（静岡市）
　　しずおかけん　しずおかし
23　愛知県　（名古屋市）
　　あいちけん　なごやし
24　三重県　（津市）
　　みえけん　つし

九州地方
きゅうしゅうちほう

40　福岡県　（福岡市）
　　ふくおかけん　ふくおかし
41　佐賀県　（佐賀市）
　　さがけん　さがし
42　長崎県　（長崎市）
　　ながさきけん　ながさきし
43　熊本県　（熊本市）
　　くまもとけん　くまもとし
44　大分県　（大分市）
　　おおいたけん　おおいたし
45　宮崎県　（宮崎市）
　　みやざきけん　みやざきし
46　鹿児島県　（鹿児島市）
　　かごしまけん　かごしまし
47　沖縄県　（那覇市）
　　おきなわけん　なはし

四国地方
しこくちほう

36　徳島県　（徳島市）
　　とくしまけん　とくしまし
37　香川県　（高松市）
　　かがわけん　たかまつし
38　愛媛県　（松山市）
　　えひめけん　まつやまし
39　高知県　（高知市）
　　こうちけん　こうちし

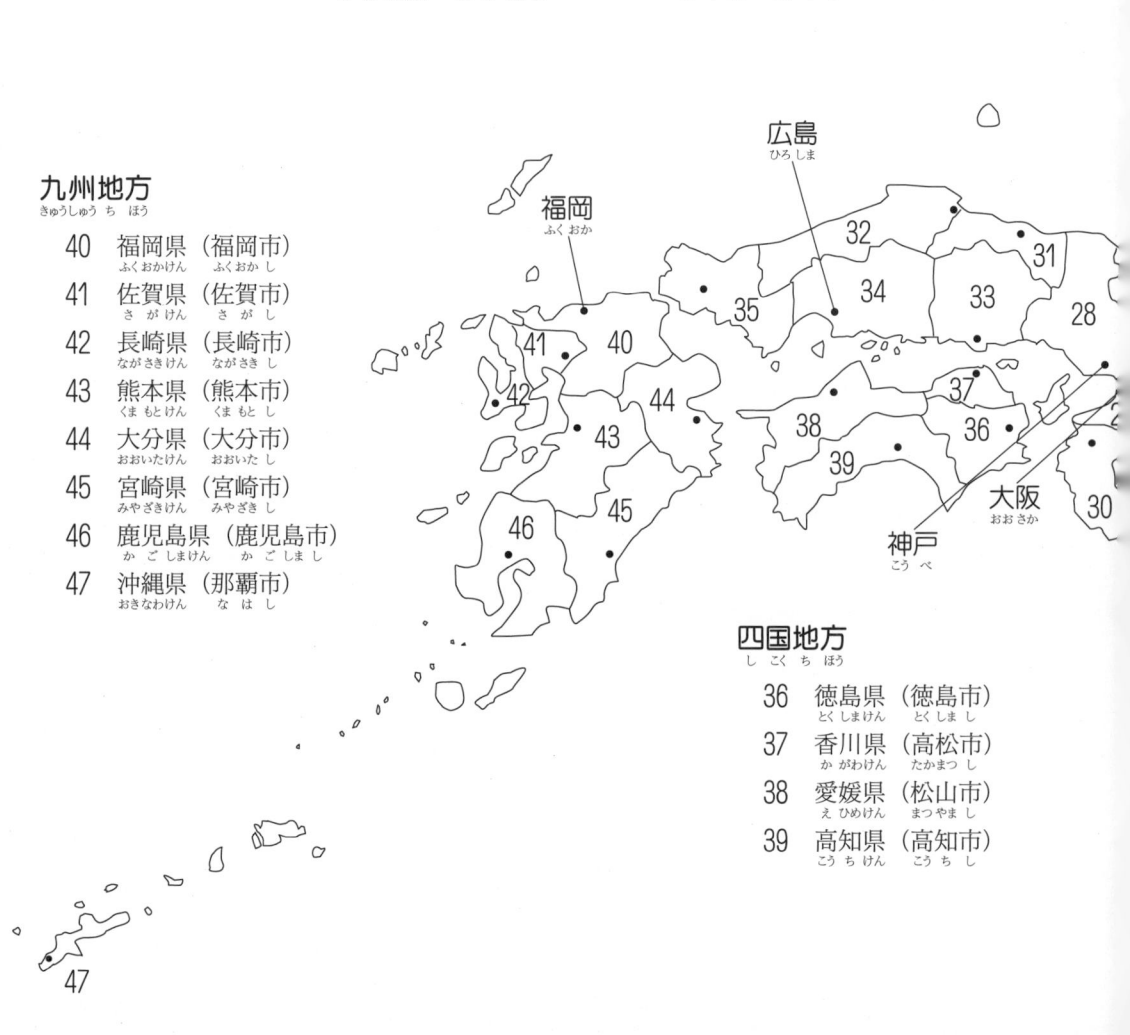